A RELIGION OF POTS AND PANS?

Number 156
A RELIGION OF POTS AND PANS?
Modes of Philosophical and Theological Discourse in Ancient Judaism
Essays and a Program

by
Jacob Neusner

A RELIGION OF POTS AND PANS?
Modes of Philosophical and Theological Discourse in Ancient Judaism

Essays and a Program

by
Jacob Neusner

Scholars Press
Atlanta, Georgia

A RELIGION OF POTS AND PANS?
Mdes of Philosophical and Theological
Discourse in Ancient Judaism

Essays and a Program

© 1988
Brown University

Library of Congress Cataloging in Publication Data

Neusner, Jacob, 1932-
    A religion of pots and pans?

    (Brown Judaic studies ; no. 156)
    Includes index.
    1. Mishnah--Theology. I. Title. II. Series.
BM497.8.N487   1989   296.1'23   88-30828
ISBN 1-55540-283-6

Printed in the United States of America
on acid-free paper

FOR MY COLLEAGUES SOMETIME STUDENTS
SOMETIME TEACHERS, AND ALL-THE-TIME FRIENDS

EUGENE V. GALLAGHER
CONNECTICUT COLLEGE

A TOKEN OF THANKS
FOR HIS HOSPITALITY
AT CONNECTICUT COLLEGE
IN CONNECTION WITH
THE REINFELD LECTURE

AND OF
REGARD FOR HIS EXCEPTIONALLY HELPFUL CONTRIBUTIONS
TO MY SUMMER SEMINAR FOR COLLEGE TEACHERS
SPONSORED BY THE NATIONAL ENDOWMENT FOR THE
HUMANITIES
AND CONDUCTED BY ME AT BROWN UNIVERSITY IN
JUNE THROUGH AUGUST, 1988

AND

GARY PHILLIPS
COLLEGE OF THE HOLY CROSS

AND A STATEMENT OF RESPECT AND ESTEEM
FOR HIS SCHOLARSHIP AND CRITICAL ACUMEN
EXPRESSED IN HIS WORK WITH ME
IN THE SAME SEMINAR

THEIR CONTRIBUTIONS TO THAT SEMINAR
WERE RICH, STIMULATING, AND PROVOCATIVE,
AND I LEARNED FROM THEM
AS MUCH AS I TREASURED THEIR PRESENCE.

Contents

Preface

This book consists of essays on a single problem, which is the religious character of the Judaism that began with the Mishnah and reached its definitive statement, for ancient times, in the Talmud of Babylonia or Bavli. I have maintained that the Judaism under description, which I call "the Judaism of the Dual Torah," after the appeal to the reception and transmission of the Torah given by God to Moses at Sinai in two media, written ("the Old Testament") and oral (now: the Mishnah, Talmuds, Midrash-compilations, and the like), is best studied through its normative statements. Those statements concern what people are supposed to do, that is, address correct behavior and therefore take the form of law. I maintain, therefore, that if we wish to understand this Judaism, we begin our work in the categories set down by that Judaism, which are categories of norms of behavior, and, further, we explore the inner structure and meaning of the law as statements of how things are to be done. Not only so, but I also hold that an appreciation for the modes of discourse, the way important ideas are set forward and analyzed, allows us to see that the authorship of the Mishnah, showing the way for all subsequent intellectuals within their ongoing formation of Judaism, took up fundamental questions of intellectual life and of the right ordering of human society.

The essays themselves are divided into two groups. In the first set I set forward the issue (Chapter One) and the evidence in the details of law for sustained discourse concerning issues of theology (Chapters Two and Three) and of philosophy (Chapters Four through Seven). Since in my forty-three volumes of the *History of the Mishnaic Law* I had already reached and set forth precisely the issues as I lay them out here, although not commonly specifying matters as I do here, I note how little of my *ouevre* has been purused by those who condemn it, such as Maccoby, Urbach, and Sanders (dealt with in Chapter One), who condemn it. There are substantial points of disagreement between me and them, and these concern matters of fact and interpretation, use of evidence and reconstruction of evidence into intelligible accounts of how things were, how people conceived the world. The only form of public discourse that is acceptable in the academy of the West is an address to issues, *sine ira et studio,* and that form defines my discourse too. But scholarship goes forward where it is supposed to, which is in the intellect and sensibility of thoughtful people, and while for a while politics may seem to settle who sits next to whom at the table, in fact, over long spans of time, in matters of learning politics makes no difference whatsoever. For in learning power is not in the politics of preferment and prejudice but in the power of the intellect. In the end, minds are made up by sound method and well-crafted argument, evidence set forth clearly and propositions laid out rationally and accessibly. I have no doubt about the future of learning in the field in which I have worked, and, if truth be told, I have few regrets even about the shape of the present.

In the second set, I place these papers into the context of my on-going research program, which, having begun in 1958 with my first sustained work on the *haburah* ("fellowship") in ancient Judaism and then on Yohanan ben Zakkai, now enters its fourth decade. The inclusion of Part Two is readily explained, not only in terms of my own intellectual autobiography, but especially in the framework of the coming chapters that I plan to write in that autobiography. At this turning, when my interests develop for an account of the social science of Judaism in its first stages, I think it worthwhile to tell people where I have been and where I am heading. That is to say, I am in process of setting forth a sustained picture of the philosophy, politics, and economics of Judaism first of the initial system, in the Mishnah, then of the successor, somewhat asymmetrical system, in the Yerushalmi and its associated writings, particularly Genesis Rabbah and Leviticus Rabbah, and finally, in the classical statement, the Bavli and its associated writings. The seventh paper is an effort to hold together a sequence of scholarly careers, now done. The eighth paper, written with my colleague and teacher and intellectual companion and co-worker, Calvin Goldscheider, spells out a yet-broader program for the study of the social foundations of Judaism. In an age in which Jews go forward in the building of a political entity, the Jewish state, and in the lands of the diaspora in the construction of communities that accomplish common goals and draw upon common resources, the relevance of research into how in the history of Judaism people have conceived and thought through the social issues of their shared religious life is self-evident.

JACOB NEUSNER

July 28, 1988
Celebrating my fifty-sixth birthday
Program in Judaic Studies
Brown University
Providence, Rhode Island U.S.A.

Introduction

What Is at Stake in the Debate on
Whether to Represent Judaism as
a Religion of Pots and Pans
or as a Religion of Sanctification and Salvation?

The central vision of the Mishnah sees humanity as formed in God's image and made after God's likeness. God is holy in heaven, and it is the task of Israel, God's Holy People, to make itself holy and to sanctify life here on earth. The human being, "in our image, after our likeness," "male and female created God them," is counterpart and partner and creation. For like God the human being has power to make worlds, in the conceptual language of the Mishnah, has the power over the status and condition of creation to put everything in its proper place, to call everything by its rightful name.

And that brings us to the meeting of theology and philosophy in the Mishnah's judgment of the nature of the power of the human being in relationship to God. The human being and God are the two beings that possess the active will. The human being is like God in that both God and the human being not only do, but form attitudes and intentions. That theory of the human being, a philosophical issue concerning the nature of will and attitude, meets the theory of God's relationship with humanity, a theological concern concerning the correspondence of God's and humanity's inner being. And all of this deep thought is precipitated by the critical issue facing Israel, the Jewish people, defeated on the battlefield and deprived of its millennial means of serving God in the Temple in Jerusalem: what, now, can a human being do?

The setting in which a Judaism laid its heaviest stress upon sanctification has then to be specified. The Mishnah is a document of the second century, written in the aftermath of the destruction of the Temple of Jerusalem in 70, and the failure of a war fought three generations later to rebuild the temple. Now with Jerusalem inaccessible to Jews, the locus of holiness for the preceding millennium had been closed off. Addressing an age of defeat and, in consequence of the permanent closure of the Temple in Jerusalem, despair, the Mishnah's framers' principal message, which makes the Judaism of this document and of its social components distinctive and cogent, is that the human being is at the center of creation, the head of all creatures upon earth, corresponding to God in Heaven, in whose image the human being is made.

The way in which the Mishnah makes this simple and fundamental statement is illustrated on nearly every page of the document. It is to impute the power, effected through an act of sheer human will or intentionality, to the human being to inaugurate and initiate those corresponding processes, sanctification and uncleanness, which play so critical a role in the Mishnah's account of reality. The will of the human being, expressed through the deed of the human being, is the active power in the world. As matters would be phrased in later writings, "Nothing whatsoever impedes the human will." But, of course, looking back on the age at hand, we know that everything did. The "Israel" of the Mishnah never achieved its stated goals, for example, in once more setting up a government of priests and kings, in once more regaining that order and stasis that, in mind at least, people imagined had once prevailed. But of course, the key is in the "once more," for these were things that, in point of fact, had not been at all. The will for "once more" encompassed nowhere and never.

So, stated briefly, the question taken up by the Mishnah and answered by Judaism is, What can a person do? And the answer laid down by the Mishnah is, the human being, through will and deed, is master of this world, the measure of all things. But that world of all things of which the human being is the measure is within: in intellect, imagination, sentient reality. Since when the Mishnah thinks of a human being, its authorship means the Israelite, who is the subject and actor of its system, the statement is clear. This is the Judaism that identifies at the center of things Israel, the Israelite person, who can do what he or she wills. In the aftermath of the two wars and defeats of millennial proportions, the message of the Mishnah cannot have proved more pertinent – or poignant and tragic. And yet the power of the message shaped the entire history of Israel, the Jewish People, and of Judaism, from then to now. For Israel, the Jewish People, understood as the answer to the ineluctable questions of frailty and defeat in society and death for everyone who walked the earth the self-evident truth that everything that matters depends upon the human will and intention: we are what in mind and imagination and sentiment and heart we hope, believe, insist, above all by act of will persist in being. So much for what I conceive to be the central concern of the Mishnah, the first document of the Judaism of the Dual Torah.

Others have seen that Judaism in a different way. They have found in the minutia of legal discourse through which the authorship of the Mishnah delivers its message not a system of sanctification, such as I have located therein, but merely an obsessive formalism. Accordingly, they have represented Judaism, that is, the Judaism that begins, beyond the Hebrew Scriptures, with the Mishnah, by drawing a contrast between legalism and formalism, on the one side, and the law of love, on the other. Citing the negative writing of Judaism by Schuerer, Billerbeck, and others in the context of his critique of some of my books, Hyam Maccoby states:

> The work of Schürer, Ferdinand Weber, and Billerbeck, representing rabbinic theology as an anxious, obsessional ritualism, was countered by George Foot Moore, James Parkes, and E.P. Sanders. However, the work of these fair-minded Christian scholars has been dismissed with scorn and abuse by Neusner, whose writings are already being quoted in support of a return to the position of German anti-Jewish scholarship that "the Pharisees were interested mainly in ritual purity." This is not merely a recondite dispute among scholars. Neusner's professed wonder that anyone should take the matter so seriously is disingenuous. If, as seemed likely until quite recently, Neusner's work were to be accepted at his own valuation as the only objective and scientific approach to rabbinic studies, this would represent a major defeat for Judaism – not in any fundamentalist sense, but in the sense that the Christian claim that the New Testament is the true heir and continuation of prophetic concepts of justice and mercy, rather than Pharisaism and rabbinic Judaism, would be vindicated.

I believe that the embarrassment at results of my research that is expressed by Maccoby and others – results showing that the rabbinic traditions about the Pharisees did concern, in important proportion, matters of cultic cleanness ("ritual purity") – misses the important point made by those rules that referred to the eating of meals as though one were a priest in the Temple.

That explains why my purpose in the essays collected here is to explain precisely how the authorship of the Mishnah conducts its public discourse, so that people will grasp the theology and philosophy implicit in the legal discussions of that important document. Then, I believe, we shall learn how to hear, within somewhat recondite discussions, how the authorship of the Mishnah has made its profound statement and its definitive judgments on issues of broad interest and general intelligibility. True, as we shall see, they talk about humble things, excretions, produce, petty criminals, mixtures of this and that, matters of doubt about nothing of consequence. But, as I shall show in these papers, at stake are fundamental principles of theology and philosophy. When, therefore, we understand how the Mishnah's authorship gives voice to its conceptions, we shall grasp why a religion that talks about pots and pans in fact addresses sanctification and salvation.

Why does it matter to make this simple point, that embedded in detail are grand concerns? It is because a profound misconstrual of the modes of discourse in the Mishnah and in successor statements within the Judaism beginning with the Mishnah has yielded a preposterous caricature of that Judaism. Because, as a matter of fact, sages in the Mishnah do not pursue the thematic program deemed appropriate by circles of Judaic and Protestant scholarship in religion, these sages are misrepresented in one of two ways. Either, as in the instance of Protestant Evangelical scholarship, they are portrayed as a bunch of nit-pickers and petty formalists, who care more for what one has for lunch than for what God wants of humanity. Or, as in the instance of Reform and Conservative Judaic scholars and Christian apologists for Judaism, they are represented as people who really were interested in precisely what Protestant scholarship thinks should have interested them. Then any account by a Jew or by a gentile of the things they said that takes seriously the program they pursued, in the language and issues that they produced, is deemed betrayal and pandering to the gentiles, if by a Jew, or mere anti-Semitism, if by a gentile.

Accordingly, Reform Judaic and Protestant Evangelical scholarship in Britain and Germany have rejected pictures of that Judaism that emphasize the importance of norms of behavior and of belief and characterized as obsessive ritualism and formalism that picture (in the case of Reform Judaism) of that religion (in the case of Protestant New Testament scholarship). But that scholarship, represented in the recent past by Hyam Maccoby (to whom we shall return in the Introduction and Chapter One) errs by utterly misunderstanding the point of public discourse in the Mishnah and its successor-writings and by a profound misreading of those writings. For if we take seriously the serious issues embedded in discourse about pots and pans, instead of dismissing as (mere) ritualism and formalism concern for what and how we eat and other humble matters, we discover discourse on perennial issues of intellect: philosophical questions, theological concerns. Rejecting the law as a source and expression of theology misses what is at stake in the concrete expression, in dietary rules for instance, of the theology of sanctification at hand. Reform Judaism, like the Protestant critics of the Pharisees whom Maccoby rightly condemns, exhibit only limited appreciation for expression, in rite, of what people hold to be right beliefs about God and what God is, about humanity and what we represent, above all, about how, in the humblest matters, inheres the presence of the commanding God of Sinai. To turn matters around, if justice and mercy, holiness and sanctification, do not take the form we can grasp in the everyday life of kitchen, bedroom, study, and workplace, then where shall we sanctify our lives? For that is where we live.

When Protestant apologists for Judaism misrepresent the Judaism to conform to what (their version of) Protestant theology approves, and when Reform Judaic polemicists criticize a Judaism that does care about pots and pans, they frame issues to conform to their construction of contemporary religion. They do not allow us to take seriously and with full appreciation the Judaism of the Mishnah and its successor-writings. My sense is that at stake in much of the Protestant critique of Judaism of the past hundred years has been an attack on Roman Catholic Christianity. Of course, at issue for the Reform and Conservative Judaic critique of portraits of a Judaism of works as well as faith (to borrow Lutheran language), that is, of pots and pans as well as of justice and mercy, is Orthodox Judaism, in all its forms, which, now as in the past, believes God cares for what goes into my mouth and also for what comes out of my mouth.

Now what if Schuerer, Weber, Billerbeck, as much as Sanders, Urbach, and Maccoby, have grossly misunderstood both the modes of discourse of the legal writings of Judaism and also the character of a religion of sanctification? If for instance we recognized the issues inhering in concern for "ritual purity," which is to say, for sanctification, should we so readily dismiss as "anxious, obsessional ritualism" what in fact was a profound exploration of ontology? I am inclined to think that a clear understanding of how the Mishnah undertakes to discuss the great issues of human existence will move us past issues as now framed. For the very categories "justice and mercy" frame discourse wrongly, when, to begin with, people are concerned with serving God, who, of course, they understand to be just and merciful; but to the service of God through everyday life, other categories prove critical as well, and sanctification in the model of the priest in the Temple forms a mode of service to God not to be dismissed.

I find strikingly pertinent to the debate at hand William Scott Green's comments, in the same symposium in *Midstream* in which Maccoby's remarks appear, about the clearly apologetic character of the approach of colleagues who see things as Maccoby does:

> From the perspective of ethnic Jewish Studies, materials are deemed interesting because they are Jewish. This school of thought is marked by a fundamentally romantic view of all things it defines as Jewish.

Ethnic scholarship tends to be avenging and celebratory. Ethnic education, at whatever level, makes learning into a ritual of attachment to the heroic people. Ethnic intellectual discourse tends to be restricted, often in Hebrew, and directed primarily to those within the ethnic group or those who share its romantic suppositions.

In short, ethnic Jewish Studies is a self-validating enterprise designed to preserve Jewish distinctiveness. Ethnic Jewish scholarship serve a powerful communal purpose and therefore is highly charged. It aims to teach the Jews about themselves and thereby to create a usable Jewish past, a workable Jewish present, and a viable Jewish future. Within this framework, reasoned intellectual dissent is all too often ignored or censored, or discounted and dismissed, as a form of disloyalty and disrespect.

Disciplinary Jewish Studies share none of these aims and suppositions. They apply to Jewish sources and materials the standardized inquiries, analytical criteria, and Cartesian skepticism of university studies in the humanities and social sciences. These disciplines attempt to address common questions to various texts, cultures, and societies and thus deny special privilege to any of them. They reject in principle private, self-validating worlds of experience whose meaning is pertinent, and can be transmitted, only to initiates. Within a disciplinary framework, the study of discrete Jewish materials is shaped by general questions about human imagination and behavior, questions extrinsic to particular Jewish needs, concerns, and preoccupations.

These descriptions are caricatures, Weberian "pure types," and no one in Jewish Studies conforms fully to either. But more deliberately than any other, Jacob Neusner has appropriated the disciplinary agenda and applied it relentlessly and methodically to the classics of Judaism. His work has subverted nearly every supposition of ethnic scholarship on the Talmud and cognate writings and has ended the academic political domination of their study by a few seminary and Israeli professors. The results and reactions have been chronicled in the pages of this magazine.

There is a surrealism to the entire dispute. Ethnic and disciplinary Jewish Studies operate in incongruous worlds, have incompatible motivations, and address disparate constituencies. The dispute between them is bitter because it is pointless. Not enough is shared between them to allow the possibility of communication, much less persuasion.

Recognition of the blatantly apologetic purpose in Maccoby's critique should not obscure the deeper problem, which is the difficulty in communication and persuasion. Should I not simply write off the other side as beyond the possibility of communication? The rules of the academy deny that option.

For at stake are not partisan politics of apologetics but issues of description, analysis, interpretation. Even though framed in an inappropriate way, the issues of use of evidence and correct category-formation, that is, analysis and interpretation, respectively, have to be joined in the setting of actual evidence, sources, or, in my language, description. I cannot dismiss, as do others, merely because I find self-evidently wrong the positions I reject. It is my task both to criticize what others have done and also to compose the correct construction, out of evidence, of the intellectual system and structure at hand. That is to say, my task must always be to describe, analyze, and interpret evidence. What validates that conviction is the axiom of academic discourse, which is that reason does prevail, and that critical thought does dispose of all questions. That, in a thirty-year career, I have come this far in my sustained inquiry into the study of religion and society for the case of Judaism, attests to the sustaining power of the academy, that is to say, of intellect in its only valid form today.

Accordingly, I present these papers because I hope, yet, to communicate, through concrete cases, how weighty a burden of theological meaning is born by the law, and why if one wishes to represent the Judaism of the Dual Torah, then and now, in accord with its authoritative sources, one must deal with those sources, in their categories, following their issues, and for their purposes. For that is how that Judaism speaks.

Part One

ESSAYS ON MODES OF DISCOURSE

Chapter One

The Debate on Pots and Pans

The contemporary chapter in the long-standing debate on whether or not Judaism is a religion of pots and pans was opened (and mostly written) by me in two ways. The first was in my reviews of books about ancient Judaism, particularly as represented in Rabbinic sources, by Ephraim E. Urbach, Hebrew University of Jerusalem, Edward P. Sanders, Oxford University, and the second, in my account of the Rabbinic traditions on the Pharisees. In the former, which I shall revisit presently, I condemned as essentially beside the point accounts of the Judaism portrayed in the Mishnah and related writings. In my view Urbach and Sanders misrepresented what matters in the Judaism they claimed to describe (there was no analysis or interpretation in either work). I do not think either one of them grasps the sources as they should be understood. In the latter, I set forth, through a sustained account of evidence, what a particular body of writings said mattered in that same Judaism.

At stake in the debate is whether or not the Judaism portrayed by the Mishnah and successor-documents concerned Providence, good and evil, life after death, and divine justice and mercy, as Maccoby, Urbach, Sanders, and the others think should form the main points of interest, or whether it focused upon pots and pans, that is to say, details of the norms of everyday conduct in humble matters. The issues are matters of the religious study of religion as well as the theological study of religion and contemporary apologetics. Contemporary apologetics for Judaism accepts the Protestant Evangelical reading of what constitutes a suitable religion and then claims that Judaism is a suitable religion (in context, I suppose, *salonfahig*). The theological study of religion insists that issues of dogmatic theology, historical theology, even systematic theology, frame the agenda for scholarship on the description, analysis, and interpretation of a religion. The religious study of religion allows the religion at hand to speak in its own terms and context, but also attempts to interpret that religion in terms and context intelligible here and now.

If apologetics predominate, then scholarship must take up a position outside the door. For as soon as considerations extrinsic to data and their interpretation intervene, no serious learning can sustain itself. If the theological study of religion defines issues, then data to begin with must be selected and organized by categories extrinsic to those data. Here too, description of data as they are, rather than as they have been reformed for a different sort of reading, cannot succeed. The first approach imputes meaning to evidence prior to the reading of the evidence; assesses stakes not intrinsic in the evidence; insists upon considerations of contemporary debate clearly anachronistic in the setting of the evidence. The second approach invokes principles of category-formation that derive from not the here and now of evidence but the world-beyond of religious belief, systematically set forth. Only the third approach proves viable for the academy, which asks this-worldly questions about evidence read as testimonies to this worldly activities. The difficulty in debating with the apologists and theological enemies of Judaism alike is that there is no shared framework of thought. Debate, therefore, has consisted of an exchange of uncomprehending opinions in an atmosphere of sustained nastiness, *odium theologicum* in its full and most repulsive stench.

The religious study of religion defines the sole arena for debate within the academy, and matters are in my view best worked out by appeal to considerations of, first, use of historical evidence, and, second, correct category-formation. If we read the evidence properly and if, further, we form our descriptive categories in the right way, then we emerge with my account of the Judaism of the Mishnah, and not the accounts of Urbach and Sanders (and the many others before them who read the same evidence in the same way to produce the same results, or, *mutatis mutandis,* results of a precisely opposite character).

The issue was raised by a British polemicist of Reform Judaism and scholar of medieval Jewish affairs, Hyam Maccoby. He objected to my results in that work on the Rabbinic traditions about the Pharisees before 70, though he did not review that book. In reviewing my *Judaism: The Evidence of the Mishnah,* where the issue of the Pharisees before 70 is not raised at all, he said so. As is clear, in my *Rabbinic Traditions about the Pharisees before 70* (which this colleague did not review), I had found that a sizable portion of those traditions concerned cultic issues of eating ordinary food in a state of priestly purity required for the eating of Holy Things of the altar of the Lord in the Temple in Jerusalem, on the one side, and carefully preparing food in accord with God's revealed laws concerning tithing, on the other. Since these rules, and their considerable position in the Rabbinic traditions on the Pharisees, corresponded to reports in

Matthew, Mark, and Luke, about the Pharisees, colleagues in New Testament studies found considerable interest in them. In my view, an interest in living everyday life as though one were a priest in the Temple represented, and today for observant Jews represents, a profound religious affirmation. In the laws of the Mishnah and related writings, therefore, I found not mere formalism, surely not a religion of pots and pans, but a sustained and courageous human aspiration for sanctification: for making the human being holy, as God is holy, and through the rules for cultic sanctification that God had set forth for the priests.

The clearest objection to my findings on the importance of purity in Pharisaism, which I take to form the source for the centrality of sanctification in Judaism, comes in the remarks of Hyam Maccoby in a symposium on my *Judaism: The Evidence of the Mishnah*. There he states,

> Jacob Neusner's remarks in reply to my essay, "Jacob Neusner's Mishnah" (*Midstream*, May, 1984) are very much off the point. I did *not* object to his treating the Mishnah on its own terms, in isolation from later commentaries on the Mishnah (i.e, the Talmudim and their medieval exegesis). This obviously needs to be done, and Maimonides gave a good example of how to do it. My objection was that Neusner was attempting to interpret the Mishnah in isolation from the aggadah (non-legal material found in all rabbinic literature, including the Mishnah itself).

> Neusner argues that since the Mishnah has its own style and program, nothing outside it is relevant to explaining it. This is an obvious fallacy. The Mishnah, as a digest, in the main, of the legal (Halakhic) aspect of rabbinic Judaism, necessarily has its own style and program. But to treat it as something intended to be a comprehensive compendium of the Oral Torah is simply to beg the question. Neusner does not answer the point, put to him by E. P. Sanders and myself, that the liturgy, being presupposed by the Mishnah, is surely relevant to the Mishnah's exegesis. Nor does he answer the charge that he ignores the aggadic material within the Mishnah itself, e.g., *Avot;* or explain why the copious aggadic material found in roughly contemporaneous works should be regarded as irrelevant. Instead, he insists that he is right to carry out the highly artificial project of deliberately closing his eyes to all aggadic material, and trying to explain the Mishnah without it.

> This leads to absurdities, such as saying that the Mishnah is not much concerned with justice, or with repentance, or with the Messiah. It also leads to Neusner's endorsement of 19th-century German anti-Jewish scholarship, the aim of which was to substantiate the New Testament charge against the Pharisees, "You pay tithes of mint and dill and cummin; but you have overlooked the weightier demands of the Law, justice, mercy and good faith" (Matthew 23:23). Neusner attempts to obfuscate the issue by expressing great admiration for the

Mishnah, and this will no doubt impress people who accept his protestations at their face value. But he admires the Mishnah for the very things that the New Testament alleges *against* the Pharisees: for formalism, attention to petty legalistic detail, and for a structuralist patterning of reality in terms of "holiness" rather than of morality, justice, and love of neighbor.

The work of Schürer, Ferdinand Weber, and Billerbeck, representing rabbinic theology as an anxious, obsessional ritualism, was countered by George Foot Moore, James Parkes, and E.P. Sanders. However, the work of these fair-minded Christian scholars has been dismissed with scorn and abuse by Neusner, whose writings are already being quoted in support of a return to the position of German anti-Jewish scholarship that "the Pharisees were interested mainly in ritual purity." This is not merely a recondite dispute among scholars. Neusner's professed wonder that anyone should take the matter so seriously is disingenuous. If, as seemed likely until quite recently, Neusner's work were to be accepted at his own valuation as the only objective and scientific approach to rabbinic studies, this would represent a major defeat for Judaism – not in any fundamentalist sense, but in the sense that the Christian claim that the New Testament is the true heir and continuation of prophetic concepts of justice and mercy, rather than Pharisaism and rabbinic Judaism, would be vindicated.

This characterization of Judaism as a religion that concerns itself with "an anxious, obsessional ritualism" represents Maccoby's evaluation of the law. For the Mishnah and its successor writings form a corpus of sustained inquiry into details of the law, and a fourth of that law concerns cultic cleanness, another sixth, rules of ritual tithing, and another sixth, rules of the Temple cult. Clearly, a vast proportion of the evidence concerning the Judaism of the Mishnah consists in discourse about ritual, temple, cult, purity, sacrifice, – pots and pans.

But the traits of mind and heart characterized as "obsessional ritualism" stand for a profound convictions concerning the nature of God and the world and the relationship of the human being to the holy. Maccoby and the others for whom he speaks simply have misunderstood the modes of discourse by which sages carry on thought and intellectual inquiry. They consequently misrepresent the evidence and misconstrue the stakes. They criticize a portrait of the Judaism of the Mishnah and related writings, because they do not like the configuration of that portrait. Not only so, but they impose upon the Judaism at hand the values and conceptions of another religion entirely, which is, the Protestant Evangelical Christianity of German Protestant theological faculties of the nineteenth and twentieth centuries, faculties that, in scholarly form, carried on Luther's critique of Roman Catholic Christianity. Speaking of Judaism, they mean the Pope. Maccoby and Sanders, in their "defense" of Judaism, judge

Judaism in the court at which Martin Luther is the presiding judge. But in that court, a religion of works and faith, of tradition and also Scripture, is bound to be condemned.

Still, the argument need not exchange theological imprecations. By the rules of the academy, it can be reconstructed on the basis of sound humanistic modes of inquiry. Specifically, we can attempt to understand discourse within the rules of discourse set forth therein. We can listen to what people are saying, without rejecting out of hand the topics they discuss. And we can, further, try to make sense of the principles at issue, gain access to the profound questions of human and social concern, that come to concrete analysis and debate in the odd form in which, in the case of the Mishnah and related writings, questions are analyzed. Then a religion in which ordinary people aspire to sustain their lives in accord with the rules governing the Temple priests may enjoy admiration and respect of those who grasp the full meaning of the sanctification of life, not the scornful (and apologetic) rejection of those who deem a life made holy by faithful loyalty to God's will, even as to pots and pans, to be mere " formalism, attention to petty legalistic detail." The issue is explicitly joined when Maccoby states explicitly, "But he admires the Mishnah for the very things that the New Testament alleges *against* the Pharisees: for formalism, attention to petty legalistic detail, and for a structuralist patterning of reality in terms of "holiness" rather than of morality, justice, and love of neighbor."

Let me now turn to the two points at stake in the debate with theology and apologetics. The first, with theology, concerns category-formation, and for that purpose, I revisit my review of Ephraim E. Urbach, *The Sages. Their Concepts and Beliefs* (Translated from the Hebrew by Israel Abrahams. Jerusalem: The Magnes Press, The Hebrew University, 1975. Two volumes – I. Text: pp. xxii and 692. II. Notes: pp. 383). Urbach claims "to describe the concepts and beliefs of the Tannaim and Amoraim and to elucidate them against the background of their actual life and environment." The work has been described by M.D. Heer in precisely those terms (*Encyclopaedia Judaica* 16:4): "He [Urbach] outlines the views of the rabbis on the important theological issues such as creation, providence, and the nature of man. In this work Urbach synthesizes the voluminous literature on these subjects and presents the views of the talmudic authorities." The topics are as follows: belief in one God; the presence of God in the world; "nearness and distance – Omnipresent and heaven;" the power of God; magic and miracle; the power of the divine name; the celestial retinue; creation; man; providence; written law and oral law; the commandments; acceptance of the yoke of the kingdom of heaven; sin, reward, punishment, suffering, etc.; the people of Israel and its sages, a chapter which encompasses the election of Israel, the status of the sages in the days of the Hasmoneans, Hillel, the regime of the sages after the destruction of the Temple, and so on; and redemption.

What is pertinent here is Urbach's plan of category-formation. We need not dwell on the obvious problems involved in his selection of sources, which is both narrowly canonical and somewhat confusing. Rather, let us ask, does the world-view of the talmudic sages emerge in a way which the ancient sages themselves would have recognized? That question directs our attention to the categories that Urbach has selected for the organization and representation of his data (however poorly selected as to sources). From the viewpoint of their organization and description of reality, their world-view, it is certain that the sages would have organized their card-files quite differently. We know that is the case because we do not have, among the chapters before us, a single one which focuses upon the theme of one of the orders, let alone tractates, within which the rabbis divided and presented their various statements on reality, e.g., Seeds, the material basis of life; Seasons, the organization and differentiation of time; Women, the status of the individual; Damages, the conduct of civil life including government; Holy Things, the material service of God; and Purities, the immaterial base of divine reality in this world. The matter concerns not merely the superficial problem of organizing vast quantities of data. The talmudic rabbis left a large and exceedingly complex, well-integrated legacy of law. Clearly, it is through that legacy that they intended to make their fundamental statements upon the organization and meaning of reality. An account of their concepts and beliefs which ignores nearly the whole of the halakhah surely is slightly awry.

In fairness to Urbach, I must stress that he shows himself well aware of the centrality of law ("*halakhah*") in the expression of the world-view of the talmudic rabbis. He correctly criticizes his predecessors for neglecting the subject and observes, "The Halakha does not openly concern itself with beliefs and concepts; it determines, in practice, the way in which one should walk... Nevertheless beliefs and concepts lie at the core of many Halakhot; only their detection requires exhaustive study of the history of the Halakha combined with care to avoid fanciful conjectures and unfounded explanations." Urbach occasionally does introduce halakhic materials. But, as is clear, the fundamental structure of his account of talmudic theology is formed in accord not with the equivalent structure of the Talmud – the *halakhah* – but with the topics and organizing rubrics treated by all nineteenth- and twentieth-century Protestant historical studies of theology: God, ethics, revelation, and the like. That those studies are never far from mind is illustrated by Urbach's extensive discussion of whether talmudic ethics was theonomous or autonomous (I, pp. 320ff.), an issue important only from the viewpoint of nineteenth-century Jewish ethical thought and its response to Kant. But Urbach's discussion on that matter is completely persuasive, stating what is certainly the last word on the subject. He can hardly be blamed for criticizing widely held and wrong opinions.

The use of evidence in the setting of flawed category-formation deserves attention. Urbach's allegation that he reads the sources historically and not theologically is fantastic, because his reading of the sources "historically" is uncritical. That is to say, he believes everything the sources allege, and hence his "historical" account is a mere paraphrase of sources and not a sifting of evidence with that Cartesian skepticism to which William Green referred in the passage cited above. True, on many specific points, Urbach contributes sporadic philological observations, interesting opinions and judgments as to the lateness of one saying as against the antiquity of another, subjective opinions on what is more representative or reliable than something else. If these opinions are not systematic and if they reveal no uniform criterion, sustainedly applied to all sources, they nonetheless derive from a mind of immense learning. But that is merely adventitious.

The simple fact is that Urbach, like the Jerusalem School of Historical Scholarship in Judaism in general, gullibly accepts as fact everything the sources say, except what, for reasons of his own, he rejects. If a source – any source, however many centuries later in redaction – says a given authority made a statement, Urbach takes that allegation as fact and uses the statement as evidence of the position of that authority, in the time and place in which that authority lived. If a story is told, then the story happened just as it is told, except in some detail Urbach, again for subjective and not systematic reasons, has decided is not true. But we must ask ourselves, if a saying is assigned to an ancient authority, how do we know that he really said it? If a story is told, how do we know that the events the story purports to describe actually took place? And if not, just what are we to make of said story and saying for historical purposes? Further, if we have a saying attributed to a first-century authority in a document generally believed to have been redacted five hundred or a thousand years later, how do we know that the attribution of the saying is valid, and that the saying informs us of the state of opinion in the first century, not only in the sixth or eleventh in which it was written down and obviously believed true and authoritative? Do we still hold, as an axiom of historical scholarship, *ein muqdam umeuhar* ["temporal considerations do not apply"] – in the Talmud?! And again, do not the sayings assigned to a first-century authority, redacted in documents deriving from the early third century, possess greater credibility than those first appearing in documents redacted in the fifth, tenth, or even fifteenth centuries? Should we not, on the face of it, distinguish between more and less reliable materials? The well-known tendency of medieval writers to put their opinions into the mouths of the ancients, as in the case of the Zohar, surely warns us to be cautious about using documents redacted, even formulated, five hundred or a thousand or more years after the events of which they speak. Urbach ignores all of these questions and the work of those who ask them. But for our purposes, the main point is that his category-formation expresses a naive and anachronistic judgment of how sages thought and of what they thought about.

Urbach's work, as I said, in the balance brings to their full realization the methods and suppositions of the past hundred years. I cannot imagine that anyone again will want, from these perspectives, to approach the task of describing all of "the concepts and beliefs of the Tannaim and Amoraim," of elucidating all of them "against the background of their actual life and environment." So far as the work can be done in accord with established methods, here it has been done very competently indeed. But when we contemplate the gross errors in category-formation, we have, as in the case of Maccoby and (as we shall see in a moment, Sanders) to revert to the blatantly apologetic purposes that sustain the work:

> The aim of our work is to give an epitome of the beliefs and concepts of the Sages as the history of a struggle to instill religious and ethical ideals into the everyday life of the community and the individual, while preserving at the same time the integrity and unity of the nation and directing its way in this world as a preparation for another world that is wholly perfect.... Their eyes and their hearts were turned Heavenward, yet one type was not to be found among them...namely the mystic who seeks to liberate himself from his ego and in doing so is preoccupied with himself alone. They saw their mission in work here in the world below. There were Sages who inclined to extremism in their thoughts and deeds, and there were those who preached the way of compromise, which they did not, however, determine on the basis of convenience. Some were severe and exacting, while others demonstrated an extreme love of humanity and altruism. The vast majority of them recognized the complexities of life with its travail and joy, its happiness and tragedy, and this life served them also as a touchstone for their beliefs and concepts.

While the values expressed here may well conform to the world-view of the National Religious Party of the State of Israel, which put Urbach up for the presidency of the State, I cannot say. But they certainly address conceptions, issues, and categories for which, in the literature at hand, it is extremely difficult to find counterparts. Accordingly, whatever Urbach says in his description of the Judaism of sages may well be so, but it remains to be demonstrated as historical fact in the way in which contemporary critical historians generally demonstrate matters of fact. It requires analysis and argument in the undogmatic and unapologetic spirit characteristic of contemporary studies in the history of ideas and of religions.

My second complaint with theological apologetics, besides the enormous flaws in category-formation, draws me to revisit my review of Edward P. Sanders's account of Rabbinic Judaism. For Sanders's effort at an apologetics for the sages of Rabbinic Judaism begins in his affirmation that a suitable religion must concern itself with weightier matters of the Torah than merely tithing dill and cummin. He therefore proposes to apologize for the many legal passages produced by the sages at hand and explains how they really were talking about other things than the things that they appeared to be talking about, so that theirs was a religion of, if not justice and mercy, then at least "covenantal nomism," which is (to his mind at least) different from, and surely better than, a religion of pots and pans. His apologetic therefore begins with an affirmation of a pattern of religion that derives from a theology of a religion that wishes to stand in judgment upon other religions and their theologies. In this regard Sanders has found a suitable voice in Maccoby.

In his *Paul and Palestinian Judaism: A Comparison of Patterns of Religion* (London: SCM Press, 1977. Pp. xviii+627), Sanders describes "Palestinian Judaism" through three bodies of evidence: Tannaitic literature, the Dead Sea Scrolls, and Apocrypha and Pseudepigrapha, in that order. I of course deal only with the treatment of the first. To each set of sources, Sanders (like Urbach, Moore, and everyone else) addresses questions of systematic theology: election and covenant, obedience and disobedience, reward and punishment and the world to come, salvation by membership in the covenant and atonement, proper religious behavior (so for Tannaitic sources); covenant and the covenant people, election and predestination, the commandments, fulfillment and transgression, atonement (Dead Sea Scrolls); election and covenant, the fate of the individual Israelite, atonement, commandments, the basis of salvation, the gentiles, repentance and atonement, the righteousness of God (Apocrypha and Pseudepigrapha, meaning, specifically: Ben Sira, I Enoch, Jubilees, Psalms of Solomon, IV Ezra). There follows a brief concluding chapter (pp. 419-28, summarizing pp. 1-418). So far as the book has a polemical charge, it is to demonstrate (pp. 420-21) that "the fundamental nature of the covenant conception... largely accounts for the relative scarcity of appearances of the term 'covenant' in Rabbinic literature. The covenant was presupposed, and the Rabbinic discussions were largely directed toward the question of how to fulfill the covenantal obligations." This proposition is then meant to disprove the conviction ("all but universally held") that Judaism is a degeneration of the Old Testament view: "The once noble idea of covenant as offered by God's grace and obedience as the consequence of that gracious gift degenerated into the idea of petty legalism, according to which one had to earn the mercy of God by minute observance of irrelevant ordinances."

Sanders' search for patterns yields a common pattern in "covenantal nomism," which, in general, emerges as follows (p. 422):

> The "pattern" or "structure" of covenantal nomism is this: (1) God has chosen Israel and (2) given the law. The law implies both (3) God's promise to maintain the election and (4) the requirement to obey. (5) God rewards obedience and punishes transgression. (6) The law provides for means of atonement, and atonement results in (7) maintenance or re-establishment of the covenantal relationship. (8) All those who are maintained in the covenant by obedience, atonement, and God's mercy belong to the group which will be saved. An important interpretation of the first and last points is that election and ultimately salvation are considered to be by God's mercy rather than human achievement.

Anyone familiar with Jewish liturgy will be at home in that statement. Even though the evidence on the character of Palestinian Judaism derives from diverse groups and reaches us through various means, Sanders argues that covenantal nomism was "the basic type of religion known by Jesus and presumably by Paul...." And again, "covenantal nomism must have been the general type of religion prevalent in Palestine before the destruction of the Temple."[1]

The stated purposes require attention. Sanders states at the outset (p. xii) that he has six aims: (1) to consider methodologically how to compare two (or more) related but different religions; (2) to destroy the view of Rabbinic Judaism which is still prevalent in much, perhaps most, New Testament scholarship; (3) to establish a different view of Rabbinic Judaism; (4) to argue a case concerning Palestinian Judaism (that is, Judaism as reflected in material of Palestinian provenance) as a whole; (5) to argue for a certain understanding of Paul; and (6) to carry out a comparison of Paul and Palestinian Judaism. Numbers (4) and (6),

---

[1]So far as I can see, Sanders is reticent about the meaning of "religion" in this context, and other "types of religion" which are not to be found in Palestine before A.D. 70, but which might have been present there, also are not defined or discussed. I find a general lack of precision in terminology. But Sanders' purpose is not to contribute to the theoretical literature of religious studies.

he immediately adds, "constitute the general aim of the book, while I hope to accomplish the others along the way." Since more than a third of the work is devoted to Rabbinic Judaism, Sanders certainly cannot be accused of treating his second goal casually. As is clear, Sanders has allowed "most" New Testament scholarship to define the issues, and, as an apologist for (a) Judaism, he has properly accepted the discipline of his chosen craft. But, as I shall show, this leads him to distort and misinterpret the evidence he pretends to portray: describe, analyze, and interpret.

For the long agendum of this book touches only occasionally upon issues of history, history of religions, and history of ideas. In fact, this is a work of historical theology: *wissenschaftliche Theologie.* The polemic against New Testament scholarship on Judaism is a powerful theme which runs through the book and takes many forms. It is difficult to locate a major unit of thought which is not in some way affected by Sanders' apologetic interest. This example should not be thought to exhaust the matter, but shows how, at the very center of the book, issues are defined in contemporary theological terms. As we shall see in a moment, the very work of description itself becomes flawed on this account.

Sanders' very good intention deserves the attention of students of religions who are not theologians, because what he wanted to achieve is in my view worthwhile. This intention is the proper comparison of religions (or of diverse expressions of one larger religion): "I am of the view...that the history of the comparison of Paul and Judaism is a particularly clear instance of the general need for methodological improvement in the comparative study of religion. What is difficult is to focus on what is to be compared. We have already seen that most comparisons are of reduced essences...or of individual motifs...." This sort of comparison Sanders rejects. Here I wish to give Sanders' words, because I believe what he wants to do is precisely what he should have done but, as I shall explain, has not succeeded in doing:

> What is clearly desirable, then, is to compare an entire religion, parts and all, with an entire religion, parts and all; to use the analogy of a building to compare two buildings, not leaving out of account their individual bricks. The problem is how to discover two wholes, both of which are considered and defined on their own merits and in their own terms, to be compared with each other.

Now let us ask ourselves whether or not Sanders has compared an entire religion, parts and all, with other such entire religions.

On the basis of my description of the contents of the book, we must conclude that he has not. The categories are all wrong for the Judaism attested by the Mishnah and related writings. As with Urbach,

Sanders has followed the requirements of apologetics, rather than the traits of the evidence, in framing his categories and so determining his hermeneutic problem. For the issues of election and covenant, obedience and disobedience, and the like, while demonstrably present and taken for granted in the diverse "Judaisms" of late antiquity, do not necessarily define the generative problematic of any of the Judaisms before us. To put matters in more general terms: Systemic description must begin with the system to be described. Comparative description follows. And to describe a system, we commence with the principal documents which can be shown to form the center of a system. Our task then is to uncover the exegetical processes, the dynamics of the system, through which those documents serve to shape a conception, and to make sense, of reality. We then must locate the critical tensions and inner problematic of the system thereby revealed: What is it about? What are its points of insistence? The comparison of systems begins in their exegesis and interpretation.

But Sanders does not come to Rabbinic Judaism (to focus upon what clearly is his principal polemical charge) to uncover the issues of Rabbinic Judaism. He brings to the Rabbinic sources the issues of Pauline scholarship and Paul. This blatant trait of his work, which begins, after all, with a long account of Christian anti-Judaism ("The persistence of the view of Rabbinic religion as one of legalistic works-righteousness," pp. 33-58), hardly requires amplification. In fact, Sanders does not really undertake the systemic description of earlier Rabbinic Judaism in terms of its critical tension. True, he isolates those documents he thinks may testify to the state of opinion in the late first and second centuries. But Sanders does not describe Rabbinic Judaism through the systemic categories yielded by its principal documents. His chief purpose is to demonstrate that Rabbinism constitutes a system of "covenantal nomism." While I think he is wholly correct in maintaining the importance of the conceptions of covenant and of grace, the polemic in behalf of Rabbinic legalism as covenantal does not bring to the fore what Rabbinic sources themselves wish to take as their principal theme and generative problem. For them, as he says, covenantal nomism is a datum. So far as Sanders proposes to demonstrate the importance to all the kinds of ancient Judaism of covenantal nomism, election, atonement, and the like, his work must be pronounced a success but trivial. So far as he claims to effect systemic description of Rabbinic Judaism ("a comparison of patterns of religion"), we have to evaluate that claim in its own terms.

What Sanders has done is to impose the pattern of one religious expression, Paul's, upon the description of another, that of the

Tannaitic-Rabbinical sources.[2] He therefore ignores the context of the sayings adduced in the service of comparison, paying little attention to the larger context in which those sayings find meaning. In this connection I point to the observation of Mary Boyce (*A History of Zoroastrianism* [Leiden, 1975], p. 246):

> Zoroaster's eschatological teachings, with the individual judgment, the resurrection of the body, the Last Judgment, and life everlasting, became profoundly familiar, through borrowings, to Jews, Christians, and Muslims, and have exerted enormous influence on the lives and thoughts of men in many lands. Yet it was in the framework of his own faith that they attained their fullest logical coherence....

What Boyce stresses is that, taken out of the Zoroastrian context, these familiar teachings lose their "fullest logical coherence." Sanders, for his part, has not asked what is important and central in the system of Tannaitic-Rabbinic writings. All he wants to know is what, in those writings, addresses questions of interest to Paul.

The work of description, first for its own purposes, then for systemic comparison, begins with not Paul or "New Testament scholarship" but the Mishnah. The issues therefore have to be set forth in terms native to that writing and those that flowed from it. Allowing "Paul" or "New Testament scholarship" to tell us what constitutes a suitable religion, then demonstrating that the sages or rabbis or the Mishnah or Rabbinic Judaism formed a suitable religion, seems to me an error, from the viewpoint of the religious study of religion, of monumental proportions. Now the Mishnah certainly is the first document of Rabbinic Judaism. Formally, it stands at the center of the system, since the principal subsequent Rabbinic documents, the Talmuds, lay themselves out as if they were exegeses of Mishnah (or, more accurately, of Mishnah-Tosefta). It follows that an account of what Mishnah is about, of the system expressed by Mishnah and of the world-view created and sustained therein, should be required for systemic comparison such as Sanders proposes. Now if we come to Mishnah with questions – and, more to the point, the values and theological convictions – of Pauline-Lutheran theology, important to

---

[2]Try to imagine the scholarly agendum if Christianity were the minority religion, Judaism the majority one. Books on "the Christian background of Judaism" and "what Paul teaches us about the world of Mishnah" surely would distort the interpretation of Paul. After all, "Paul and the dietary laws" would not focus upon an issue at the center of Paul's thought, though it might be a principal point of interest to theological faculties. Proof that Jesus made important contributions to Judaism through his disciple, Hillel, or that Jesus was a Pharisee, would seem still more ridiculous, except that, the apologetic mind being what it is, they are written even here and now.

Sanders and New Testament scholarship, we find ourselves on the peripheries of Mishnaic literature and its chief foci. True, the Mishnah contains a very few relevant, accessible sayings, for example, on election and covenant. But on our hands is a huge document which does not wish to tell us much about election and covenant and which does wish to speak about other things.

Description of the Mishnaic system is not easy. It took me twenty-two volumes to deal with the sixth of Mishnah's six divisions. Still, we have to wonder whether Sanders has asked of himself the generative and unifying questions of the core of Mishnah at all: Has he actually sat down and studied (not merely "read") one document, even one tractate, beginning to end, and analyzed its inner structure, heart, and center? By this question I do not mean to ask whether Sanders has mastered Rabbinic writings. The evidence in his book is that he can look things up, presumably with Billerbeck's help. He knows Hebrew and is competent, if no expert (!). The question is, Does Sanders so grasp the problematic of a Rabbinic compilation that he can accurately state what it is that said compilation wishes to express – its generative problematic? Or does he come to the Rabbinic literature with a quite separate and distinct set of questions, issues in no way natural to, and originating in, the Rabbinic writings themselves? Just now we noticed that Sanders' theological agendum accords quite felicitously with the issues of Pauline theology. To show that that agendum has not been shaped out of the issues of Rabbinic theology, I shall now adduce negative evidence on whether Sanders with equal care analyzes the inner structure of a document of Rabbinic Judaism.

First, throughout his "constructive" discussions of Rabbinic ideas about theology, Sanders quotes all documents equally with no effort at differentiation among them. He seems to have culled sayings from the diverse sources he has chosen and written them down on cards, which he proceeded to organize around his critical categories. Then he has constructed his paragraphs and sections by flipping through those cards and commenting on this and that. So there is no context in which a given saying is important in its own setting, in its own document. This is Billerbeck-scholarship, possible only in a field in which partisanship replaces the hard work of learning.

Of greater importance, the diverse documents of Rabbinism are accorded no attention on their own. Let me expain what I mean. Anyone who sits down and studies Sifra, in a large unit of its materials, for example, can hardly miss what the redactor of the document wants to say. The reason is that the polemic of that document is so powerfully stated and so interminably repeated as to be inescapable. What Sifra wishes to say is this: the Mishnah requires an exegetical foundation.

But Mishnah notoriously avoids scriptural prooftexts. To Sifra none of the Mishnah's major propositions is acceptable solely upon the basis of reason or logic. All of them require proper grounding in exegesis – of a peculiarly formal sort – of Scripture. One stratum of the Talmuds, moreover, addresses the same devastating critique to the Mishnah. For once a Mishnaic proposition will be cited at the head of a talmudic pericope, a recurrent question is, What is the source of this statement? And the natural and right answer (from the perspective of the redactor of this sort of pericope) will be, As it is said..., followed by a citation of Scripture.

Now if it is so that Sifra and at least one stratum of Talmud so shape their materials as to make a powerful polemical point against the Mishnah's autonomous authority ("logic"), indifferent as the Mishnah is to scriptural authority for its laws, then we must ask how we can ignore or neglect that polemic. Surely we cannot cite isolated pericopae of these documents with no attention whatsoever to the intention of the documents which provide said pericopae. Even the most primitive New Testament scholars will concur that we must pay attention to the larger purposes of the several evangelists in citing sayings assigned to Jesus in the various Gospels. Everyone knows that if we ignore Matthew's theory of the law and simply extract Matthew's versions of Jesus' sayings about the law and set them up side by side with the sayings about the law given to Jesus by other of the evangelists and attitudes imputed to him by Paul, we create a mess of contradictions. Why then should the context of diverse Rabbinic sayings, for example, on the law, be ignored? In this setting it is gratuitous to ask for an explanation of Sanders' constant reference to "the Rabbis," as though the century and a half which he claims to discuss produced no evidence of individuals' and ideas' having distinct histories. This is ignorant.

Still more telling evidence that Sanders does not succeed in his systemic description comes when he gives one concrete example (in the entire 238 pages of discussion of "Tannaitic" Judaism) of what a document wishes to tell us. I shall focus on the matter because Sanders raises it. He states (p. 71):

> Rabbinic discussions are often at the third remove from central questions of religious importance. Thus the tractate Mikwaoth, "immersion pools," does not consider the religious value of immersion or the general reason for purity, much less such a large topic as why the law should be observed. It simply begins with the classification of the grades among pools of water. This does not mean that there were no religious principles behind the discussion; simply that they (a) were so well understood that they did not need to be specified and (b) did not fall into the realm of halakah.

The next chapters of this book will refute that ignorant judgment that "religious principles...did not fall into the realm of halakah." Nothing could be further from the truth. But let us focus upon the issue at hand.

Specifically, on the basis of this statement we must conclude that Sanders has looked at M. Miqvaot 1:1, perhaps even the entire first chapter of the document. It is true that tractate Miqvaot does begin with classification of the grades among pools of water. But a study of the tractate as a whole reveals that it certainly has its own issues, its own critical concerns, indeed, its own generative problematic. In fact the shank of the tractate – M. Miq. 2:4-5:6 – asks about collections of diverse sorts of water and how they effect purification. A secondary development of the same theme follows: the union of pools to form a valid collection of water, and yet a tertiary development, mixtures of water with other liquids (wine, mud). Therefore the primary interest of the tractate is in water for the immersion pool: What sort of water purifies? Now anyone interested in the document must wonder, Why is it that, of all the possible topics for a tractate on purification, the one point of interest should be the definition of effective water? And the first observation one might make is that Scripture, for its part, would be surprised by the datum of Mishnah-tractate Miqvaot.[3] For, in the

---

[3]This is worked out in my *History of the Mishnaic Law of Purities*, vols. 13, *Miqvaot. Commentary*, and 14, *Miqvaot. Literary and Historical Problems* (Leiden, 1976). One of the most complex problems of Mishnah-study is the relationship of the diverse tractates of Mishnah to Scripture. I have dealt with this problem in "From Scripture to Mishnah: The Origins of Mishnah-tractate Niddah," *Journal of Jewish Studies*; "From Scripture to Mishnah: The Exegetical Origins of Maddaf," *Festschrift for the Fiftieth Anniversary of the American Academy for Jewish Research*; "From Scripture to Mishnah: The Case of Mishnah's Fifth Division," *Journal of Biblical Literature* (March 1979); "The Meaning of Torah shebe al peh, with Special Reference to Kelim and Ohalot," *AJS Review* I (1976): 151-70; and in the various volumes of *Purities, Holy Things,* and *Women.* I do not understand why Sanders does not begin his work of description with an account of the Old Testament legacy available to all the groups under discussion as well as with an account of how, in his view, each group receives and reshapes that legacy. Everyone claimed, after all, to build upon the foundations of Mosaic revelation ("covenantal nomism"), indeed, merely to restate what Moses or the prophets had originally said. It seems to me natural to give the Old Testament a central place in the description of any system resting upon an antecedent corpus of such authority as the Mosaic revelation and the prophetic writings. Systemic comparison on diverse relationsips to, and readings of, Scripture certainly is invited. In this context I must reject Sanders' critique of Vermes (pp. 25-29). His omission of reference to the Targumim because they are "generally late" is self-serving. The

opinion of the priestly authorities of Leviticus and Numbers, still water by itself – not spring water, not standing water mixed with blood or ashes, for example – does not effect purification. Water may remove uncleanness, but the process of purification further requires the setting of the sun. Water mixed with blood may purify the leper; water mixed with the ashes of a red cow may purify one made unclean by a corpse. But water by itself is inadequate to complete purification. At best, Scripture knows running water as a means of purification. But Mishnah-tractate Miqvaot stresses the purificatory properties of still water, and explicitly excludes spring water from the center of its discussion.

My own conception of what it is that Mishnah wishes to say in this tractate is at best a guess, but it is worth repeating so that the full character of Sanders' "defense" of this particular tractate may become clear:

> What is the fundamental achievement of our tractate? The Oral Torah [Mishnah] provides a mode of purification different from that specified in the Written Torah for the Temple, but analogous to that suitable for the Temple. Still water serves for the table, living water [approved by Scripture] cleans the Zab, and, when mixed with blood or ashes, the leper and the person unclean by reason of touching a corpse. All those other things cleaned by the setting of the sun, the passage of time, in the Oral Torah [Mishnah-tractate Miqvaot] are cleaned in the still water [of the immersion pool, which, Mishnah makes clear, must be] gathered in the ground, in the rains which know no time, but only the eternal seasons.[4]

Targumim are diverse and hard to use; not all are in English. Sanders chokes on the gnat of the Targums and swallows the camel of the Midrashim. Sanders says, "Even if generally late, the Targums may, to be sure, contain early traditions. But these must now be sought out one by one." True indeed. And the same is so for the whole of Tannaitic literature! By "Tannaitic literature," Sanders means literature containing sayings attributed to Tannaim, or authorities who are assumed to have flourished before A.D. 200. As I shall suggest in a moment, such "early traditions" as occur in the name of first- and second-century authorities in documents of the third and later centuries also must be sought out, one by one. Sanders' more honest reason follows: "In general, the present state of Targumic studies does not permit the Targums to be used for our purposes." That is, I suppose, they are hard to use as he wants to use them. My argument is that the same is self-evidently true of the earlier Rabbinic documents. But Sanders successfully answers his own objection, with his stress on systemic -- therefore diachronic -- as against merely synchronic, comparison. Omission of the Targums is less damaging than failure to exploit the sizable legacy of the Old Testament, which surely is available, all parties concur, by the first century B.C. That omission is incomprehensible.

[4]*Purities*, 14:204-5.

What follows is my conception of the world-constructing meaning of the laws just now summarized:

> In an age in which men and women immersed themselves in spring-fed lakes and rushing rivers, in moving water washing away their sins in preparation for the end of days, the Pharisees observed the passing of the seasons, which go onward through time, immersing in the still, collected water which falls from heaven. They bathe not in running water, in the anticipation of the end of days and for the sake of eschatological purity, but in still water, to attain the cleanness appropriate to the eternal Temple and the perpetual sacrifice [of the very real, physical Temple of Jerusalem]. They remove the uncleanness defined by the Written Torah for the holy altar, because of the conviction of the Oral Torah [Mishnah] that the hearth and home, table and bed, going onward through ages without end, also must be and can be cleaned, in particular, through the rain: the living water from heaven, falling in its perpetual seasons, trickling down the hills and naturally gathering in ponds, ditches, and caverns, for time immemorial. As sun sets, bringing purification for the Temple, so rain falls, bringing purification for the table.[5]

Now I cite this passage to juxtapose it to Sanders' judgment that Miqvaot "does not consider the religious value of immersion or the general reason for purity." I think it does exactly that – in its own way.

In my view, Sanders finds in Mishnah-tractate Miqvaot no answers to questions of religious value because he has not asked how Miqvaot asks its questions to begin with. And that is because he has not allowed the tractate to speak for itself, out of its own deepest stratum of conceptions. He has brought to the tractate an alien set of questions and, finding nothing in the tractate to deal with those questions – that is, no sayings explicitly addressed to them – he has gone his way. It is true that the tractate does not consider "the religious value of immersion," and that is because it has quite separate, and, if I am right, more profound, issues in mind. To say, "This does not mean that there were no religious principles behind the discussion" is not only patronizing, it also is ignorant.[6] To claim that the "principles were so

---

[5]*Ibid.*, p. 205.

[6]I must concede that it is asking much of scholars to sit patiently to master the details of the Mishnaic (and other Rabbinic) law and only then to raise the questions of the deeper range of meanings of that law. But the work of interpretation begins in exegesis and only ends in the formation and history of ideas. If people find too arduous, or merely dull, the work of patient exegesis, then of the recombinant history of small ideas, let them write on some subject other than earlier Rabbinic Judaism. The legal materials are not easy to understand. They are still more difficult to interpret as statements of philosophical or metaphysical conceptions. My message is that only in the work of exegesis is that task of interpretation to be undertaken, and it is only

well understood that they did not need to be specified" is true but beside the point, if Sanders cannot accurately tell us what these principles were. Granted that we deal with a system of "convenantal nomism," what is it that that covenant was meant to express? And how did the ancient rabbis interpret that covenant and its requirements for their own trying times? Answering these questions requires Sanders to take Judaism seriously in its own terms. But this he does not do.

The claim, in this very context, that religious principles cannot be discussed in the Mishnah because of the character of Mishnah, would be more persuasive if there were substantial evidence that Mishnah to begin with has been studied in its own framework. Sanders says (p. 71):

> We should at least briefly refer to another characteristic of the literature which makes a small-scale analysis of basic religious principles impossible: they are not discussed as such. Rabbinic discussions are often at the third remove from central questions of religious importance.

There follows the treatment of Miqvaot cited above. I contend that it begs the question to say "basic religious principles" are not "discussed as such." In the chapters that follow, I shall show what it takes to move

---

through interpretation that the meaning of the law is to be attained. Nobody begged Sanders to come and defend the Jews.

Anyhow, why should "the religious value" of immersion be spelled out by the second-century rabbis in terms immediately accessible to a twentieth-century theologian? Mishnah's audience is second-century rabbis. How can we expect people to explain to outsiders ("why the law should be kept" indeed!) answers to questions which do not trouble insiders to begin with. The whole statement of the question is topsy-turvy. I find deplorable Sanders' failure to object to the notion of "central questions of religious importance" and "religious principles." Taken for granted is the conception that what are central questions to us are central questions to all "worthwhile" religious literature. It follows that if we cannot locate what to us are "religious principles," then we have either to condemn or to apologize for the documents which lack them. Stated in this way, the implicit position takes for granted "we all know" the meaning of "religion," "religious importance," "religious principles." In the case of the vast halakhic literature, we do not find readily accessible and immediately obvious "religious principles." When, moreover, we do find those conceptions, subject to generalization and analysis, which do address issues of common, even contemporary concern, we sometimes discover a range of topics under analysis more really philosophical than religious (in the contemporary sense of these words). An apology for Rabbinic Judaism bypassing the whole of the halakhic corpus which constitutes its earliest stratum is cosmically irrelevant to the interpretation of Rabbinic Judaism, therefore to the comparison of that system to others in its own culture.

from that "third remove" backward to "central questions of religious importance."

The upshot may be stated very simply. The diverse Rabbinic documents require study in their own terms. The systems of each – so far as there are systems – have to be uncovered and described. The way the several systems relate and the values common to all of them have to be spelled out. The notion that we may cite promiscuously everything in every document (within the defined canon of "permitted" documents) and then claim to have presented an account of "the Rabbis" and their opinions is not demonstrated and not even very well argued. We hardly need dwell on the still more telling fact that Sanders has not shown how systemic comparison is possible when, in point of fact, the issues of one document, or of one system of which a document is a part, are simply not the same as the issues of some other document or system. That is, he has succeeded in finding Rabbinic sayings on topics of central importance to Paul (or Pauline theology). He has not even asked whether these sayings form the center and core of the Rabbinic system or even of a given Rabbinic document. To state matters simply, How do we know that "the Rabbis" and Paul are talking about the same thing, so that we may compare what they have to say? And if it should turn out that "the Rabbis" and Paul are not talking about the same thing, then what is it that we have to compare?

Even by 1973, when Sanders completed this work,[7] it was clear that the issue of historical dependability of attributions of sayings to particular rabbis had to be faced, even though, admittedly, it had not been faced in most of the work on which Sanders was able to draw. I do not wish to dwell upon the problem of why we should believe that a given rabbi really said what is attributed to him, because I have already discussed that matter at some length.[8] Still, it seems to me that the issues of historical evidence should enter into the notion of the

---

[7]And on the problem at hand, there has been no other by him. He ignored all of the criticism of his work, except as it pertained to his theological position on Paul and the law, in his book in reply to critics of *Paul and Palestinian Judaism*, in which my review is not even listed in the bibliography. In his work on *Jesus and Judaism* he shows that he has learned nothing about the halakhah, about which he proposes to expatiate so learnedly, and misrepresents specific cases in many of the passages in which he invokes halakhic materials in the interpretation of Jesus's actions. I have shown how grossly he misconstrues the matter of the money-changers in the temple in my article on that subject in *New Testament Studies* (December, 1989), and Bruce Chilton and I have addressed his misinterpretation of purity-law in a joint article now in press.

[8]"The History of Earlier Rabbinic Judaism: Some New Approaches," *History of Religions* 16 (1977): 216-36.

comparison of systems. If it should turn out that "the Rabbis'" ideas about a given theological topic respond to a historical situation subject to fairly precise description, then the work of comparison becomes still more subtle and precarious. For if "the Rabbis" address their thought – for example, about the right motive for the right deed – to a world in which, in the aftermath of a terrible catastrophe, the issue of what it is that human beings still control is central, the comparison of their thought to that of Paul requires us to imagine what Paul might have said if confronted by the situation facing "the Rabbis."

As I said in the introduction, a powerful motif in sayings assigned to authorities who lived after the Bar Kokhba war is the issue of attitude: the surpassing power of human intention in defining a situation and judging it. In many ways diverse tractates of Mishnah seem to want to say that there are yet important powers left in the hands of defeated, despairing Israelites. The message of much of Mishnaic *halakhah* is that there is an unseen world, a metaphysical world, subject to the will of Israel. Given the condition of defeat, the despair and helplessness of those who survived the end of time, we may hardly be surprised at the message of authorities who wish to specify important decisions yet to be made by people totally subjugated to the will of their conquerors. Now if we ignore that historical setting, the dissonances of theology and politics, in which the message concerning attitude and intention is given, how are we properly to interpret and compare "the Rabbis'" teachings on the effects of the human will with those of Paul, or those assigned to Jesus, for that matter? If they say the same thing, it may be for quite divergent reasons. If they say different things, it may be that they say different things because they speak of different problems to different people.

Now these observations seem to me to be obvious and banal. But they are necessary to establish the urgency of facing those simple historical questions Sanders wishes to finesse (by quoting me, of all people!). If we have a saying assigned to Aqiba how do we know it really was said by him, belonging to the late first and early second century? If we cannot show that it does go back to A.D. 100, then we are not justified in adducing such sayings as evidence of the state of mind of one late-first- and early-second-century authority, let alone of all the late-first- and early-second-century authorities – and let alone of "the Rabbis" of the later first and whole of the second centuries. I cannot concede that Sanders' notion of systemic description, even if it were wholly effected, has removed from the critical agendum these simple questions of historical study we have yet to answer.

Nor should we ignore the importance in the work, not only of comparison, but also of interpreting a given saying, of establishing the historical context in which the saying was said (or at least in which it was important to be quoted). Sanders many times cites the famous saying attributed to Yohanan b. Zakkai that the corpse does not contaminate, nor does purification water purify, but the whole thing is hocus-pocus. That saying first occurs in a later, probably fourth-century, Midrashic compilation. Surely we might wonder whether, at the time of the making of that compilation, issues of magic were not central in Rabbinic discourse. The denial of efficacy, *ex opere operato*, of a scriptural purification rite, addressed to a world in which magic, including Torah magic, was deemed to work *ex opere operato*, may be interpreted as a powerful polemic against a strong current of the fourth-century Palestinian and Babylonian Jews' life, a time at which Rabbinical circles, among others, were deeply interested in the magical powers inherent in Torah. Now I do not mean to suggest that the proper interpretation of the saying is in accord with this hypothesis, nor do I even propose the stated hypothesis for serious consideration here. I only offer it as an example of one context in which the saying is credibly to be interpreted and, more important, as evidence of the centrality of context in the interpretation of each and every saying. If we do not know where and when a saying was said, how are we to interpret the saying and explain its meaning?

In my view the meaning of a saying is defined, at the outset, by the context in which it is meaningful. To be sure, the saying may remain meaningful later on, so that, cited for other purposes, the saying takes on new meanings. No one denies that obvious proposition, which, after all, is illustrated best of all by the history of the interpretation, but, of greater systemic consequence, the deliberate misinterpretation, of the Old Testament in Judaism and Christianity. If that is so, then we surely should not reduce to a fundamentalistic and childish hermeneutical framework the interpretation by sayings attributed to rabbis in Rabbinic documents of diverse periods, put together, as I said earlier, for diverse purposes and therefore addressed, it seems to me self-evident, to historically diverse circumstances. So, in all, I think Sanders pays too much attention to the anti-Judaism of New Testament scholars. It is true, I suppose, that there is a built-in bias on the part of some of Christian scholarship on Rabbinic Judaism, leading to negative judgments based upon fake scholarship (Sanders' attack on Billerbeck is precise and elegant). But the motive for a major scholarly project must be constructive. One must love one's subject, that is, one's sources and scholarly setting. But then, the beginning of love is "never having to say you're sorry," and apologetics hardly frames a worthwhile reading of a religion.

Still, in Sanders' behalf it must be repeated that he has defined the work to be done in terms which I think are valid and fructifying. All contemporary scholarship on Judaism is carried forward in the shadow of the murder of nearly six million Jews in Europe ("the Holocaust"), and one fundamental factor in that catastrophe was the systematic dehumanization of the Jews by means of the degradation of their religion. In that context, Sanders has laid forth an apologetic for Rabbinic Judaism and a powerful critique of ignorant or malicious or out-and-out anti-Semitic reports of, and judgments on, Rabbinic Judaism (or simply "Judaism"). Even though that theological enterprise cannot be deemed consequential for the study of the history of the religious world of ancient Judaism, it surely is not irrelevant to the context in which that history is written. Sanders' insistence that when Judaism is studied by Christian scholars, it must be considered without the endemic anti-Judaism characteristic of earlier work, is important for both social and academic reasons. The sort of people who believed that Judaism was depraved also maintained, like Kittel in 1933, that the best solution (if inexpedient) to the Jewish problem was to exterminate the Jews. In its apologetic aspect, Sanders' book addresses itself to a considerable social problem of our age. But, alas, it also is a service to scholarship in the history of religions to insist, as Sanders does, that religions, including Judaism, be studied *sine ire et studio.* So as it is a document of the times, Sanders' book is on the side of life if not of learning.

This reprise of the errors deriving from misconstruction of principles of category-formation by Urbach and misunderstanding, because of an apologetic bias, of what is at stake in the study of religion by Sanders, brings us back to the papers at hand. In representing the religion of the Judaism set forth, first of all, by the authorship of the Mishnah, I claim to work within the categories of the Mishnah. I begin with the topical program the authorship has set forth. But, as is clear, I do not permit their program to dictate my questions; category-formation derives from negotiation among two worlds, theirs, set forth in their categories, ours, composed by our categories. From the negotiation between the one and the other a sound account derives. And all scholarship of an interpretive character emerges from a sustained process of interpretation, translation, mediation, represented by the work of negotiation. Second, I am not bound by the terms of an apologetic program. On the contrary, my contract is with my sources, and my task is to tease out of those sources a picture of how people were thinking and about what they were reflecting.

The upshot in my view is that we deal with deep thought about critical issues of theology, on the one hand, and perennial issues of philosophy, on the other. Whether or not a religion that sets forth theological and philosophical positions on these issues, rather than on other ones, is then appropriate and suitable or subject to condemnation is not at stake. What matters to me, and all that counts in the academy, where I work, is whether I have accurately described, analyzed, and interpreted the world-view of the writings, the Judaism of which I claim to set forth. So there is the issue: a religion of pots and pans? or a religion of theology and philosophy? To settle the question, we have to see whether, as I maintain, when they talked of pots and pans, they worked out principles of theology and philosophy. And to find the answer to that fundamental question of analysis and interpretation, we have faithfully and patiently and accurately to read the sources themselves. That is what I shall now do in the chapters that complete this part of the book.

Chapter Two

How the Mishnah Expresses its Theology [1]: From Ritual to Theology in the Systemic Statement of the Mishnah's Law on Burning the Red Cow

While some religions, Christianity and Islam for example, are rich not only in law but also in theological writings, and others in myth, still others make their systemic statements about the nature of being and the realm of the sacred primarily through law. Accordingly, we have to ask details of rite to teach us about the systemic myth, that is, move backward from way of life to world-view. In the case of early rabbinic Judaism we have a considerable corpus of laws which prescribe the way things are done but make no effort to interpret what is done. These constitute ritual entirely lacking in mythic, let alone theological, explanation. Accordingly, the processes and modes of thought of earlier Rabbinic Judaism turn out to be encapsulated in descriptions of ritual. Yet much of the law contained in the Mishnah in fact was not practiced; indeed, the earlier rabbis scarcely claim that it was. Further, the laws about ritual cleanness or purity, so far as they had to be kept so that a person could enter the Temple, bore no more concrete relevance to everyday life than did the cultic laws, and only a small part of the Jewish population of Palestine was expected to keep those laws outside of the cult. Accordingly, we have before us the paradox presented by most serious effort to create a corpus of laws to describe a ritual life which did not exist. The processes of making those laws themselves constituted the rabbis' – and their predecessors' – mode of thinking about the same issues investigated, in other circumstances, through rigorous theological thought, on the one side, or profound mythic speculation, on the other. *So far as the laws describe a ritual, the ritual itself is myth,* in two senses.

First, the ritual is myth or world-view in the sense that it was not real, was not carried out.

Second, while lacking mythic articulation, the ritual expresses important ideas and points of view on the structure of reality.

What is lacking, specifically, is not myth, but articulated and explicit articulation of myth or world-view. The law contains myth and so serves as an artifact of a world-view in that it encompasses cognitive content. The law does not explicitly articulate the content in a particular form of abstract discourse, but leaves its content embedded in ritual. What people are supposed to do, without a stage of articulation of the meaning of what they do, itself expresses what they think. The explanation of the ritual, the drawing out of that explanation of some sort of major cognitive statement, is skipped. The world therefore is mapped out through gesture. The boundaries of reality are laid forth through norms on how the boundaries of reality are laid forth. Accordingly, we deal with laws made by people who never saw or performed the ritual described by those laws. It is through thinking about the laws that they shape and express their ideas, their judgments upon transcendent issues of sacred and profane, clean and unclean. It follows that thinking about the details of the law turns out to constitute reflection on the nature of being and the meaning of the sacred. The form – the ritual – lacking myth or world-view is wholly integrated to the content, the mythic substructure. The structure of the ritual is its myth and conveys the systemic way of life.

We turn to the particular ritual in hand, the burning of the red cow for the preparation of ashes, to be mixed with water and sprinkled upon a person who has become unclean through contact with a corpse. Let us first consider once again the way in which the priestly author of Numbers 19:1-10 describes the rite, the things he considers important to say about it:

> Tell the people of Israel to bring you a red cow without defect, in which there is no blemish, and upon which a yoke has never come. And you shall give her to Eleazar the priest, and she shall be taken outside the camp and slaughtered before him. And Eleazar the priest shall take some of her blood with his finger and sprinkle some of her blood toward the front of the tent of meeting seven times. And the heifer shall be burned in his sight; her skin, her flesh, and her blood, with her dung, shall be burned; and the priest shall take cedarwood and hyssop and scarlet stuff and cast them into the midst of the burning of the heifer. Then the priest shall wash his clothes and bathe his body in water, and afterwards he shall come into the camp, and the priests shall be unclean until evening. And a man who is clean shall gather up the ashes of the heifer and deposit them outside the camp in a clean place; and they shall be kept for the congregation of the people of Israel for the water for impurity, and for the removal of sin. And he who gathers the ashes of the heifer shall wash his clothes and be unclean until evening (Num. 19:1-10a).

How is the ash used? Num. 19:17 states:

For the unclean they shall take some ashes of the burnt sin-offering
and running water shall be added in a vessel; then a clean person shall
take hyssop and dip it in the water and sprinkle it upon the tent...(in
which someone has died, etc.).

Let us now ask, what to the biblical writer are the important traits
of the rite of the burning of the cow and the mixing of its ashes into
water? The priestly author stresses, first of all, that the rite takes
place outside of the camp, which is to say, in an unclean place. He
repeatedly tells us that anyone involved in the rite is made unclean by
his participation in the rite, thus, 19:7, the priest shall wash his
clothes; Num. 19:8, the one who burns the heifer shall was his clothes;
Num. 19:10, and he who gathers the ashes of the heifer shall wash his
clothes and be unclean until evening. The priestly legislator therefore
takes for granted that the rules of purity which govern rites in the
Temple simply do no apply to the rite of burning the cow. Not only are
the participants *not* in a state of cleanness, but they are in a state of
uncleanness, being required to wash their clothes, remaining unclean
until the evening only then allowed back into the camp which is the
Temple. Accordingly, the world outside the Temple is by definition not
subject to the Temple's rules and is not going to be clean.

What is interesting, when we turn to Mishnah-tractate Parah,
which deals with the same topic, the burning of the red cow, is its
distinctive agendum of issues and themes. The predominant concerns of
Mishnah-tractate Parah, deriving from the period before 70, are two:
first, the degree of cleanness required of those who participate in the
rite and how these people become unclean; second, how the water used
for the rite is to be drawn and protected, with special attention
directed to not working between the drawing of the water and the
mixing of the ashes referred to in Num. 19:17. The theoretical concerns
of Mishnah-tractate Parah thus focus upon two important matters of no
interest whatever to the priestly author of Numbers 19:1-10, because
the priestly author assumes the rite produces uncleanness, is conducted
outside of the realm of cleanness, and therefore does not involve the
keeping of the Levitical rules of cleanness required for participation in
the Temple cult.

By contrast, Mishnah-tractate Parah is chiefly interested in that
very matter. An important body of opinion in our tractate demands a
degree of cleanness higher than that required for the Temple cult itself.
Further, the whole matter of drawing water, protecting it, and mixing
it with the ash, is virtually ignored by the priestly author, while it
occupies much of our tractate and, even more than in quantity, the
quality and theoretical sophistication of the laws on that topic form
the apex of our tractate. Accordingly, the biblical writer on the rite of

burning the red cow wishes to tell us that the rite takes place outside
the camp, understood in Temple-times as outside the Temple. The rite
is conducted in an unclean place. And it follows that people who are
going to participate in the rite, slaughtering the cow, collecting its
ashes, and the like, are not clean. The Mishnaic authorities stress
exactly the opposite conception, that people who will participate in
the rite must be clean, not unclean, as if they were in the Temple. And
they add a further important point, that the water which is to be used
for mixing with the ashes of the cow must be mixed with the ashes
without an intervening act of labor, not connected with the rite.

The authorities of the Mishnah describe a ritual which, in fact,
they have never seen, and about which they claim to have few
traditions. The ritual under description is a myth or world-view in two
senses. First, the ritual is something which is not part of observed
reality. Second, the laws of the ritual themselves contain important
expressions about the nature of the sacred and the clean. The
articulation of the laws, through the standard legal disputes of the
late first- and second-century authorities, contains within itself
statements about the most fundamental issues of reality, statements
which, in describing the form of the ritual, also express the content of
the ritual, its myth. These statements, it goes without saying, further
carry forward the conceptions of the period before 70.

For the purpose of the present discussion, we have now to review
familiar materials. The first dispute concerns which hand one uses for
sprinkling the blood toward the door of the Holy of Holies; the second
asks about how we raise the cow up to the top of the pyre of wood on
which it is going to be burned; and the third deals with whether
intending to do the wrong thing spoils what one actually does. The first
is at M. Parah 3:9:

> They bound it with a rope of bast and place it on the pile of wood, with
> its head southward and its face westward.
>
> The priest, standing at the east side, with his face turned toward the
> west, slaughtered it with his right (northern) hand and received the
> blood with his left (southern) hand.
>
> R. Judah says, "With his right hand did he receive the blood and he
> put it into his left hand, and he sprinkled with (the index finger of) his
> right hand."

Before analyzing the pericope, we call to mind the corresponding
Toseftan supplement (T. Parah 3:9):

> They bound it with a rope of bast and put it onto the wood pile.
>
> And some say, "It went up with a mechanical contraption."

R. Eliezer b. Jacob says, "They made a causeway on which it ascended."

Its head was to the south and its face to the west.

In the present set, therefore, are which hand we use for sprinkling the blood, and how we raise the cow to the top of the pyre of wood. Let us notice, first of all, the placing of the cow and the priest. The rite takes place on the Mount of Olives, that is, to the east and north of the Temple mount in Jerusalem. Accordingly, we set up a north-south-east-west grid. The cow is placed with its head to the south, pointing in the direction of the Temple Mount, slightly to the south of the Mount of Olives, and its face is west – that is, toward the Temple. The priest then is set east of the cow, so that he too will face the Temple. He faces west – toward the Temple. When he raises his hand to slaughter the cow, he reaches over from north and east to south and west, again, toward the Temple. We have, therefore, a clear effort to relate the location and slaughter of the red cow, which takes place outside the Temple, toward the Temple itself. In fact each gesture is meant to be a movement toward the Temple. Just as Scripture links the cow, outside the camp, to the camp, by having the blood sprinkled in the direction of the camp (a detail which the Mishnah takes for granted), so that the sprinkling of the blood, which is the crucial and decisive action which effects the purpose of the rite – accomplishes atonement, or *kapparah*, in Mishnaic language – so all other details of the rite here are focused upon the Temple.

This brings us to Judah's opinion, which disagrees about slaughter with the left hand. We have set up a kind of mirror to the Temple, with the whole setting organized to face and correspond to the Holy Place. The priest in the Temple slaughtered with his right hand, and received the blood in his left. Likewise, the anonymous rule holds, the priest now does the same. In other words, our rite in all respects replicates what is done in the Temple setting: What is done there is done here. Judah, by contrast, wants the blood received with the right hand and slaughtered with the left. Why? Because we are not *in* the Temple itself. We are facing it. Thus if we want to replicate the cultic gestures, we have to do each thing in exactly the opposite direction. Just as, in a mirror, one's left is at the right, and the right is at the left, so here, we set up a mirror. Accordingly, he says, if in the Temple the priest receives the blood in his left hand, on the Mount of Olives and facing the Temple, he receives the blood in his right hand. All parties to the dispute, therefore, agree on this fundamental proposition, that the effort is to replicate the Temple's cult in every possible regard.

This brings us to the dispute about how we get the beast up to the top of wood pile. The anonymous rule, shared by the Mishnah and

Tosefta, is that we bind the sacrificial cow and somehow drag it up to the top. But in the Temple the sacrifices were not bound; they would be spoiled if they were bound. Accordingly, Eliezer b. Jacob, a contemporary of Judah, imposes the same rule. He says that there was a causeway constructed from the ground to the top of the wood pile on which the cow will be slaughtered and burned, and the cow walks up on its own. Self-evidently, both parties cannot be right, and the issue is not what really was done in "historical" times – let us say, seventy-five years earlier. As in the dispute between Judah and the anonymous narrator, the issue is precisely how we shall do the rite, on the Mount of Olives, so as to conform to the requirements of the rite on the Temple Mount itself.

To state matters in general terms, it is taken for granted by all parties to the present pericope that the rite of the cow is done in the profane world, outside the cult, *as if* it were done in the sacred world constituted by the Temple itself. How is the contrary viewpoint expressed? The simplest statement is in Mishnah Parah 2:3B-D:

> B.   The harlot's hire and the price of a dog – it is unfit.

That is to say, if the red cow is purchased with funds deriving from money spent to purchase the services of a prostitute or to buy a dog, the cow is unfit for the rite. The pericope continues:

> C.   R. Eliezer declares fit,
> D.   since it is said, *You will not bring the harlot's hire and the price of a dog to the house of the Lord your God* (Deut. 23:18). But this (cow) does not come to the house (of the Lord, namely, the Temple).

The issue could not be drawn more clearly than does the glossator (D). Eliezer holds that since the burning of the cow takes place outside of the Temple, the Temple's rules as to the acquisition of the cow simply do not apply.

A more subtle question appears at Mishnah-tractate Parah 4:1 and Mishnah-tractate Parah 4:3. The first item, Mishnah-tractate Parah 4:1, is as follows:

> The cow of purification which one slaughtered not for its own name (meaning, not as a cow of purification, but for some other offering), or the blood of which one received and sprinkled not for its own name, etc., is unfit.
>
> R. Eliezer (Eleazar) declares fit.

What is at issue? In the sanctuary, we have correctly to designate the purpose of a sacrifice. Eleazar holds that this is not a rite subject to the rule of the Temple cult. The rule continues,

> And if this was done by a priest whose hands and feet were not washed, it is unfit.
>
> R. Eliezer declares fit.

Priests in the Temple of course had to be properly washed. Since the rite is not in the Temple. Eliezer says that the priest need not even be washed. In this connection, Tosefta supplies:

> If one whose hands and feet were not washed burned it, it is unsuitable.
>
> And R. Eleazar b. R. Simeon declares fit,
>
> as it is said, *When they come to the Tent of Meeting, they will wash in water and not die* (Ex. 30:20) – lo, the washing of the hands applies only inside (the Temple, and not on the Mount of Olives).

The issue is fully articulated, and the glosses in both the matter of the harlot's hire and the matter of washing spell out the implications. The law which describes the ritual – the *structure* of the ritual itself – also expresses the *meaning* of the ritual. The form imposed upon the ritual fully and completely states the content of the ritual. If now we ask, What is this content? we may readily answer: The ritual outside of the cult is done in a state of cleanness, as is the ritual done inside the cult. The laws of the cult, furthermore, apply no only to the conduct of the slaughtering of the cow (the cases given here), but also to the preservation of purity by those who will participate in the slaughtering.

The authorship of the Mishnah presupposes what Scripture takes for granted is not possible, namely, that the rules of purity apply outside of the Temple, just as the rules of Temple slaughter apply outside of the Temple. And the reason is, of course, that the Mishnah derives, in part, from the Pharisees, whose fundamental conviction is that the cleanness-taboos of the Temple and its priesthood apply to the life of all Israel, outside of the Temple and not of priestly caste. When Israelites eat their meals in their homes, they must obey the cleanness-taboos as if they were priests at the table of God in the Temple. This larger conception is expressed in the acute laws before us.

Let us now proceed to a matter which is by no means self-evident, and which was not understood in the way in which I shall explain it even by the second-century authorities. It concerns the issue of drawing the water. The rule, as we know, is that if I draw water for mixing with the ashes of the red cow, and, before actually accomplishing the mixture, I do an act of labor not related to the rite of the mixing of the ashes, I spoil the water. This is stated very succinctly, "An act of extraneous labor spoils the water." This conception is likely to originate before the destruction of the Second Temple in 70, because taken for granted at Mishnah-tractate 7:6-7 is the principle, evidently deriving from Pharisaism before 70, that an act of extraneous labor done between the drawing of the water and the mixing of ashes and water spoils the drawn water. The rule lies far beyond the imagination of the priestly writer of Numbers, because he tells us virtually nothing about the water into which the ashes are to be mixed. But that is of no consequence. As we observed earlier, what is interesting is the language which is used, *unfit*, not *unclean*. So the matter of the cleanness of the water – its protection against sources of contamination – is not at issue. Some other consideration has to be involved. The drawing of the water is treated as intrinsic to the rite. That is: I burn the cow. I go after water for mixing with the ashes of the cow. That journey – outside of the place in which the cow is burned – is assumed to be part of the larger rite.

Now this matter of extraneous labor is exceedingly puzzling. We have to ask, to begin with, for some sort of relevant analogy. Do we know about other rites in which we distinguish between acts of labor which are intrinsic and those which are not? And on what occasion is such a distinction made? The answer to these questions is obvious. We do distinguish between acts of labor required for the conduct of the sacrificial cult, and those which are not required for the conduct of the sacrificial cult; in particular we make that distinction on the *Sabbath*. On the Sabbath-day labor is prohibited. But the cult is continued. How? Labor intrinsic to the sacrifices required on the Sabbath is to be done, and that which is not connected with the sacrifice is not to be done.

When we introduce the issue of extraneous labor (and the issue extends to the burning of the cow itself, but I think this is secondary), what do we say about the character of the sanctity of the rite? Clearly, we take this position: The rite is conducted by analogy to the sacrifices which take place in the Temple, so that the place of the rite and all its participants in the Temple sacrifices must be clean. So too with the matter of labor. When we impose the Temple's taboos, we state that the rite is to be conducted in *clean space*. When we introduce the issue of labor, we forthwith raise the question of *holy time*, the Sabbath. For it is solely to the Sabbath that the matter of labor or no labor, labor which is intrinsic or labor which is extrinsic, applies. When we impose the taboos applicable to the Temple on the Sabbath, we state that the rite is to be conducted in holy time – wherever it is done.

The cleanness-laws in the present instance create in the world outside of the cult a *place of cleanness* analogous to the cult. The Sabbath-laws in the present instance create in the world outside of the cult a *time of holiness* analogous to the locus of the cult. The ritual constructs a structure of clean cultic space and holy Sabbath time in the world to which, by the priestly definition, neither cleanness nor holiness (in the limited sense of the present discussion) apply. The laws, it is clear, do not contain explanations. The issues themselves are trivial, ritualistic; yet even the glossators at the outset introduced, into the consideration of legal descriptions of ritual, extra-legal conceptions of fundamental importance. Accordingly, the processes of thought which produce the rabbis' legal dicta about ritual matters also embody the rabbis' judgments about profound issues.

The final stage is to consider other sorts of sayings, in which the rabbis speak more openly and directly about matters we should regard as theological, not ritual, in character. These are general, not specific, theologic-mythic sayings which lack ritual altogether and treat questions of salvation, not the conduct of rite. They constitute a quite distinct mode of expression about the same questions answered by the Mishnah through law. These theological sayings contrast, therefore, to the ones about ritual law, showing a separate way in which the authorities of the same period form and express their ideas.

The issue at hand, in particular, is the relationship between cleanness and holiness. We have already considered the matter in our interpretation of the ritual laws, showing that cleanness is distinct from holiness, and the two are related to and expressed by the laws about burning the red cow. Pinhas b. Yair gives us a statement (M. Sot. 9:15, translated following Kaufman) which links the issues of cleanness and holiness to salvation:

> R. Pinhas b. Yair says, "Attentiveness leads to (hygienic) cleanliness, cleanliness to (ritual) cleanness, cleanness to holiness, holiness to humility, humility to fear of sin, fear of sin to piety, and piety to the holy spirit, the holy spirit to the resurrection of the dead, and the resurrection of the dead to Elijah of blessed memory."

Pinhas therefore sees cleanness as a step in the ladder leading to holiness, thence to salvation: The resurrection of the dead and the coming of the Messiah. Maimonides, much later, introduces into the Messianic history the burning of the cow of purification. Referring to the saying that nine cows in all were burned from the time of Moses to the destruction of the Second Temple (Mishnah-tractate Parah 3:5), he states (*Red Heifer* 3:4):

> Now nine red heifers were prepared from the time this commandment was received until the Temple was destroyed the second time...and a tenth will King Messiah prepare – may he soon be revealed.

Maimonides thus wishes to link the matter of burning the red cow which produces water for ritual purification to the issue of the coming of the Messiah. Both sayings, those of Pinhas b. Yair and Maimonides, show that it is entirely possible to speak directly and immediately, not through the language of ritual law, about fundamental questions. And when we do find such statements, we no longer are faced with ritual laws at all, but have theology: *myth without ritual.* Yet it seems to be clear that Pinhas b. Yair and Maimonides saw in the issues of purity, in the very specific questions addressed by the rabbinic lawyers who provide the ritual law, matters of transcendent, even salvific, weight and meaning. Having seen the issues of the tractate in episodic form, let us now turn back to examine how these same matters are set out in context, examining the relevant chapters whole and complete.

Mishnah-tractate Parah

4:1

A.	The cow of purification which one slaughtered not for its name [not as a cow of purification but for some other offering],
B.	[the blood of which] one received and [or] sprinkled
C.	not for its own name,
D.	or [which one received] for its own name and [sprinkled] not for its own name,
E.	or [which one received] not for its own name and [sprinkled] for its own name,
F.	is unfit.
G.	R. Eliezer (Pa., Katsh, Plate 106, PB, P, N, M, K, C: Leazar) declares fit. [Since it is done outside the sanctuary, it is distinguished from the sin-offering.]
H.	And [if this was done by one] whose hands and feet were not washed, it is unfit.
I.	R. Eliezer (Katsh, Plate 106, PB, P, N, M, K, C: Leazar) declares fit.
J.	And [if it was done] not by the high priest, it is unfit.
K.	R. Judah declares fit.
L.	And by one not wearing proper garments – it is unfit.
M.	And it was done in the white garments.

Mishnah-tractate Parah 4:1
(b. Zeb. 20a)

We have three disputes, A-F vs. G, H vs. I, J vs. K, and a law phrased as a simple declarative sentence, L, spelled out by Mishnah-tractate Parah. M. Zeb. 1:1 states that all animal-offerings slaughtered under the name, that is, for the purpose of some other offering, are valid, except for a Passover-offering and a sin-offering, understood as the purification-offering of the red cow. That is to say, in all but the named cases one may nonetheless toss the blood against the altar-base and burn the sacrificial portions on the altar. A repeats that law, adding the matter of the receiving and sprinkling of the blood, B, which is completed by C in the model of A, then spelled out in D-E with reference to the two separate acts of B. Eliezer's view, unlike Judah's in Mishnah-tractate Parah 3:9, is that this is not a rite subject to the rule of the Temple cult, since it is performed outside the cult. He therefore rejects A-F as well as M. Zeb. 1:1, at which point he will delete the reference to the sin-offering. His view is carried forward at Mishnah-tractate Parah 4:3. The same issue recurs at H-I. M. Zeb. 2:1 insists that the priest be properly washed. Eliezer says the rule differs for the rite of the cow, as against Mishnah-tractate Parah 3:1-7 (!). J-K then reverse the matter. Sacrifices do not have to be done by the high priest. This one, J insists, does. Judah differs, consistent with his view that this is like all other sacrifices. M defines L. The point is that even a high priest carries out the rite in white garments, which are four, worn by any priest, and not in the eight of the high priest (M. Yoma 7:5). It follows from Judah's opinion in K, but, if L does not continue Judah's saying, the absence of a differing view tells us that the authority behind J (A-F, H) at this point concedes the rite is comparable to any held in the Temple itself.

Mishnah-tractate Parah

4:2

A. (1) [If] one burned it outside of its pit,

     (2) or [divided it and burned it] in two pits,

     (3) or [if] one burned two [cows] in one pit – it is unfit.

B. [If] one sprinkled and did not aim at the door [of the Holy of Holies], it is unfit.

C. [If] one sprinkled from the sixth for the seventh, and went and sprinkled the seventh time, it is unfit.

D. [If one did so] from the seventh for the eighth and went back and sprinkled for the eighth, it is fit.

Mishnah-tractate Parah 4:2

We have three rules, all stated in simple declarative sentences, A, B, and C-D. The point of A is that the burning must take place in the pit, and the pit has to be designated for the particular cow for which it is used. We cannot burn part of a cow in one pit, part in another, or two in a single one. The principle is the same, Albeck (p. 266) observes, as Mishnah-tractate Parah 3:7. M. 3:9 has told us that the sprinkling is toward the Holy of Holies. B repeats that rule and tells us it is a requirement. C-D further expand Mishnah-tractate Parah 3:9, which says that there must be a dipping of the finger for each sprinkling. C says that if we sprinkle twice – the sixth, the seventh – with one dipping, it is unacceptable, and repeating the gesture does not help. The count has been broken off. Or C wishes to say that if we lost count, we cannot make it up. D clarifies C. Maimonides assumes that "unfit" refers to the whole rite, which is then worthless, not merely to a single aspect of the rite. Rahab holds only the sprinkling is unfit. For C-D, Maimonides (*Red Heifer* 4:7) gives:

Mishnah-tractate Parah

4:3

A.   [If] one burned it without wood,
        or [burned it] with any sort of wood,
        even with straw or with stubble,
        it is fit.

B.   If one flayed and cut it up, it is fit.

C.   If one slaughtered it on condition of eating some if its meat or of drinking some of its blood, it is fit [or: unfit] (Fit/KSR: K, T, Pa., P; Unfit/PSWL: C, V, N, M, Katsh Plate 106, PB).

D.   R. Eliezer (T, Pa., P, PB: Eleazar) says, "Intention does not render unfit in the case of the cow."

Mishnah-tractate Parah 4:3 (A:
vs. Sifré. Num. 124E)

Again we have three rules, A, B, and the dispute of C-D. A brings us back to Mishnah-tractate Parah 3:8. There we are told the specific sorts of wood which are to be used. Now we learn the opposite – no wood or any sort of wood is needed to burn the cow. B is autonomous. T. 3:12F, on Mishnah-tractate Parah 3:10A, has already told us that it does not matter how the cow bursts of is made to burst. C ends either *fit* or *unfit*. If *fit*, then D explains C. If *unfit*, then D disputes the rule of C. Eliezer is consistent with Mishnah-tractate Parah 4:1, where he says that whatever one's intention, the sacrifice is valid. Mishnah-tractate Parah 4:1, 2, and 3 go over the thematic ground of Mishnah-tractate Parah 3:7-10.

Mishnah-tractate Parah

4:4

A.   All those who are engaged in the work of the cow from the beginning to the end [of the process]

(1) render clothing [or other utensils which they touch] unclean, and (2) render it [the rite] unfit through [other]work.

B.   If an invalidity happened to it in its slaughter, it does not render clothing unclean.

C.   If it happened to it in its sprinkling [= of the blood toward the Holy of Holies],

all who participate in the work involving it before its unfitness – it renders clothing unclean.

D.   And [those who do so] after its unfitness – it does not render clothing unclean.

E.   It turns out that its strict rule is its lenient rule. [Danby: Thus wherein stringency applies leniency applies also.]

F.   At all times –

(1) do they commit sacrilege against it;

(2) and do they add wood to it.

G.   (1) And its rites are done by day;

(2) and by a priest.

H.   (1) And [other] work [done by those involved in the rite] renders it unfit,

(2) until it is made into ashes.

I.   (1) And [other] work [done by those involved in the rite] renders the water unfit,

(2) until they will put the ashes into it.

Mishnah-tractate Parah 4:4 (b.
Hul. 29b, b. Yoma 42b)

The present pericope contains the fundamental laws of our tractate (Maimonides, Mishnah-commentary). First, a person involved in the rite renders utensils unclean (A1). But this depends upon the proper completion of the rite. If the cow was not properly slaughtered, then those occupied in the rite are not going to make clothing unclean. (B). C further qualifies. If the rite was properly carried out to the point of slaughter, then the uncleanness will apply to all matters affecting the cow before it was discovered to be unfit, but not afterward. A further basic principle, A2, is that a person who carries out the rite must pay close attention and not do any other work whatsoever, which is repeated at H-I, with appropriate qualifications. The point of H-I is that the act of preparing the ashes and mixing them with water ends the rite, and thereafter the participants may engage in other work. This applies to the making of the ashes, H, and the mixing of the water, I.   The observation of E is that we are strict as to the invalidation of the rite, but thus also lenient when it comes to rendering utensils unclean.

The set, F-I, is formed of four rules, each divided into two parts. F's *all times* applies to F1 and 2. G is clear; T. will qualify this rule in the light of H-I, that is, until the act of mixing the rite is done by day and by a priest. Other actions may be done by night and by a layman. H-I are clear as stated. The whole is phrased in simple declarative sentences, but, self-evidently, these are of two sorts, fully spelled out sentences, A-E, a complete unit, and rather abbreviated, but completely clear ones, in the second unit. That we have two distinct units is clear, and the repetition of the issue of work (A2) in H-I confirms that the stylistic distinctiveness also is substantive. Having dealt with the matter of the rite itself, we turn to the still more suggestive discussion of the prohibition against performing any act of servile labor along with the drawing of the water, Mishnah-tractate Parah Chapter Seven.

Mishnah-tractate Parah

7:5

A.   He who draws [water] [both] for himself and for a purification-rite

B.   draws for himself first and ties it [the bucket] to the carrying-yoke, and afterward he draws the water from the purification-rite.

C.   And if he drew [water] for the purification-rite first, and afterward drew for himself, it is unfit.

D.   He places his own [bucket of water] behind him, and that of the purification-rite before him.

E.   And if he put that of the purification-rite behind him, it is unfit.

F.   [If] both of them are for the purification-rite, [if] he places one before him and one behind him, it is fit,

G.   because it is not possible [to do otherwise] (T, Pa., C, V: 'Y 'PSR; P, PB, K, M, Katsh, Plate 108: [Y]PSR).

Mishnah-tractate Parah 7:5

This simple pericope contains no surprises. A-C tell us that a person should not do any work extrinsic to the rite. He therefore draws his own water and puts it in its place on the carrying yoke, then draws the water for the rite. He can carry both together since the water-bucket of his own is needed to balance that of purification-water. C is self-evident. D opens a new discussion, based on B. The water for the rite must be guarded at all times. Accordingly, it must be given the front position on the yoke. E, like C, is self-evident. F-G goes over familiar ground (Mishnah-tractate Parah 6:1). Since in the present circumstance there is no alternative, the man is allowed to put one bucket of purification-water at the rear.   Here the reading *impossible (to do otherwise)* is the only possible one.   Maimonides (*Red Heifer* 10:4) states D-G as follows:

> If a man is conveying water to be sanctified...he must sling the vessel not behind him but in front of him, for it is said, *as a thing to be watched over, as a water of sprinkling* (Num. 19:9): thus so long as it is watched over, it is valid as water of sprinkling; otherwise it becomes invalid. If one has drawn water in two jars, he may put one before him and one behind him, because otherwise it is not possible (to balance them on his yoke).

Mishnah-tractate Parah

7:6

A.   He who brings the [borrowed] rope in his hand [after drawing the water with a bucket suspended on a rope, intending to return the rope to the owner] –

B.   if it is on his way [to the rite of adding ashes], it is suitable.

C.   And if it is not on his way, it is unfit.

D.   On [this issue, concerning the rope] one went to Yavneh three festival-seasons (MW'DWT), and at the third festival-season, they declared it fit for him – as a special dispensation [instruction of the interim (HWR'T S'H)].

Mishnah-tractate Parah 7:6

After the man drew the water but before adding ashes to it, he wishes to take the rope with him, intending to return it to the owner. If en route he gives the rope back, it is all right, but if he has to take an indirect route to do so, it invalidates the water. D's gloss of the rule stresses that this is a special dispensation concerning water which has already been mixed. But it does not apply in the future.   Why should it, since even carrying the rope is extrinsic to the rite, not merely going aside to return it? Maimonides (*Red Heifer* 7:8) has the man carrying the rope, "and on his way he meets the owner of the rope and gives it to him as he goes along."

Mishnah-tractate Parah

7:7

A.   He who [when raising the bucket] wraps the rope hand over hand [little by little] – it [the water] is suitable.

B.   And if he arranged it [wrapping it around his hand] at the end, it is unfit.

C.   Said R. Yosé, "*This* [and not Mishnah-tractate Parah 7:6] did they declare fit as a special dispensation [an instruction of the interim]."

Mishnah-tractate Parah 7:7

The reason for B is clear. Wrapping the rope up after the water is drawn is not part of the process of drawing water; the extraneous work renders the water unfit. But why should it be permissible to wrap the rope little by little while drawing the water? Presumably because this part of the labor is involved in the actual drawing of water. The reference of C seems to be A.

Mishnah-tractate Parah

7:8

A.   He who puts away the bucket [in connection with drawing water] so that it should not be broken,

B.   or who turned it upside down so as to dry it off [for future use in the same mixture (MA)],

C.   [if he did so] so as to draw with it – it is suitable. [Maimonides, *Red Heifer* 7:10: "Since this serves the need of the water-drawing."]

D.   [If he did so] in order to convey the mixture [of water and ashes already prepared] with it – it is unsuitable.
[ibid.: "Since he performs an act of work which does not serve the need of the water-drawing."]

E.   He who clears out sherds from the trough so that it may hold a larger quantity of water – it is suitable.

F.   And if [he did so] so that they should not hinder him when he empties out the [mixed] water [into flasks for sprinkling],

G.   it is unfit.

Mishnah-tractate Parah 7:8

Putting away the bucket, A, or drying it off, B, is intrinsic to the act of drawing of water (Maharam). But if one puts away the bucket or dries it off so as to carry in it the already sanctified, or mixed, water, the water is made unfit; this now has nothing to do with drawing the water. E and F-G make the same point, now in connection with the trough. All this is obvious and hardly requires specification. The main point is that if the specific actions concern the present act of drawing water and mixing it, then they do not spoil the rite.

Mishnah-tractate Parah

7:9

A.   He whose water was on his shoulder,

B.   and he taught a lesson,

C.   and showed others the way,

D.   and killed a snake or a scorpion,

E.   took foodstuffs to put them aside [for storage] –

F.   it [the water] is unfit.

G.   [If he took] food in order to eat it – it is suitable.

H.   [If he killed] the snake and the scorpion who were standing in his way – it is suitable.

I.   Said R. Judah, "This is the principle: Anything which is done on account of work [Slotki: "any act that is in the nature of work"], "whether he stood still [to do it] or did not stand [to do it] – "it is unfit. "And anything which is not on account of work – "if he stood still [interrupting his journey to do it], it is unfit. "And if he did not stand still, it is suitable.

Mishnah-tractate Parah 7:9 (y. Ber. 2:5)

The principle of A-H is simple and familiar. Anything in the category of work which one does before casting on the ashes renders the water invalid. the development of the pericope is somewhat complex. G tells us that essential to A-E is simply E. The contrast is storing food as against eating it forthwith. If one does the former, this is work which has nothing to do with the rite. D is contradicted by H. D makes no distinction between killing a snake which is preventing one from passing and killing a snake which is not preventing him from passing. Doing so under any circumstances is going to render the water unfit (F). H qualifies this rule, therefore contradicts it, in line with G. Fundamental to the pericope are A, a necessary superscription, E, F, and G. Once D was added, then H was necessary; or D originally invited the gloss, "which were not standing in his way." B-C are ignored and have no clear place, until we reach I.

Judah's saying is even more difficult to place in the present construction. Up until now we have had no discussion of standing still or not standing still – that is, interrupting the journey. We can hardly hold that that distinction applies at D/H, and it is not suggested by E/G, unless we impose the requirement of eating while actually walking. Judah's point is that any sort of work renders the water unfit. Anything which is not in the nature of work need not render the water unfit. If the man can do it on the move, the water remains fit. This "general principle" is relevant only to B and C, and perhaps they have been separated from their natural conclusion in I. But B-C do not lead to I, unless it is self-evident that teaching a lesson or showing others the way are not "acts which are in the nature of work," in Slotki's felicitous translation. But I, as I said, can have nothing to do with D or E, and B and C would have to add, "if he stood still, it is unfit, if he did not stand still, it is fit." Then Judah spells out that distinction, on the one hand, and distinguishes between any sort of work, which may not be done, and actions – such as teaching – which are not in the nature of work, on the other. Essentially what we see in the present group are various ways of saying a single thought; we can hardly regard the cases themselves as illuminating or suggestive. The sole problem is the obvious disorganization of the pericope. T. greatly improves the pericope.

Mishnah-tractate Parah

7:10

A.   He who gave [entrusted] his water over to someone who was unclean it is unfit.

B.   [If he gave the water to] someone who was clean – it is fit.

C.   R. Eliezer (*Eliezer:* Katsch, Plate 109, C, PB, M, V, N; *Eleazar:* Maimonides, K, P, Pa.) says, "Even [if he gave then] to someone who was unclean they are acceptable, "so long as the owner of the water did not [in the interim] perform any work [which would have distracted his attention from the actions of the unclean person]."

Mishnah-tractate Parah 7:10

This simple dispute, A-B *vs.* C, introduces the issue of keeping watch over the water. If a person is unclean, A-B hold, he cannot keep watch. If the person is clean, however, he may watch over the water. The one who gives them over may now perform work, since the guard takes possession of the water. Eliezer rejects this view, introducing a new consideration: the water remains in the possession of the owner. So it does not matter whether the watchman is clean or unclean. If the owners did work, the water is unfit. But if they did not work, then the unclean person may watch over the water. The owners, not working, will keep an eye on the guard. Two issues therefore are intertwined, the *clean vs. unclean guardian,* and the question of whether the water passes out of the possession of the owner and into that of the guardian. Therefore the guardian must be clean. Mishnah-tractate Parah 7:2-3 cannot concur, but at some points T. 6:4ff. can and do. If A-B are right, then we see no distinction between mixing and drawing, for the water passes out of the possession of the owner. Therefore the guardian must be clean. But the owner *may* work. Eliezer says the owner always possesses the water. But he may not work.

Mishnah-tractate Parah

7:11

A.   Two who were drawing water for the purification-rite and they raised [the bucket] with one another –

B.   or one took out the thorn from the other,

C.   in connection with a single mixing [Slotki: "if there is to be only one mixture"], it is suitable.

D.   And in connection with two mixings [emptying the water, with ashes into two jars], it is unfit.

E.   R. Yosé says, "Even in connection with two mixings, it is fit, if they made a condition with one another [that each will assist the other in the drawing of water, in which case the assistance to the second is regarded as for the purpose of the drawing of water for the first]."

Mishnah-tractate Parah 7:11

The issue is extraneous work. If the two men are drawing water for a single act of mixing, then what one does for the other is deemed to be done for himself. Raising the bucket is part of the rite, and pulling a thorn from the other's hand or body is necessary in drawing of water to do work for the other, and the water is fit. But if it is for two drawings – each planning to mix for himself – then, in doing work for the other, the person interrupts the drawing with extraneous work – unconnected with *his* drawing of the water – and he renders his water unfit. Yosé's gloss points out that they may agree in advance that each will work in both drawings, in which case assistance to the second is deemed necessary for his own drawing. Rosh says the condition is that each will serve as watchman of the water of the other – thus (plausibly) reading Mishnah-tractate Parah 7:11 in the light of Mishnah-tractate Parah 7:10. B's addition does not change the picture, TYY (N. 72) explains: A involves only a brief interruption, yet, if it is for separate mixings, that suffices; B says that even though removing the thorn is only remotely connected to drawing water, in a single rite it is all right. Given the nature of the rule, A, C-D, E is phrased succinctly; no other form would have served the dispute better.

Mishnah-tractate Parah

7:12

A.   He who [while carrying water] breaks down [a fence] on condition of putting up a fence [afterward] – it is suitable.

B.   But if [before mixing] he [actually] built a fence – it [the water] is unfit.

C.   He who eats on condition of storing [up dates of figs, that is, if someone gave him figs on condition of his doing some work to earn them] – it is suitable.

D.   But if he [actually] stored [some of them], it is unfit.

E.   If he was eating and left over some food and threw what he left in his hand under the fig tree or among drying figs, so that it should not be wasted – it is unfit.

Mishnah-tractate Parah 7:12

The point is that intention to do work does not spoil the water, but actually doing work does. Thus if a person intends to restore a fence he broke through in order to carry water to its destination, he does not spoil the water. But if he stops and puts the fence back together, he does. Destruction to be sure, is preparatory to building, but is essential in carrying out the rite (GRA). C-D repeat this point intending to store up food – which is familiar from Mishnah-tractate Parah 7:9. E makes exactly the same point a third time. So much for the law as it is set forth in situ.

Let us now return to the issues raised at the outset and summarize the entire argument. It is now clear that the Mishnaic rabbis express their primary cognitive statements, their judgments upon large matters, through ritual law, not through myth or world-view or theology, neither of which is articulated at all. Indeed, we observe a curious disjuncture between ritual laws and theological sayings concerned with the *heilsgeschichtliche* meanings of the laws. Since the ritual was not carried out by the authorities of the law, the purpose and meaning of legislation in respect to the ritual of burning the cow are self-evidently not to describe something which has been done, but to create – if only in theory – something which, if done, will establish limits and boundaries to sacred reality. The issue of the ritual is *cleanness* outside of the Temple, and, if I am right about the taboo connected with drawing the water, *holiness* outside of the Temple as well.

The lines of structure, converging upon, and emanating from, the Temple, have now to be discerned in the world of the secular, the unclean, and the profane. Where better to discern, to lay out these lines of structure, than in connection with the ritual of sacrifice not done in the Temple but outside of it, in that very world of the secular, unclean, and profane. As I have stressed, the priestly author of Numbers cannot imagine that cleanness is a perquisite of the ritual. He says the exact opposite. The ritual produces contamination for those who participate. The second century rabbis who debated the details of the rite held that the rite is performed just as it would have been done in the Temple. The laws which describe the ritual therefore contain important judgments upon its meaning. With remarkably little eisegesis of those laws – virtually none not coming to us from the glossators themselves – we are able to see that their statements about law deal with metaphysical reality, revealing their effort to discern and to define the limits of both space and time.

The structure of the ritual contains its meaning. Form and content are wholly integrated. Indeed, we are unable to dissociate form from content. It follows that what is done in the ritual, the sprinkling with one hand or the other, the binding of the cow or the use of a causeway to bring it to the pyre, the purchase of cows with the wrong sort of money, the employment of unwashed priests, the exclusion of the issue of the wrong intention – all of these matters of rite and form alone contain whatever the rabbis will tell us about the meaning of the rite and its forms. The reason, as I have stressed, is that the rabbis before us think about transcendent issues primarily through rite and form. When, as I showed at the end, they choose another means of discourse and a different mode of thought entirely, matters of rite and form fall away. Theological and mythic considerations to which ritual is irrelevant take their place. Judah, Eleazar b. R. Simeon, Eliezer b. Jacob, and the others cited, however, refer to no myth or world-view, make use of neither mythic nor theological language, because they think about reality and speak about it through the norms of the law. Since, as I have stressed, the law concerns a ritual which these authorities have never seen and certainly would never perform, *the law itself constitutes its own myth:* (1), the fabulous myth of a ritual no one has ever done; and (2) the transcendent myth or world-view of the realm of the clean and the sacred constructed through ritual and taboo in the world of the unclean and the secular. The ritual *is* the myth. What people are told to do is what they are supposed to think. The gestures and taboos of the rite themselves express the meaning of the rite, without the mediation of myth or world-view.

Chapter Three

How the Mishnah Expresses its Theology [2]:
The Mishnah's Theology of History

i.
History and the Laws of History:
Rosh Hashanah Chapter Four, Taanit Chapter Four,
Zebahim Chapter Fourteen, and Sotah Chapter Nine

The framers of the Mishnah present us with a kind of historical thinking quite different from the one that they, along with all Israel, had inherited in Scripture. The legacy of prophecy, apocalypse, and mythic-history handed on by the writers of the books of the Hebrew Scriptures of ancient Israel, for instance, Jeremiah, Daniel, and Genesis, Exodus, and Deuteronomy, respectively, exhibits a single and quite familiar conception of history. First of all, history refers to events seen whole. Events bear meaning, form a pattern, and, therefore, deliver God's message and judgment. The upshot is that every event, each one seen on its own, must be interpreted in its own terms, not as part of a pattern but as significant in itself. What happens is singular, therefore an event to be noted and points toward lessons to be drawn for where things are heading and why.

If things do not happen at random, they also do not form indifferent patterns of merely secular, social facts. What happens is important because of the meaning contained therein. That meaning is to be discovered and revealed through the narrative of what has happened. So for all Judaisms until the Mishnah, the writing of history serves as a form or medium of prophecy. Just as prophecy takes up the interpretation of historical events, so historians retell these events in the frame of prophetic theses. And out of the two – historiography as a mode of mythic reflection, prophecy as a means of mythic construction – emerges a picture of future history, that is, what is going to happen. That picture, framed in terms of visions and supernatural symbols, in the end focuses, as much as do prophecy and history-writing, upon the here and now.

The upshot is simple. History consists of a sequence of one-time events, each of them singular, all of them meaningful. These events move from a beginning somewhere to an end at a foreordained goal. History moves toward eschatology, the end of history. The teleology of Israel's life finds its definition in eschatological fulfillment. Eschatology therefore constitutes not a choice *within* teleology, but the definition *of* teleology. That is to say, a theory of the goal and purpose of things (teleology) is shaped solely by appeal to the account of the end of times (eschatology). History done in this way then sits enthroned as the queen of theological science. Events do not conform to patterns. They form patterns. What happens matters because events bear meaning, constitute history. Now, as is clear, such a conception of mythic and apocalyptic history comes to realization in the writing of history in the prophetic pattern or in the apocalyptic framework, both of them mythic modes of organizing events. We have every right to expect such a view of matters to lead people to write books of a certain sort, rather than of some other. In the case of Judaism, obviously, we should expect people to write history books that teach lessons or apocalyptic books that through pregnant imagery predict the future and record the direction and end of time. And in antiquity that kind of writing proves commonplace among all kinds of groups and characteristic of all sorts of Judaisms but one. And that is the Judaism of the Mishnah. Here we have a Judaism that does not appeal to history as a sequence of one-time events, each of which bears meaning on its own. What the Mishnah has to say about history is quite different, and, consequently, the Mishnah does not conform in any way to the scriptural pattern of representing, and sorting out, events: history, myth, apocalypse.

The first difference appears right at the surface. The Mishnah contains no sustained narrative whatsoever, a very few tales, and no large-scale conception of history. It organizes its system in non-historical and socially unspecific terms. That is to say, there is no effort at setting into a historical context, e.g., a particular time, place, a circumstance defined by important events, any of the laws of the Mishnah. The Mishnah's system is set forth out of all historical framework, as we observed in Chapter One. That is a medium for the presentation of a system that has no precedent in prior systems of Judaism or in prior kinds of Judaic literature. The law codes of Exodus and Deuteronomy, for example, are set forth in a narrative framework, and the Priestly Code of Leviticus, for its part, appeals to God's revelation to Moses and Aaron, at specific times and places. In the Mishnah we have neither narrative nor setting for the representation of law.

Instead of narrative which, as in Exodus, spills over into case-law, the Mishnah gives description of how things are done in general and universally, that is, descriptive laws. Instead of reflection on the meaning and end of history, it constructs a world in which history plays little part. Instead of narratives full of didactic meaning, the Mishnah's authorship as we shall see in a moment provides lists of events so as to expose the traits that they share and thus the rules to which they conform. The definitive components of a historical-eschatological system of Judaism – description of events as one-time happenings, analysis of the meaning and end of events, and interpretation of the end and future of singular events – none of these commonplace constituents of all other systems of Judaism (including nascent Christianity) of ancient times finds a place in the Mishnah's system of Judaism. So the Mishnah finds no precedent in prior Israelite writings for its mode of dealing with things that happen. The Mishnah's way of identifying happenings as consequential and describing them, its way of analyzing those events it chooses as bearing meaning, its interpretation of the future to which significant events point – all those in context were unique. In form the Mishnah represents its system outside of all historical framework.

Yet to say that the Mishnah's system is ahistorical could not be more wrong. The Mishnah presents a different kind of history. Its authorship revises the inherited conception of history and reshapes that conception to fit into its own system. When we consider the power of the biblical myth, the force of its eschatological and messianic interpretation of history, the effect of apocalypse, we must find astonishing the capacity of the Mishnah's framers to think in a different way about the same things. By "history," as the opening discussion makes clear, I mean not merely events, but how events are so organized and narrated as to teach (for them, theological, for us, religious-historical or social) lessons, reveal patterns, tell us what we must do and why, what will happen to us tomorrow. In that context, some events contain richer lessons than others; the destruction of the Temple of Jerusalem teaches more than a crop failure, being kidnapped into slavery more than stubbing one's toe. Furthermore, lessons taught by events – "history" in the didactic sense – follow a progression from trivial and private to consequential and public.

The framers of the Mishnah explicitly refer to very few events, treating those they do mention within a focus quite separate from what happened – the unfolding of the events themselves. They rarely create or use narratives. More probative still, historical events do not supply organizing categories or taxonomic classifications. We find no tractate devoted to the destruction of the Temple, no complete chapter detailing the events of Bar Kokhba, nor even a sustained celebration of the events of the sages' own historical life. When things that have happened are mentioned, it is neither in order to narrate, nor to interpret and draw lessons from, the event. It is either to illustrate a point of law or to pose a problem of the law – always *en passent*, never in a pointed way. So when sages refer to what has happened, this is casual and tangential to the main thrust of discourse. Famous events, of enduring meaning, such as the return to Zion from Babylonia in the time of Ezra and Nehemiah, gain entry into the Mishnah's discourse only because of the genealogical divisions of Israelite society into castes among the immigrants (M. Qiddushin 4:1). Where the Mishnah provides little tales or narratives, moreover, they more often treat how things in the cult are done in general than what, in particular, happened on some one day. It is sufficient to refer casually to well known incidents. Narrative, in the Mishnah's limited rhetorical repertoire, is reserved for the narrow framework of what priests and others do on recurrent occasions and around the Temple. In all, that staple of history, stories about dramatic events and important deeds, in the minds of the Mishnah's jurisprudents provide little nourishment. Events, if they appear at all, are treated as trivial. They may be well-known, but are consequential in some way other than is revealed in the detailed account of what actually happened. Let me now show some of the principal texts that contain and convey this other conception of how events become history and how history teaches lessons.

Sages' treatment of events determines what in the Mishnah is important about what happens. Since the greatest event in the century and a half, from ca. 50 to ca. 200, in which the Mishnah's materials came into being, was the destruction of the Temple in 70, we must expect the Mishnah's treatment of that incident to illustrate the document's larger theory of history: what is important and unimportant about what happens. The treatment of the destruction occurs in two ways. First, the destruction of the Temple constitutes a noteworthy fact in the history of the law. Why? Because various laws about rite and cult had to undergo revision on account of the destruction. The following provides a stunningly apt example of how the Mishnah's philosophers regard what actually happened as being simply changes in the law. We begin with Mishnah-tractate Rosh Hashanah Chapter Four.

Rosh Hashanah Chapter Four

4:1-3

A.   The festival day of the New Year which coincided with the Sabbath –

B.   in the Temple they would sound the *shofar*.

C.   But not in the provinces.

D.   When the Temple was destroyed, Rabban Yohanan ben Zakkai
      made the rule that they should sound the *shofar* in every locale in
      which there was a court.

E.   Said R. Eleazar, "Rabban Yohanan b. Zakkai made that rule only
      in the case of Yabneh alone."

F.   They said to him, "All the same are Yabneh and every locale in
      which there is a court.

                                                    M. Rosh Hashanah 4:1

A.   And in this regard also was Jerusalem ahead of Yabneh:

B.   in every town which is within sight and sound [of Jerusalem], and
      nearby and able to come up to Jerusalem, they sound the *shofar*.

C.   But as to Yabneh, they sound the *shofar* only in the court alone.

                                                    M. Rosh Hashanah 4:2

A.   In olden times the *lulab* was taken up in the Temple for seven
      days, and in the provinces, for one day.

B.   When the Temple was destroyed, Rabban Yohanan ben Zakkai
      made the rule that in the provinces the *lulab* should be taken up
      for seven days, as a memorial to the Temple;

C.   and that the day [the sixteenth of Nisan] on which the *omer* is
      waved should be wholly prohibited [in regard to the eating of new
      produce] [M. Suk. 3:12].

                                                    M. Rosh Hashanah 4:3

First, let us examine the passage in its own terms, and then point to
its consequence for the argument about history. The rules of sounding
the *shofar* run to the special case of the New Year which coincides
with the Sabbath, M. 4:1A-C. Clearly, we have some diverse
materials here since M. 4:1A-D (+ E-F), are formally different from M.
4:3. The point of difference, however, is clear, since M. 4:3A has no
counterpart at M. 4:1A-C, and this is for redactional reasons. That is, to
connect his materials with what has gone before, the redactor could not
introduce the issue of M. 4:1A-C with the formulary, *In olden times...
When the Temple was destroyed....* Consequently, he has used the more
common, mild apocopation to announce his topic, and then reverted to
the expected formulary pattern, which, I think, characterized M. 4:1A-
C as much as M. 4:3. M. 4:2A assumes a different antecedent construction
from the one we have, a formulary which lists points in which
Jerusalem is ahead of Yabneh, and, perhaps, points in which Yabneh is
ahead of Jerusalem. But M. 4:2 clearly responds to M. 4:1E's view. The
meaning of the several entries is clear and requires no comment.

But the point as to the use and meaning of history does. What we
see is that the destruction of the Temple is recognized and treated as
consequential – but only for the organization of rules. The event forms

division between one time and some other, and, in consequence, we sort
out rules pertaining to the Temple and synagogue in one way rather
than in another. That, sum and substance, is the conclusion drawn from
the destruction of the Temple, which is to say, the use that is made of
that catastrophe: an indicator in the organization of rules. What we
see is the opposite of an interest in focusing upon the one-time meaning
of events. Now it is the all-time significance of events in the making of
rules. Events are now treated not as irregular and intrinsically
consequential but as regular and merely instrumental.

4:4

A.   At first they would receive testimony about the new moon all day
long.

B.   One time the witnesses came late, and the Levites consequently
were mixed up as to [what] song [they should sing].

C.   They made the rule that they should receive testimony [about the
new moon] only up to the afternoon offering.

D.   Then, if witnesses came after the afternoon-offering, they would
treat that entire day as holy, and the next day as holy too.

E.   When the Temple was destroyed, Rabban Yohanan b. Zakkai
made the rule that they should [once more] receive testimony
about the new moon all day long.

F.   Said R. Joshua b. Qorha, "This rule too did Rabban Yohanan b.
Zakkai make:

G.   "Even if the head of the court is located somewhere else, the
witnesses should come only to the location of the council [to give
testimony, and not to the location of the head of the court]."

M. Rosh Hashanah 4:4

A-C form a complete unit. E is distinctly secondary. The long
antecedent narrative, A-D is formally out of phase with M. 4:3. The
appendix supplied at F-G is thematically appropriate.

The passages before us leave no doubt about what sages selected as
important about the destruction: it produced changes in synagogue rites.
Although the sages surely mourned for the destruction and the loss of
Israel's principal mode of worship, and certainly recorded the event of
the ninth of Ab in the year 70, they did so in their characteristic way:
they listed the event as an item in a catalogue of things that are like
one another and so demand the same response. But then the destruction
no longer appears as a unique event. It is absorbed into a pattern of like
disasters, all exhibiting similar taxonomic traits, events to which the
people, now well-schooled in tragedy, knows full well the appropriate
response. So it is in demonstrating regularity that sages reveal their
way of coping. Then the uniqueness of the event fades away, its
mundane character is emphasized. The power of taxonomy in imposing

order upon chaos once more does its healing work. The consequence was reassurance that historical events obeyed discoverable laws. Israel's ongoing life would override disruptive, one-time happenings. So catalogues of events, as much as lists of species of melons, served as brilliant apologetic by providing reassurance that nothing lies beyond the range and power of ordering system and stabilizing pattern. Here is yet another way in which the irregular was made regular and orderly, subject to rules:

Mishnah-tractate Taanit 4:6-7

4:6

A.   Five events took place for our fathers on the seventeenth of Tammuz, and five on the ninth of Ab.

B.   On the seventeenth of Tammuz

(1) the tablets [of the Torah] were broken,

(2) the daily whole offering was cancelled,

(3) the city wall was breached,

(4) Apostemos burned the Torah, and (5) he set up an idol in the Temple.

C.   On the ninth of Ab

(1) the decree was made against our forefathers that they should not enter the land,

(2) the first Temple,

(3) the second [Temple] were destroyed,

(4) Betar was taken,

(5) the city was ploughed up [after the war of Hadrian].

D.   When Ab comes, rejoicing diminishes.

M. Taanit 4:6

4:7

A.   In the week in which the ninth of Ab occurs it is prohibited to get a haircut and to wash one's clothes.

B.   But on Thursday of that week these are permitted,

C.   because of the honor due to the Sabbath.

D.   On the eve of the ninth of Ab a person should not eat two prepared dishes, nor should one eat meat or drink wine.

E.   Rabban Simeon b. Gamaliel says, "He should make some change from ordinary procedures."

F.   R. Judah declares people obligated to turn over beds.

G.   But sages did not concur with him.

M. Taanit 4:7,

I include M. Taanit 4:7 to show the context in which the list of M. 4:6 stands. The stunning calamities catalogued at M. 4:6 form groups,

reveal common traits, so are subject to classification. Then the laws of
M. 4:7 provide regular rules for responding to, coping with, these
untimely catastrophes, all (fortuitously) in a single classification. So
the raw materials of history are absorbed into the ahistorical,
supernatural system of the Mishnah. The process of absorption and
regularization of the unique and one-time moment is illustrated in the
passage at hand.

A still more striking example of the reordering of one-time events
into all-time patterns derives from the effort to put together in a
coherent way the rather haphazard history of the cult inherited from
Scripture, with sacrifices made here and there and finally in
Jerusalem. Now, the entire history of the cult, so critical in the larger
system created by the Mishnah's lawyers, produced a patterned,
therefore sensible and intelligible, picture. As is clear, everything
that happened turned out to be susceptible of classification, once the
taxonomic traits were specified. A monothetic exercise, sorting out
periods and their characteristics, took the place of narrative, to
explain things in its own way: first this, and then that, and, in
consequence, the other. So in the neutral turf of holy ground, as much as
in the trembling earth of the Temple mount, everything was absorbed
into one thing, all classified in its proper place and by its appropriate
rule. Indeed, so far as the lawyers proposed to write history at all,
they wrote it into their picture of the long tale of the way in which
Israel served God: the places in which the sacrificial labor was
carried on, the people who did it, the places in which the priests ate
the meat left over for their portion after God's portion was set aside
and burned up. This "historical" account forthwith generated precisely
that problem of locating the regular and orderly, which the
philosophers loved to investigate: the intersection of conflicting but
equally correct taxonomic rules, as we see at M. Zebahim 14:9, below.
The passage that follows therefore is history, so far as the Mishnah's
creators proposed to write history: the reduction of events to rules
forming compositions of regularity, therefore meaning. We follow
Mishnah-tractate Zebahim Chapter Fourteen.

14:4-8

I. A.   Before the tabernacle was set up, (1) the high places were
          permitted, and (2) [the sacrificial] service [was done by] the first
          born [Num. 3:12-12, 8:16-18].

    B.   When the tabernacle was set up, (1) the high places were
          prohibited, and (2) the [sacrificial] service [was done by] priests.

    C.   Most Holy Things were eaten within the veils, Lesser Holy Things
          [were eaten] throughout the camp of Israel.

                            M. Zebahim 14:4

II.   A.   They came to Gilgal.

      B.   The high places were prohibited.

      C.   Most Holy Things were eaten within the veils, Lesser Holy Things, anywhere.

M. Zebahim 14:5

III.   A.   They came to Shiloh.

      B.   The high places were prohibited.

      C.   (1) There was no roof-beam there, but below was a house of stone, and hangings above it, and (2) it was 'the resting place' [Deut. 12:9].

      D.   Most Holy Things were eaten within the veils, Lesser Holy Things and second-tithe [were eaten] in any place within sight [of Shiloh].

M. Zebahim 14:6

IV.   A.   They came to Nob and Gibeon.

      B.   The high places were permitted.

      C.   Most Holy Things were eaten within the veils, Lesser Holy Things, in all the towns of Israel.

M. Zebahim 14:7

V.   A.   They came to Jerusalem.

      B.   The high places were prohibited.

      C.   And they never again were permitted.

      D.   And it was 'the inheritance' [Deut. 12:9].

      E.   Most Holy Things were eaten within the veils, Lesser Holy Things and second-tithe within the wall.

M. Zebahim 4:8

Let us rapidly review the formal traits of this lovely composition, because those traits justify my insistence that we deal with a patterning of events. This set of five formally balanced items bears remarkably few glosses. The form is best revealed at M. 14:5, 7. M. 14:6C is the only significant gloss. M. 14:4 sets up a fine introduction, integral to the whole despite its interpolated and extraneous information at A2, B2. M. 14:8C is essential; D is a gloss, parallel to M. 14:6C2. The unitary construction is self-explanatory. At some points it was permitted to sacrifice on high places, at others, it was not, a neat way of harmonizing Scripture's numerous contradictions on the subject. M. 14:4B depends upon Lev. 17:5. M. 14:5 refers to Joshua 4:19ff.; M. 14:6, to Joshua 18:1. The 'resting place' of Deut. 12:9 is identified with Shiloh. At this point the obligation to separate second tithe is incurred, which accounts for the conclusion of M. 14:4D. M. 14:7 refers to I Samuel 21:2, 7, after the destruction of Shiloh, and to I Kings 3:4. M.

14:8 then identifies the 'inheritance' of Deut. 12:9 with Jerusalem. The 'veils' are familiar at M. 5:3, 5, and the walls of Jerusalem, M. 5:6-8.

14:9

A.   All the Holy Things which one sanctified at the time of the prohibition of the high places and offered at the time of the prohibition of high places
outside –

B.   lo, these are subject to the transgression of a positive commandment and a negative commandment, and they are liable on their account to extirpation [for sacrificing outside the designated place, Lev. 17:8-9, M. 13:1A].

C.   [If] one sanctified them at the time of the permission of high places and offered them up at the time of the prohibition of high places,

D.   lo, these are subject to transgression of a positive commandment and to a negative commandment, but they are not liable on their account to extirpation [since if the offerings had been sacrificed when they were sanctified, there should have been no violation].

E.   [If] one sanctified them at the time of the prohibition of high places and offered them up at the time of the permission of high places,

F.   lo, these are subject to transgression of a positive commandment, but they are not subject to a negative commandment at all.

M. Zebahim 14:9

Now we see how the Mishnah's sages turn events into rules and show the orderly nature of history. The secondary expansion of M. 14:4-8 is in three parts, A-B, C and E-F, all in close verbal balance. The upshot is to cover all sorts of circumstances within a single well-composed pattern. This is easy to represent by simple symbols. We deal with two circumstances and two sets of actions: The circumstance of the prohibition of high places, (-), and that of their permission (+), and the act of sanctification of a sacrifice (A) and offering it up, (B), thus:

A: –A –B = negative, positive, extirpation

C: +A +B = negative, positive

E: –A +B = positive only.

We cannot have +A +B, since there is no reason to prohibit or to punish the one who sanctifies and offers up a sacrifice on a high place when it is permitted to do so(!). Accordingly, all possible cases are dealt with.

In the first case, both sanctification and offering up take place at the time that prohibition of high places applies. There is transgression of a positive commandment and a negative commandment. The negative is Deut. 12:13, the positive, Deut. 12:14. *Take heed that you do not offer your burnt-offerings at every place that you see; but at the place which the Lord will choose in one of your tribes, there you shall offer your burnt-offerings...* The mixtures, C and E, then go over the same ground. If sanctification takes place when it is permitted to sanctify animals for use in high places, but the offering up takes place when it is not allowed to do so (e.g., the former for M. 14:4, the latter, M. 14:6), extirpation does not apply (Lev. 17:5-7). When we then reverse the order (e.g., M. 14:6, M. 14:7), there is no negative (Deut. 12:13), but the positive commandment (Deut. 12:14) has been transgressed. C surely conforms to Simeon's theory, M. 14:2P, but sages, M. 14:2Q, need not differ. But matters do not stop here. The rule-making out of the raw materials of disorderly history continues unabated.

14:10

A. These are the Holy Things offered in the tabernacle [of Gilgal, Nob, and Gibeon]:

B. Holy Things which were sanctified for the tabernacle.

C. Offerings of the congregation are offered in the tabernacle.

D. Offerings of the individual [are offered] on a high place.

E. Offerings of the individual which were sanctified for the tabernacle are to be offered in the tabernacle.

F. And if one offered them up on a high place, he is free.

G. What is the difference between the high place of an individual and the high place of the community?

H. (1) Laying on of hands, and (2) slaughtering at the north [of the altar], and (3) placing [of the blood] round about [the altar], and (4) waving, and (5) bring near.

I. R. Judah says, "there is no meal-offering on a high place [but there is in the tabernacle]" –

J. and (1) the priestly service, and (2) the wearing of garments of ministry, and (3) the use of utensils of ministry, and (4) the sweet-smelling savor and (5) the dividing line for the [tossing of various kinds of] blood, and (6) the rule concerning the washing of hands and feet.

K. But the matters of time, and remnant, and uncleanness are applicable both here and there [by contrast to M. 14:3F-I].

M. Zebahim 14:10

When M. 14:4-8 refer to a high place which was permitted, and refer also to the presence of veils, it is assumed that there were both a tabernacle (hence the veils) and also high places. This must mean

Gilgal, M. 14:5 and Nob and Gibeon, M. 14:7. Now the issue is, if there are both a tabernacle and a high place, which sorts of offerings belong to which kind of altar? It follows that the pericope treats the situations specified at M. 14:5, 7, a secondary expansion. A is answered by B. C-F go on to work out their own interests, and cannot be constructed to answer A, because they specify *are offered in the tabernacle* as a complete apodosis, which A does not require and B clearly does not want. B tells us that even though it is permitted to offer a sacrifice on a high place, a sacrifice which is set aside for the tabernacle (obviously) is to be offered there. Then C-F work the matter out. C and D are clear as stated. Holy Things which are sanctified for the tabernacle are offerings of the congregation (C). It is taken for granted that they are meant for the tabernacle, even when not so designated as specified by B. Individuals' sacrifices are assumed to be for high places unless specified otherwise (D). Obviously, if they are sanctified for the tabernacle, E, they are sacrificed there. But there is no reason to inflict liability if they are offered on a high place, F. The whole is carefully worked out, leaving no unanswered questions.

G then asks what difference there is between the high place which serves an individual, and "the high place" – the tabernacle – which serves the congregation, that is, the ones at Gilgal, Nob, and Gibeon. H specifies five items, J, six more, and Judah brings the list up to twelve. K completes the matter. *Time* refers to the improper intention to the flesh or burn the sacrificial parts after the appropriate time, thus *refuse*. The word-choice is unexpected. The inclusion of M. Zeb. 14:9, structurally matching M. Taanit 4:7, shows us the goal of the historical composition. It is to set forth rules that intersect and produce confusion, so that we may sort out confusion and make sense of all the data. The upshot may now be stated briefly: the authorship at hand had the option of narrative, but chose the way of philosophy: generalization through classification, comparison and contrast.

The Mishnah absorbs into its encompassing system all events, small and large. With what happens the sages accomplish what they do with everything else: a vast labor of taxonomy, an immense construction of the order and rules governing the classification of everything on earth and in Heaven. The disruptive character of history – one-time events of ineluctable significance – scarcely impresses the philosophers. They find no difficulty in showing that what appears unique and beyond classification has in fact happened before and so falls within the range of trustworthy rules and known procedures. Once history's components, one-time events, lose their distinctiveness, then history as a didactic intellectual construct, as a source of lessons and rules, also loses all pertinence. So lessons and rules come from sorting things out and classifying them, that is, from the procedures and modes of thought of the philosopher seeking regularity. To this labor of taxonomy, the historian's way of selecting data and arranging them into patterns of meaning to teach lessons, proves inconsequential. One-time events are not what matters. The world is composed of nature and supernature. The repetitious laws that count are those to be discovered in Heaven and, in Heaven's creation and counterpart, on earth. Keep those laws and things will work out. Break them, and the result is predictable: calamity of whatever sort will supervene in accordance with the rules. But just because it is predictable, a catastrophic happening testifies to what has always been and must always be, in accordance with reliable rules and within categories already discovered and well explained. That is why the lawyer-philosophers of the mid-second century produced the Mishnah – to explain how things are. Within the framework of well-classified rules, there could be messiahs, but no single Messiah.

Up to now I have contrasted "history" with "philosophy," that is, disorderly and unique events as against rules governing all events and emerging inductively from them. I therefore have framed matters in such a way that the Mishnah's system appears to have been ahistorical and anti-historical. Yet in fact the framers of the Mishnah recognized the past-ness of the past and hence, by definition, laid out a conception of the past that constitutes a historical doctrine. Theirs was not an anti-historical conception of reality but a deeply historical one, even though it is a different conception of the meaning of history from the familiar one. It was, in a single word, social scientific, not historical in the traditional sense of history-writing. Let me explain this difference, since it is fundamental to understanding the Mishnah's system as essentially philosophical and, in our terms, scientific.

To express the difference, I point out that, for modern history-writing, what is important is to describe what is unique and individual, not what is ongoing and unremarkable. History is the story of change, development, movement, not of what does not change, develop, or move. For the thinkers of the Mishnah, historical patterning emerges as today scientific knowledge does, through taxonomy, the classification of the unique and individual, the organization of change and movement within unchanging categories. That is why the dichotomy between history and eternity, change and permanence, signals an unnuanced exegesis of what was, in fact, a subtle and reflective doctrine of history. That doctrine proves entirely consistent with the large perspectives of scribes, from the ones who made omen-series in ancient Babylonia to the ones who made the Mishnah.

How, then, in the Mishnah does history come to full conceptual expression? History as an account of a meaningful pattern of events, making sense of the past and giving guidance about the future, begins with the necessary conviction that events matter because they form series, one after another. And when we put a series together, we have a rule, just as when we put cases together, we can demonstrate the rule that governs them all. The Mishnah's authorship therefore treats historical events just as they sort out anything else of interest to them: correct composition of contracts, appropriate disposition of property, proper conduct on a holy day, all things imputed through specific events, formed so that we can derive out of the concrete the abstract and encompassing rule, just as I pointed out in Chapter One. What we see, therefore, is the congruence of language and thought, detail and main point, subject-matter and sheltering system.

That is why we may not find surprising the Mishnah's framers' reluctance to present us with an elaborate theory of events, a fact fully consonant with their systematic points of insistence and encompassing concern. Events do not matter, one by one. The philosopher-lawyers exhibited no theory of history either. Their conception of Israel's destiny in no way called upon historical categories of either narrative or didactic explanation to describe and account for the future. The small importance attributed to the figure of the Messiah as an historical-eschatological figure, therefore, fully accords with the larger traits of the system as a whole. Let me speak with emphasis: If what is important in Israel's existence is sanctification, an ongoing process, and not salvation, understood as a one-time event at the end, then no one will find reason to narrate history.

By this point the reader must wonder where, if at all, the Mishnah's system attends to the events of the preceding century, which, after all, changed for all time the conditions of Israel's existence. If my thesis about the meaning and uses of history in the Mishnah's Judaism is valid, then we should see a head-on confrontation with the great events of the age. And so we do, but we must be prepared for the identification of what matters. To the framers of the Mishnah, a great sage is an event, as much as a battle is noteworthy, and the destruction of the Temple finds its counterpart in the death of a sage. In both instances, we shall see a pattern, and it is the same pattern. With the decline in the holiness of the Temple and the cult, changes took place, leading to disaster. With the death of the great sages (most of them second century figures, as a matter of fact), changes took place, leading to social disaster. That is the message conveyed by the details of Mishnah-tractate Sotah Chapter

Nine, to which we now turn. Let us first outline the chapter in its own terms.

The concluding chapter of Mishnah-tractate Sotah takes up the rite of breaking the heifer's neck (Deut. 21:1ff.). An effort is made at M. 9:1A-B to link the matter to M. 7:1-2's interest in the use of Hebrew in the rite, but, in fact, the relevant pericope is M. 9:6, which covers the ground of the formula spoken in the rite. So the whole unit – M. 9:1-8 – is essentially autonomous of its larger setting. A fair proportion of the whole is devoted to the exegesis of the relevant Scriptures, specifically, M. 9:1, 2, 3, 5, and 6. M. 9:2-4 present what seems to be a triplet of rulings assigned to Eliezer. M. 9:7-8 provide materials more natural to Mishnah, e.g., a triplet on how we dispose of the heifer if the murderer should be found at various points in the rite (M. 9:7), and a treatment of various kinds of evidentiary situations (M. 9:8).

The chapter's second half, M. 9:9-15, carries us to our point of interest, for it proceeds in a quite different direction, providing reflections on the decline of the times in general (M. 9:9-12), the catastrophes which followed the destruction of the Temple (M. 9:12-14), and, finally, a very long potpourri of sayings on the equivalent catastrophes attendant upon the death of sages, principally of the second century (M. 9:15). The link of these materials to the coherent half of the chapter comes at the outset, M. 9:9: the rite of breaking the heifer's neck was cancelled because there were so many murders, and, still more germane to the tractate, as a whole, the rite of the bitter water was annulled because there were so many adulterers. I am inclined to think that this excellent conclusion at M. 9:9 has been constructed to link the formally unified materials which follow, M. 9:9, 11-12, to the foregoing – both to Chapter Nine and to the tractate as a whole – and then the further pericopae, M. 9:12-15, were carried in the wake of what, if left alone, would have formed a rather deft conclusion to the work of redacting both the tractate and the chapter.

9:1

A.   The rite of the heifer whose neck is to be broken is said in the Holy Language,

B.   since it is said, *If one be found slain in the land lying in the field...*

C.   *then your elders your judges shall come forth* (Deut. 21:1-2).

D.   Three from the high court in Jerusalem went forth.

E.   R. Judah says, "Five, since is is said, *Your elders* – thus, two, and *your judges,* thus, two, and there is no such thing as a court made up of an even number of judges, so they add to their number yet one more."

M. Sotah 9:1

The pericope is in two units, A-B, and C-E. The former revert to the theme of M. 7:1-2, but it is only at M. 9:6 that what must be said in Hebrew plays a role. The cited verse, then, should be Deut. 21:7. There is no point at which the prooftext begun at B serves the purposes of A. It follows that A is a superscription attached as part of the redactional work. The use of B indeed is in connection with C-E. The anonymous view is that three go forth, but Judah shows that the cited verse requires five.

9:2-4

A. [If] it was found hidden under a heap of rocks or hanging from a tree or floating on the surface of water, they did not break the neck of a heifer,

B. since it is said, *On the ground* {Deut. 21:1] – not hidden under a pile of rock.

C. *Lying* – not hung on a tree.

D. *In the field* – not floating on the water.

E. [If] it was found near the frontier, near a town which had a gentile majority, or near a town which had no court, they did not break a heifer's neck.

F. They measure only from a town which has a court.

I. G. "[If] it was found exactly between two such towns, then the two of them bring two heifers," the words of R. Eliezer.

H. And Jerusalem does not have to bring a heifer whose neck is to be broken.

M. Sotah 9:2

II. A. "[If] its head is found in one place and its body in another place, they bring the head to the body," the words of R. Eliezer.

B. R. Aqiba says, "They bring the body to the head."

M. Sotah 9:3

III. A. From what point did they measure?

B. R. Eliezer says, "From his belly-button."

C. R. Aqiba says, "From his nose."

D. R. Eliezer b. Jacob says, "From the place at which he was turned into a corpse – from his neck."

M. Sotah 9:4

We apparently have a triplet involving Eliezer and Aqiba, but if that is the case, then M. 9:2G is defective. The material at the beginning, M. 9:2A-F, H, is clear as given. The law is stated in Mishnah's usual way, A, then given an exegetical foundation, B-D. E does not enjoy similar exegetical support. Its apodosis may be, *They did not measure.* The opinion contrary to Eliezer's will say that there is no

breaking of the heifer's neck at all. The dispute of M. 9:3 concerns
where the parts of the corpse are to be buried. Eliezer has the corpse
buried where the larger part is located. Aqiba wants the corpse to be
buried where the head is located. Then, M. 9:4, they dispute the point
at which the measuring began. The belly-button is the middle of the
body. The nose is the point from which the soul exits. Eliezer b. Jacob's
contribution to the dispute ignores the antecedent form and reasoning.

9:5

A.   The elders of Jerusalem took their leave and went away.

B.   The elders of that town bring *a heifer from the herd with which*
      labor had not been done and which had not drawn the yoke
      (Deut. 21:3).

C.   But a blemish does not invalidate it.

D.   They brought it down into a rugged valley (and *rugged* is meant
      literally, hard, but even if it is not rugged, it is valid).

E.   And they break its neck with a hatchet from behind.

F.   And its place is prohibited for sowing and for tilling, but permitted
      for the combing out of flax and for quarrying stones.

M. Sotah 9:5

Narrative style characterizes A-D. The Jerusalemites measure the
distance between the corpse and the surrounding towns, M. 9:1. They
then go home, and the elders of the town which has to carry out the rite
do their duty. The place in which the rite takes place, F, cannot be used
for agricultural purposes.

9:6

A.   The elders of that town wash their hands in the place in which the
      neck of the heifer is broken, and they say,

B.   *Our hands have not shed this blood, nor did our eyes see it* (Deut.
      21:7).

C.   Now could it enter our minds that the elders of a court might be
      shedders of blood?

D.   But [they mean:] He did not come into our hands and we sent him
      away without food.

E.   And we did not see him and let him go along without an escort.

F.   And [it is] the priests [who] say, *Forgive O Lord, your people Israel,*
      whom you have redeemed, and do not allow innocent blood in the
      midst of your people, Israel (Deut. 21:8).

G.   They did not have to say, *And the blood shall be forgiven them*
      (Deut. 21:8).

H.   But the Holy Spirit informs them, "Whenever you do this, the
      blood shall be forgiven to you."

M. Sotah 9:6

The narrative concludes here, with two more legal-analytical pericopae to come. A-B, as we noticed, are the point at which M. 9:1-8 are relevant to M. 7:1-2. C-E are a secondary interpolation, making an interesting point. Then the exposition of the Scriptures is concluded. The differentiation, within the cited verse, among the several voices provokes T. to provide us with numerous examples of the same phenomenon of various voices' speaking at a single point in Scripture.

9:7

I.	A.	[If] the murderer was found before the neck of the heifer was broken, it [simply] goes forth and pastures in the herd.
II.	B.	[If the murderer is found] after the neck of the heifer is broken, it is to be buried in its place.
	C.	For to begin with it was brought in a matter of doubt. It has atoned for the matter of doubt on which account it was brought and which has gone its way.
III.	D.	[If] the neck of the heifer was broken and afterward the murderer was found, lo, this one is put to death.

M. Sotah 9:7

The triplet bears a gloss at C. Otherwise it is in excellent form. Once the heifer is killed, the place in which it was killed remains prohibited and the heifer's carcass cannot be used for any gain. The murderer in any event will be punished (Deut. 21:9).

9:8

I.	A.	[If] one witness says, "I saw the murderer," and one witness says, "you did not see him."
	(B.	[If] one woman says, "I saw him," and one woman says, "You did not see him,")
	C.	they would go through the rite of breaking the neck of the heifer.
II.	D.	[If] one witness says, "I saw," and two say, "You did not see," they would break the neck of the heifer.
III.	E.	[If] two say, "We saw," and one says to them, "You did not see," they did not break the neck of the heifer.

M. Sotah 9:8

The rite of breaking the heifer's neck is performed when there is no sound evidence as to who has killed him. Here we run a parallel to M. 6:4. At A, B, we have testimony which is cancelled out. At D the evidence is inadequate for conviction. But at E we have ample evidence for punishing the murderer.

9:9

I.   A   When murderers became many, the rite of breaking the heifer's neck was cancelled.

        B.   [This was] when Eleazar b. Dinai came along, and he was also called Tehinah b. Perishah. Then they went and called him, " Son of a murderer."

II.   C.   When adulterers became many, the ordeal of the bitter water was cancelled.

        D.   And Rabban Yohanan b. Zakkai cancelled it, since it is said, *I will not punish your daughters when they commit whoredom, nor your daughters-in-law when they commit adultery, for they themselves go apart with whores* (Hosea 4:14).

III.   E.   When Yosé b. Yoezer of Seredah and Yosé b. Yohanan of Jerusalem died, the grape-clusters were cancelled,

        F.   since it is said, There is no cluster to eat, my soul desired the first ripe fig (Micah 7:1).

M. Sotah 9:9

The formal construction constituted by M. 9:9, 11, 12, is joined to the foregoing because of the obvious connection at A, the rite of breaking the heifer's neck. Once we establish the pattern of accounting for the end of one or another of the rites, then a whole sequence will follow in natural order. This pericope gives us a triplet, M. 9:9A, glossed at B, C, glossed at D, and E, bearing a prooftext at F.

        A   Yohanan, high priest, did away with the confession concerning tithe.

        B.   Also: He cancelled the rite of the Awakeners and the Stunners.

        C.   Until his time a hammer did strike in Jerusalem.

        D.   And in his time no man had to ask concerning doubtfully tithed produce.

M. Sotah 9:10

The general theme of accounting for the cessation of ancient rites accounts for the inclusion of this obviously irrelevant item, which ignores the established form and also is uninterested in the basic notion of the construction as a whole, which is the decline of the generations. Yohanan's time, by contrast, is represented in a positive light.

9:11-13

IV.   A   When the Sanhedrin was cancelled, singing at wedding feasts was cancelled, since it is said, *They shall not drink wine with a song* (Is. 24:9).

M. Sotah 9:11

V. A.   When the former prophets died out, the Urim and Tummim were cancelled.

VI. B.   When the sanctuary was destroyed, the Shamir-worm ceased and [so did] the honey of *supim.*

    C.   And faithful men came to an end,

    D.   since it is written, *Help, O Lord, for the godly man ceases* (Ps. 12:2).

    E.   Rabban Simeon b. Gamaliel says in the name of R. Joshua, "From the day on which the Temple was destroyed, there is no day on which there is no curse, and dew has not come down as a blessing. The good taste of produce is gone."

    F.   R. Yosé says, "Also: the fatness of produce is gone."

                        M. Sotah 9:12

    A.   R. Simeon b. Eleazar says, "[When] purity [ceased], it took away the taste and scent; [when] tithes [ceased], they took away the fatness of corn."

    B.   And sages say, "Fornication and witchcraft made an end to everything."

                        M. Sotah 9:13

We now revert to the established form and theme, with three more entries, M. 9:11, M. 9:12A, and M. 9:12B+C. Once the destruction of the Temple is introduced, M. 9:12B-C, we shall turn from the general theme of the decline of the generations to the specific one of the change in the world effected by the catastrophe of A.D. 70.

9:14

I.   A.   In the war against Vespasian they decreed against the wearing of wreaths by bridegrooms and against the wedding-drum.

II. B.   In the war against Titus they decreed against the wearing of wreaths by brides.

     C.   And [they decreed] that a man should not teach Greek to his son.

III. D.   In the last war [Bar Kokhba's] they decreed that a bride should not go out in a palanquin inside the town.

     E.   But our rabbis [thereafter] permitted the bride to go out in a palanquin inside the town.

                        M. Sotah 9:14

The triplet, A, B, and D, bears glosses at C and E. *Titus* had best be replaced by Quitus, in the time of Trajan, which makes better sense for our form. The decline of the generation in general and the affect, upon the public welfare, of the destruction of Jerusalem in particular now yield to the third and final theme in this unit, the decline of the generations in consequence of the passing of the great age of the sages.

Now the composition makes its great point, that the destruction of the Temple and the death of great sages mark the movement of time and impart to an age the general rules that govern life therein. That is the "lesson of history," and it is not drawn from a single event but from patterns exhibited by many like events, and these then are of two classifications: what happens in respect to holiness in the cult, and to holiness in the sage.

9:15

A.   When R. Meir died, makers of parables came to an end.

B.   When Ben Azzai died, diligent students came to an end.

C.   When Ben Zoma died, exegetes came to an end.

D.   When R. Joshua died, goodness went away from the world.

E.   When Rabban Simeon b. Gamaliel died, the locust came, and troubles multiplied.

F.   When Eleazar b. Azariah died, wealth went away from the sages.

G.   When R. Aqiba died, the glory of the Torah came to an end.

H.   When R. Hanina b. Dosa died, wonder-workers came to an end.

I.   When R. Yosé Qatnuta died, pietists went away.

J.   (And why was he called *Qatnuta*? Because he was the least of the pietists.)

K.   When Rabban Yohanan b. Zakkai died, the splendor of wisdom came to an end.

L.   When Rabban Gamaliel the Elder died, the glory of the Torah came to an end, and cleanness and separateness perished.

M.   When R. Ishmael b. Phabi died, the splendor of the priesthood came to an end.

N.   When Rabbi died, modesty and fear of sin came to an end.

O.   R. Pinhas b. Yair says, "When the Temple was destroyed, associates became ashamed and so did free men, and they covered their heads.

P.   "And wonder-workers became feeble. And violent men and big takers grew strong.

Q.   "And none expounds and none seeks [learning] and none asks.

I.   R.   "Upon whom shall we depend? Upon our Father in heaven."

S.   R. Eliezer the Great says, "From the day on which the Temple was destroyed, sages began to be like scribes, and scribes like ministers, and ministers like ordinary folk.

T.   "And the ordinary folk have become feeble.

U.   "And none seeks.

II.   V.   "Upon whom shall we depend? Upon our Father in heaven."

W.   With the footprints of the Messiah: presumption increases, and dearth increases.

X.   The Vine gives its fruit and wine at great cost.

Y.   And the government turns to heresy.

Z.   And there is no reproof.

AA.   The gathering place will be for prostitution.

BB.   And Galilee will be laid waste.

CC.   And the Gablan will be made desolate.

DD.   And the men of the frontier will go about from town to town, and none will take pity on them.

EE.   And the wisdom of scribes will putrefy.

FF.   And those who fear sin will be rejected.

GG.   And the truth will be locked away.

HH.   Children will shame elders, and elders will stand up before children.

II.   *For the son dishonors the father and the daughter rises up against her mother, the daughter-in-law against her mother-in-law; a man's enemies are the men of his own house* (Mic. 7:6).

JJ.   The face of the generation in the face of a dog.

KK.   A son is not ashamed before his father.

III. LL. Upon whom shall we depend? Upon our Father in heaven.

MM.   R. Pinhas b. Yair says, "Heedfulness leads to cleanliness, cleanliness leads to cleanness, cleanness leads to abstinence, abstinence leads to holiness, holiness leads to modesty, modesty leads to the fear of sin, the fear of sin leads to piety, piety leads to the Holy Spirit, the Holy Spirit leads to the resurrection of the dead, and the resurrection of the dead comes through Elijah, blessed be his memory, Amen."

M. Sotah 9:15

The pericope is divided into the following components: A-N, thirteen names, O-R, with its parallel at S-V, W-LL – a potpourri, joined, if at all, only by LL, and MM. It would appear, however, that W-LL yield thirteen clearcut and distinct stichs. Pinhas, MM, has ten. So perhaps there is some effort at presenting a formally interesting construction. The point of it all requires no comment in the present context.

The theology of the Mishnah encompasses history and its meaning, but, we now realize, history and the interpretation of history do not occupy a central position on the stage of Israel's life portrayed by the Mishnah. The critical categories derive from the modalities of holiness. What can become holy or what is holy? These tell us what will attract the close scrutiny of our authorship and precipitate sustained thought, expressed through very concrete and picayune cases. If I had to identify the two most important foci of holiness in the Mishnah, they would be, in the natural world, the land, but only The Holy Land, the Land of Israel, and, in the social world, the people, but only The People of Israel. In the interplay among Land, People, and God, we see the inner workings of the theological vision of the sages of the Mishnah. In Martin Jaffee's exposition of the main points of Mishnah-tractate Maaserot and of Chapter One of that tractate, we are able to discern, in discourses about details, the main principles of the theology of the Mishnah that flows from the sanctity of Land and People in the everyday encounter with God.

Chapter Four

How the Mishnah Expresses its Philosophy:
A Theory of Intentionality or (Mere) Obsession
with Whether Wheat Gets Wet?

One fundamental principle of the system of Judaism attested in the Mishnah is that God and the human being share traits of attitude and emotion. They want the same thing. For example, it is made clear in Mishnah-tractate Maaserot, man and God respond in the same way to the same events, since they share not only ownership of the Land but also viewpoint on the value of its produce. When the farmer wants the crop, so too does God. When the householder takes the view that the crop is worthwhile, God responds to the attitude of the farmer by forming the same opinion. The Mishnah's theological anthropology that brings God and the householder into the same continuum prepares the way for understanding what makes the entire Mishnaic system work. But in what kind of language, and precisely through what sort of discourse, does the authorship of the Mishnah set forth principles that motivate the entire system of the Mishnah? Here I shall show that through little that authorship says much, and in discourse on matters of no consequence at all, indeed, matters that, in the setting of the writers of the document, had no practical bearing at all, principal conceptions emerge.

At stake in this presentation is not the particular proposition, but the mode of discourse in which the proposition is set forth. I maintain we have philosophy and theology in a very odd idiom; others find here nothing more than obsessive formalism expressing a religion of pots and pans, and so they want the authorship of the Mishnah to be represented in other ways than in the way in which I have described them. What we shall see in striking ways is a way of expressing a principle and of exploring conflicting positions that is quite odd. Our authorship, specifically, talks only in picayune details. Great issues of philosophy are spelled out in exchanges on matters of no consequence. Only when we see the whole do we perceive that, through arguments about nothing very much, our authorship has laid forth a variety of positions on a fundamental issue, a concern that animates the entire system they propose to construct. Let me first spell out the positions, then we shall turn to a sustained and concrete example of the manner in which these positions are laid out in the to us unfamiliar mode of discourse at hand.

The Mishnah's authorship's discussion on intention works out several theories concerning not God and God's relationship to humanity but the nature of the human will, a decidedly philosophical topic. The human being is defined as not only sentient but also a volitional being, who can will with effect, unlike beasts and, as a matter of fact, angels (which do not, in fact, figure in the Mishnah at all). On the one side, there is no consideration or will or attitude of animals, for these are null. On the other side, will and attitude of angels, where these are represented in later documents, are totally subservient to God's wishes. Only the human being, in the person of the farmer, possesses and also exercises the power of intentionality. And it is the power that intentionality possesses that forms the central consideration. Because a human being forms an intention, consequences follow, whether or not given material expression in gesture or even in speech. An account of the Mishnah's sages' philosophical anthropology – theory of the structure of the human being – must begin with the extraordinary power imputed by the Mishnah's system to the will and intentionality of the human being.

But that view comes to expression with regard to human beings of a particular sort. The householder-farmer (invariably represented as male) is a principal figure, just as the (invariably male) priest in the Temple is another. The attitude of the one toward the crop, like that of the other toward the offering that he carries out, affects the status of the crop. It classifies an otherwise unclassified substance. It changes the standing of an already classified beast. It shifts the status of a pile of grain, without any physical action whatsoever, from one category to another. Not only so, but as we shall now show, the attitude or will of a farmer can override the effects of the natural world, e.g., keeping in the status of what is dry and so insusceptible to cultic uncleanness a pile of grain that in fact has been rained upon and wet down. An immaterial reality, shaped and reformed by the householder's attitude and plan, overrides the material effect of a rain-storm. And that example brings us to the way in which these profound philosophical issues are explored. It is in the remarkable essay on theories of the relationship between action and intention worked out in Mishnah-tractate Makhshirin and exemplified by Chapter Four of that tractate.

The subject-matter that serves as medium for sages' theories of human will and intention hardly appears very promising. Indeed, the topic of the tractate before us on its own hardly will have led us to anticipate what, in fact, will interest sages. The subject matter of tractate Makhshirin, to which we now turn, is the affect of liquid upon produce. The topic derives from the statement of Lev. 11:37: "And if any part of their carcass [a dead creeping thing] falls upon any seed for sowing that is to be sown, it is clean; but if water is put on the seed and any part of their carcass falls on it, it is unclean for you." Sages understand this statement to mean that seed that is dry is insusceptible to uncleanness, while seed that has been wet down is susceptible. They further take the view – and this is the point at which intention or human will enters in – that if seed, or any sort of grain, is wet down without the assent of the farmer who owns the grain, then the grain remains insusceptible, while if seed or grain is wet down with the farmer's assent, then the grain is susceptible to uncleanness. The upshot is that that grain that a farmer wets down and that is touched by a source of uncleanness, e.g., a dead creeping thing, is then deemed unclean and may not be eaten by those who eat their food in a state of cultic cleanness in accord with the laws of the book of Leviticus pertaining to the priests' food in the Temple.

Once we agree that what is deliberately wet down is susceptible and what is wet down not with the farmer's assent or by his intention is insusceptible, then we work out diverse theories of the interplay between intention and action. And that is the point, over all, at which the authorship of Mishnah-tractate Makhshirin enters in and sets forth its ideas. Tractate Makhshirin is shown to be formed of five successive layers of generative principles, in sequence:

1. Dry produce is insusceptible, a notion which begins in the plain meaning of Lev. 11:34, 37.

2. Wet produce is susceptible only when intentionally wet down, a view expressed in gross terms by Abba Yosé as cited by Joshua.

3. Then follow the refinements of the meaning and effects of intention, beginning in Aqiba's and Tarfon's dispute, in which the secondary matter of what is tangential to one's primary motive is investigated.

4. This yields the contrary views, assuredly belonging to second-century masters, that what is essential imparts susceptibility and what is peripheral to one's primary purpose does not; and that both what is essential and what is peripheral impart susceptibility to uncleanness. (A corollary to this matter is the refinement that what is wet

down under constraint is not deemed wet down by deliberation.)

5.   The disputes on the interpretation of intention – Is it solely defined by what one actually does or modified also by what one has wanted to do as well as by what one has done? – belonging to Yosé and Judah and his son Yosé.

We see from this catalogue of successive positions, assigned to authorities who lived in successive generations, that the paramount theme of the tractate is the determination of the capacity of the eligible liquids to impart susceptibility to uncleanness. The operative criterion, whether or not the liquids are applied intentionally, obviously is going to emerge in every pericope pertinent to the theme. If I now summarize the central and generative theme of our tractate, we may state matter as follows.

First, liquids are capable of imparting susceptibility to uncleanness only if they are useful to men, e.g., drawn with approval, or otherwise subject to human deliberation and intention. The contrary view is that however something is wet down, once it is wet, it falls within the rule of Lev. 11:34, 38, and is subject to uncleanness.

Second, if we begin with the fundamental principle behind the tractate, thus: it is

1.   that which is given in the name of Abba Yosé-Joshua (M. Makhsirin 1:3M):   Water imparts susceptibility to uncleanness only when it is applied to produce intentionally or deliberately. This yields a secondary and derivative rule:

2.   Aqiba's distinction at M. Makhsirin 4:9 and M. Makhsirin 5:4:   Water intrinsic to one's purpose is detached with approval, but that which is not essential in accomplishing one's primary purpose is not under the law, If water be put. What Aqiba has done is to carry to its logical next stage the generative principle. If water applied with approval can impart susceptibility to uncleanness, then, it follows, only *that part* of the detached and applied water is essential to one's intention is subject to the law, If water be put. Items in the name of second-century authorities that develop Aqiba's improvement of Abba Yosé's principle raise an interesting question:

3.   What is the relationship between intention and action? Does intention to do something govern the decision in a case, even though one's action has produced a different effect?

For example, if I intend to wet down only part of an object, or make use of only part of a body of water, but then wet down the whole or dispose of the whole, is the whole deemed susceptible? Does my consequent action revise the original effects of my intention?

The deep thought on the relationship between what one does and what one wants to see happen explores the several possible positions. Judah and his son, Yosé, take up the position that ultimate deed or result is definitive of intention. What happens is retrospectively deemed to decide what I wanted to happen (M. Makhsirin 3:5-7). Other Ushans, Yosé in particular (M. Makhsirin 1:5), maintain the view that, while consequence plays a role in the determination of intention, it is not exclusive and definitive. What I wanted to make happen affects the assessment of what actually has happened. Now the positions on the interplay of action and intention are these:

1.   Judah has the realistic notion that a person changes his mind, and therefore we adjudge a case solely by what he does and not by what he says he will do, intends, or has intended, to do. If we turn Judah's statement around, we come up with the conception predominant throughout his rulings: *A case is judged in terms solely of what the person does.* If he puts on water, that water in particular that he has deliberately applied imparts susceptibility to uncleanness. If he removes water, only that water he actually removes imparts susceptibility to uncleanness, but water that he intends to remove but that is not actually removed is not deemed subject to the person's original intention. And, it is fair to add, we know it is not subject to the original intention, because the person's action has not accomplished the original intention or has placed limits upon the original intention. What is done is wholly determinative of what is originally intended, and that is the case whether the result is that the water is deemed capable or incapable of imparting susceptibility to uncleanness.

2.   Yosé at M. Makhsirin 1:5 expresses the contrary view. Water that has been wiped off is detached with approval. But water that has remained on the leek has not conformed to the man's intention, and that intention is shown by what the man has actually done. Accordingly, the water remaining on the leek is not subject to the law, If water be put. The upshot is to reject the view that what is done is

wholly determinative of what is originally intended. We sort things out by appeal to nuances of effect.

3.   Simeon's point at M. Makhsirin 1:6 is that the liquid in the breath or left on the palm of the hand is not wanted and not necessary to the accomplishment of one's purpose. Simeon's main point is that liquid not essential in accomplishing one's purpose is not taken into account and does not come under the law, If water be put. Why not? Because water is held to be applied with approval *only* when it serves a specific purpose. That water which is incidental has not been subjected to the man's wishes and therefore does not impart susceptibility to uncleanness. Only that water that is necessary to carry out the farmer's purpose imparts susceptibility to uncleanness. If a pile of grain has been wet down, then water that the farmer has deliberately applied effects susceptibility to uncleanness to that part of the grain-pile that it has touched. But water that is incidental and not subject to the farmer's initial plan has no effect upon the grain, even though, as a matter of fact, grain at some other point in the pile may be just as wet as grain the farmer has deliberately watered.

Simeon and Yosé deem water to have been detached and applied with approval only when it serves a person's essential purpose, and water that is not necessary in accomplishing that purpose is not deemed subject to the law, If water be put. That is why Simeon rules as he does. Yosé states a different aspect of the same conception. Water that actually has dripped on the leek in no way has fallen under the person's approval. This is indicated by the facts of the matter, the results of the person's actual deed. And this brings us to the concrete exposition of the chapter at hand. With the positions and principles just now outlined, the reader can follow the discussion with little difficulty. We begin with the simple distinction between water that I want for the accomplishment of my purpose, and water that I do not want, and that category of water does not have the power to impart susceptibility to uncleanness.

The recurrent formula, "If water be put," alludes to Lev. 11:34, 37, and refers to the deliberate watering down of seed or produce. But at stake is the classification of the water. The kind of water to which allusion is made is in the category of "If water be put," meaning that that water, having served the farmer's purpose, has the power to impart susceptibility to uncleanness should it fall on grain. Water that is not in the category of "If water be put," should it fall on grain by some sort of accident, does not impart susceptibility to uncleanness to grain that is otherwise kept dry. It remains to observe that the reason the farmer wets down grain is that the grain is going to be milled, and milling grain requires some dampening of the seed. Accordingly, we have the counterpart to the issue of tithing. When the farmer plans to make use of the (now-tithed) grain, and indicates the plan by wetting down the grain, then the issue of cultic cleanness, that is, preserving the grain from the sources of cultic uncleanness listed in Leviticus Chapters Eleven through Fifteen, is raised. Before the farmer wants to use the produce, the produce is null. The will and intentionality of the farmer, owner of the grain, are what draws the produce within the orbit of the immaterial world of uncleanness and cleanness.

Now to the actual texts I have chosen for illustrating not only the issues but the way in which the issues are set forth and analyzed: arguments about very picayune questions indeed, and, furthermore, questions lacking all concrete relevance in the world in the second century in which the Mishnah's philosophers actually lived.

4:1

A.   He who kneels down to drink –

B.   the water that comes up on his mouth and on his moustache is under the law, If water be put. [That water imparts susceptibility to uncleanness should it drip on a pile of grain, since the farmer has accomplished his purpose – getting a drink – by stirring up that water and getting it into his mouth or on his moustache.]

C.   [The water that comes up] on his nose and on [the hair of] his head and on his beard is not under the law, "If water be put." [That water does not have the power to impart susceptibility to uncleanness should it fall on a pile of dry produce.]

D.   He who draws [water] with a jug –

E.   the water that comes up on its outer parts and on the rope wound round its neck and on the rope that is needed [in dipping it] – lo, this is under the law, If water be put on.

F.   And how much [rope] is needed [in handling it]?

G.   R. Simeon b. Eleazar says, "A handbreadth."

H.   [If] one put it under the water-spout, [the water on its out parts and on the rope, now not needed in drawing water] is not under the law, If water be put.

M. Makhshirin 4:1

What must get wet in order to accomplish one's purpose is deemed wet down by approval. But water not needed in one's primary goal is not subject to approval. The pericope consists of A-C and D-H, the latter in two parts, D-E + F-G, and H. The point of A-C is clear. Since, D-E, in dipping the jug into the water, it is not possible to draw water without wetting the outer parts and the rope, water on the rope and the outer parts is deemed affected by one's wishes. Simeon b. Eleazar glosses. At H one does not make use of the rope and does not care to have the water on the outer parts, since he can draw the water without recourse to either. Accordingly, water on the rope and on the outer parts does not impart susceptibility to uncleanness.

4:2

A   He on whom rains fell,

B.   even [if he is] a Father [principal source] of uncleanness –

C.   it [the water] is not under the law, If water be put [since even in the case of B, the rainfall was not wanted].

D.   But if he shook off [the rain], it [the water that is shaken off] is under the law, If water be put.

E.   [If] he stood under the water-spout to cool off,

F.   or to rinse off,

G.   in the case of an unclean person [the water] is unclean.

H.   And in the case of a clean person, [the water] is under the law, If water be put.

M. Makhshirin 4:2

. The pericope is in two parts, A-D and E-H, each in two units. The point of A + C is that the rain does not come under the person's approval. Therefore the rain is not capable of imparting susceptibility to uncleanness. If by some action, however, the person responds to the rain, for example, if he shook off his garments, then it falls under his approval. B is certainly a gloss, and not an important one. The principal source of uncleanness, e.g., the *Zab* of Leviticus, Chapter Fifteen, derives no benefit from the rain and therefore need not be explicitly excluded. At E, however, the person obviously does want to make use of the water. Therefore it is rendered both susceptible to uncleanness and capable of imparting susceptibility to other things. G makes the former point, H, the latter. Perhaps it is G that has generated B, since the distinction between unclean and clean is important at G-H and then invites the contrast between A + B and E + G, that is, falling rain *versus* rain-water pouring through the waterspout and deliberately utilized.

4:3

A   He who puts a dish on end against the wall so that it will rinse off, lo, this [water that flows across the plate] is under the law, If water be put.

B.   If [he put it there] so that it [rain] should not harm the wall, it [the water] is not under the law, If water be put.

M. Makhshirin 4:3

The established distinction is repeated once more, with reference to an inanimate object. Now we make use of the water for rinsing off the plate. Accordingly, the water is detached with approval. But if the plate is so located as to protect the wall, then the water clearly is not wanted and therefore does not have the capacity to impart susceptibility to uncleanness.

4:4-5

I. A.   A jug into which water leaking from the roof came down –

     B.   The House of Shammai say, "It is broken."

     C.   The House of Hillel say, "It is emptied out."

     D.   And they agree that he puts in his hand and takes pieces of fruit from its inside, and they [the drops of water, the pieces of fruit] are insusceptible to uncleanness.

M. Makhshirin 4:4

II. F.   A trough into which the rain dripping from the roof flowed [without approval] –

     G.   [water in the trough and (GRA)] the drops [of water] that splashed out and those that overflowed are not under the law, If water be put.

     H.   [If] one took it to pour it out –

     I.   The House of Shammai say, "It is under the law, If water be put." [Since he poured the water away only when the tub was moved to another place, it may be said that he did not object to the water when the tub was in its original place.]

     J.   The House of Hillel say, "It is not under the law, If water be put." [His pouring away showed that he did not want the water even in the tub's original place.]

III. K.   [If] one [intentionally] left it out so that the rain dripping from the roof would flow into it –

     L.   the drops [of water] that splashed out and those that overflowed –

     M.   The House of Shammai say, "They are under the law, If water be put" [all the more so what is in the trough].

     N.   The House of Hillel say, "They [the drops that splashed or overflowed] are not under the law, If water be put.

     O.   [If] one took it in order to pour it out, these and those agree that [both kinds of water] are under the law, If water be put. [For since the owner did not empty it where it stood, the water is deemed to be detached with his approval.]

     P.   He who dunks the utensils, and he who washes his clothing in a cave [pond] –

     Q.   the water that comes up on his hands is under the law, If water be put.

R.   [And the water that comes up] on his feet is not under the law, If
            water be put.

S.   R. Eleazar says, "If it is impossible for him to go down [into the
            water] unless his feet become muddy, even [the drops of water]
            that come up on his feet are under the law, If water be put [since
            he wants to clean his feet]."

                                                            M. Makhshirin 4:5

The composite is in the following parts: A-D, a complete and well-
balanced Houses' dispute, in which the apodosis exhibits exact balance
in the number of syllables, F-G, which set the stage for the second
Houses' dispute, at H-J; K-L, the protasis for the third dispute, which
depends upon F (+ G = L) – a trough that happens to receive rain *versus*
one deliberately left out to collect rain, and the standard apodosis, M-
N; and a final agreement, O, parallel to D. R-S form a separate
pericope entirely. The issue of A-D is this: We have left a jug
containing fruit in such a position that water leaking from the roof fills
it. We want to empty the fruit out of the jug. But we want to do so in
such a way that the water in the jug does not receive the capacity to
impart susceptibility to uncleanness to the fruit contained in the jug.
There are these considerations.

1.   Clearly, in its present location, the water is insusceptible.
            Why? Because it did not fall into the jug with approval.

2.   If then we break the jug, we accomplish the purpose of
            treating the water as unwanted and this is what the
            Shammaites say we should do (B).

3.   But if we merely empty out the fruit, we stir the water
            with approval; the fruit in the jug forthwith is wet down
            by the water, with approval, and becomes susceptible.

The Hillelites (C) say that if we pour out the fruit, that suffices.
Why? Because the man wants the fruit, not the water. So the water
does not have the capacity to impart susceptibility to uncleanness. In
its original location it is not subject to approval. The Shammaites and
Hillelites agree that, so long as the fruit in the jug is unaffected by the
water, the fruit is insusceptible to uncleanness. It is not made
susceptible even by the water which is removed with the fruit.
Maimonides (*Uncleanness of Foodstuffs*, 12:7) at the italicized words
adds a valuable clarification:

If a jar is full of fruit and water leaking from the roof drips into it, the
owner may pour off the water from the fruit, and it does not render the
fruit susceptible, *even though it was with his approval that the water
remained in the jar until he should pour it off the fruit.*

Accordingly, Maimonides not only follows the Hillelite position but (quite reasonably) imposes that position upon the Shammaite agreement at D.

The second Houses' dispute, F-J, goes over the ground of the first. There is no significant difference between water that has leaked into the jug and water that has fallen into the trough, A/F. But the issue, G, is different. Now we ask about water that overflows. Does this water flow with approval? Certainly not, both parties agree. None of this water is wanted. What if the man then takes up the trough with the intention of pouring the water out? We already know the Hillelite position. It is the same as at C. There is no reason to be concerned about moving the trough in order to empty it. The man pours out the water. By his deed he therefore indicates that he does not want it. The Shammaites are equally consistent. The man has raised the trough to pour out the water. In moving the water, he (retrospectively) imparts the stamp of approval on the original location of the water. The reference at G is only to set the stage for K-L, since the water in the trough of F itself is insusceptible.

At K the problem is that the man deliberately does collect the water. Accordingly, he certainly has imparted his approval to it. The problem of L is that part of the water splashes out or overflows. Clearly, the man wanted the water and therefore, what overflowed or splashed out has not conformed to his original wishes. That is, if he shook the tree to bring down the water, all parties agree that the water that falls is subject to the man's approval. But the water that does not fall is a problem. Here too the Shammaites say that what has been in the trough and overflowed has been subject to the man's intention. Therefore, like the water in the trough, the drops that splash out or overflow are under the law, If water be put. But the House of Hillel maintain that the water not in the location where the man has desired it is not subject to his wishes, and therefore does not impart susceptibility to uncleanness.

O completes the elegant construction by bringing the Hillelites over to the Shammaite position. If the man lifted up a trough of water that he *himself* has collected, then his is water that at one point in its history has surely conformed to the man's wishes and therefore has the capacity to impart insusceptibility to uncleanness. The Hillelites of N clearly will agree that the water in the trough is subject to the law, If water be put, just as the Shammaites at L-M will maintain the same. The dispute of M-N concerns only the liquid referred to at L. P-R go over the ground of M. 4:1. That is, water necessary to accomplish the man's purpose is subject to the law, If water be put. That which is not important in the accomplishment of his purpose is not subject to the law. Eleazar's gloss, S, adds that if the man's feet grow muddy in the process of getting the water, then he will want to clean his feet, and even the water on his feet therefore is subject to the law, If water be put. There is nothing surprising in this unit, but the exposition is elegant indeed.

4:6

A.   A basket that is full of lupines and [that happens to be] placed into an immersion-pool –

B.   one puts out his hand and takes lupines from its midst, and they are insusceptible to uncleanness.

C.   [If] one took them out of the water [while still in the basket] –

D.   the ones that touch the [water on the sides of the] basket are susceptible to uncleanness.

E.   And all the rest of the lupines are insusceptible to uncleanness.

F.   A radish that is in the cave-[water] –

G.   a menstruant rinses it off, and it is insusceptible to uncleanness.

H.   [If] she brought it out of the water in any measure at all, [having been made susceptible to uncleanness in the water], it is unclean.

M. Makhshirin 4:6

We go over the point at which the Houses agree at M. Makhshirin 4:4D. The lupines in the basket are wet on account of the water in the pool, but that does not render them susceptible to uncleanness. Accordingly, since the water is not detached with approval, when one takes the lupines out of the basket, they remain insusceptible. The water on the basket, however, is detached with approval, since presumably the basket has been immersed to render it clean from uncleanness. (The lupines – being food – in any event cannot be cleaned in the pool.) Accordingly, at C, the ones in the basket that touch the sides of the basket are in contact with water capable of imparting susceptibility to uncleanness, having been used with approval. The others, however, although wet, remain clean. Why? Because they have not touched water that has been detached with approval. The sentence-structure is slightly strange, since A sets the stage for a thought, but the thought begins afresh at B. This is then extreme apocopation at A-B, less clear-cut apocopation at C-D.

The same form is followed at F-H. The radish in the water is insusceptible to uncleanness. The menstruant rinses it off. While the radish is in the water, it remains insusceptible. But the woman has rinsed her hands and the radish. Accordingly, the water on the radish is detached with approval. It renders the radish susceptible to uncleanness, and as soon as the radish is taken out of the water, the woman's touch imparts uncleanness.

4:7

A.   Pieces of fruit that fell into a water-channel –

B.   he whose hands were unclean reached out and took them –

C.   his hands are clean, and the pieces of fruit are insusceptible to uncleanness.

D.   But if he gave thought that his hands should be rinsed off [in the water], his hands are clean, and the [water on the] pieces of fruit is under the law, If water be put.

M. Makhshirin 4:7

The pericope is in the severe apocopation characteristic of the present set, A, B, and C being out of clear syntactical relationship to one another. We should have to add, at A *as to pieces...*, then at B, *if he whose hands...*, and C would follow as a complete sentence. But A is not continued at B-C. Rather, we have apocopation. We have a further illustration of the principle of the foregoing. The owner wants to retrieve the fruit. Even though his hands are unclean, he reaches out and takes the fruit. What is the result? The hands are made clean by the water-flow. But the fruit remains insusceptible to uncleanness. Why? Because it was not the man's intent to rinse off his hands in the water channel and so to clean them. If, D adds, that was his intent, then his hands of course are clean, but the fruit now has been rendered susceptible to uncleanness.

4:8

A.   A [clay] dish that is full of water and placed in an immersion-pool,

B.   and into [the airspace of] which a Father of uncleanness put his hand,

C.   is unclean [but the water remains clean].

D.   [If he was unclean only by reason of] contact with unclean things, it is clean.

E.   And as to all other liquids – they are unclean.

F.   For water does not effect cleanness for other liquids.

M. Makhshirin 4:8

The present pericope is not phrased in the expected apocopation, for C refers to the dish and so completes the thought of A. We have an exercise in several distinct rules. First, a clay pot is made unclean only by a Father of uncleanness. Second, it is not cleaned by immersion in the pool but only by breaking. But the sides of the pot are porous, as at M. Makhshirin 3:2. Therefore, third, the water in the pot is deemed in contact with the immersion-pool. The dish is touched by a Father of uncleanness and is therefore made unclean. But, D, someone in the first remove of uncleanness is not able to contaminate the pot. The liquid in

the pot is not referred to at A-D, but E demands that we understand the
liquid in A-C and D to be clean. Why? Because the water referred to at
A certainly is cleaned and kept clean in the pool, along the lines of M.
Makhshirin 4:6-7. E then simply registers the fact that liquids apart
from those enumerated at M. Makhshirin 6:4 are not cleaned in an
immersion-pool. E-F should also tell us that if other liquids are in the
pot, the pot also is unclean, because liquids in the first remove of
uncleanness do impart uncleanness to clay or earthenware utensils.
Accordingly, E-F form either a slightly awry gloss, taking for granted
that A-C have said *the water is clean, even though it* [the pot] *is
unclean*, or they belong to a pericope other than the present one, which
is highly unlikely.

4:9

A.   He who draws water with a swape-pipe [or bucket] [and pieces of
         fruit later fell into the moisture or water remaining in the pipe or
         bucket],

B.   up to three days [the water] imparts susceptibility to uncleanness.
         [Afterward it is deemed to be unwanted (Maimonides).]

C.   R. Aqiba says, "If it has dried off, it is forthwith incapable of
         imparting susceptibility to uncleanness, and if it has not dried off,
         up to thirty days it [continues to] impart susceptibility to
         uncleanness."

M. Makhshirin 4:9

The dispute poses A-B against C. We deal now with a wooden pipe
or bucket. Do we deem the bucket to be dried off as soon as it is empty?
No, B says, the water in the bucket, detached with approval (by
definition) remains able to impart susceptibility for three days. Aqiba
qualifies the matter. If the water drawn with approval was dried out
of the bucket, whatever moisture then is found in the bucket is not
wanted; the man has shown, by drying out the bucket or pipe, that he
does not want moisture there. If it is not dried out, then whatever
liquid is there is deemed to be detached from the pool with approval
and therefore able to impart uncleanness for a very long time. Only
after thirty days do we assume that the wood is completely dry of the
original water detached with approval.

4:10

A.   Pieces of wood on which liquids fell and on which rains fell –

B.   if [the rains] were more [than the liquids], [the pieces of wood] are
         insusceptible to uncleanness.

C.   [If] he took them outside so that the rains might fall on them, even
         though they [the rains] were more [than the liquids], they [the
         pieces of wood] are [susceptible to uncleanness and] unclean.

D.   [If] they absorbed unclean liquids, even though he took them outside so that the rains would fall on them, they are clean [for the clean rain has not had contact with the unclean absorbed liquid].

E   But he should kindle them only with clean hands alone [to avoid contaminating the rain-water of D].

F.   R. Simeon says, "If they were wet [freshly cut] and he kindled them, and the liquids [sap] that exude from them were more than the liquids that they had absorbed, they are clean"

M. Makhshirin 4:10

The pericope is in the following parts: A-B balanced by C; and D, qualified by E. F is an important gloss of D-E. The point of A-B is familiar from M. Makhshirin 2:3. If we have a mixture of unclean and clean liquids, we determine matters in accord with the relative quantity of each. If the clean liquids are the greater part, the whole is deemed clean. Accordingly, since the rain, which is insusceptible and does not impart susceptibility to uncleanness unless it falls with approval, forms the greater part, B, the liquids on the pieces of wood are deemed clean. But if, C, the man deliberately arranged for the rain to fall on the pieces of wood, then the rain falls on the wood with approval, is susceptible to uncleanness, and is made unclean by the unclean liquids already on the wood.

D raises a separate question. What if pieces of wood have absorbed unclean liquids? The answer is that what is absorbed does not have contact with what is on the surface – that is the meaning of absorption. Therefore if rain falls on wood that has absorbed unclean liquids, the rain does not impart susceptibility to uncleanness if it has not fallen with approval. D does not treat that matter; it wishes to say something additional. Even if the rain falls with approval, the wood remains clean. Why? Because nothing has made the rain unclean. That secondary point then invites E – or E imposes the detail, *even if*, on D: Even though he took them outside, so the rain falls with approval, E adds, since the rain *has* fallen with approval, it is susceptible to uncleanness. Accordingly, the man should kindle the wood only with clean hands, lest he make the rain-water unclean.

Simeon deals then with a still further point. If the wood is freshly cut when kindled, then the unclean absorbed liquids are deemed neutralized by the sap. If the exuded liquid caused by the heat is more than the still-absorbed liquid, then the clean, exuded liquid forms the greater part, and the whole is clean, just as at A-B. Simeon, Maimonides says, differs from D (+ E). We hold, as at A-D, that if unclean liquids are absorbed by the wood, they are deemed clean and do not impart uncleanness to the oven, *only* in the case in which the wood is wet. Then, when it is heated, it produces sap in greater quantity than the unclean liquids that it absorbed. But if not, the wood imparts uncleanness to the oven when it is heated because of the unclean liquid that has been absorbed.

Now if we reflect on the detailed rules we have observed, one thing will have struck the reader very forcefully. What Scripture treats as unconditional the authorship of the Mishnah has made contingent upon the human will. Specifically, when Scripture refers at Lev. 11:34, 37, to grain's being made wet, it makes no provision for the attitude of the owner of the grain, his intention in having wet the grain, or his will as to its disposition. What is wet is susceptible, what is dry is insusceptible. The effect of the water is *ex opere operato*. Yet, as we see, that very matter of the attitude of the householder toward the grain's being made wet forms the centerpiece of interest. The issue of intentionality thus forms the precipitating consideration behind every dispute we have reviewed, and, it is clear, the Priestly authors of Leviticus could not have conceived such a consideration. The introduction of that same concern can be shown to characterize the Mishnah's treatment of a variety of biblical rules and to form a systemic principle of profound and far-reaching character. We may draw a simple and striking contrast, for instance, between the following bald statements:

1.   "Whatever touches the altar shall become holy" (Ex. 29:37)

It would be difficult to find a less ambiguous statement. But here is the rule of the Mishnah's sages:

2.   "The altar sanctifies that which is appropriate to it" (M. Zebahim 9:1)...." And what are those things which, even if they have gone up, should go down [since they are not offered at all and therefore are not appropriate to the altar]? "The flesh for the priests of Most Holy Things and the flesh of Lesser Holy Things [which is designated for priestly consumption]" (M. Zeb. 9:5).

To understand the conflict between statement No. 1 and statement No. 2 we have to understand how an animal enters the category of Most Holy Things or Lesser Holy Things. It is by the action of the farmer, who owns the beast and designates it for a purpose, within the cult, that imparts to the beast that status of Most Holy Things or Lesser Holy Things. In both cases, the rule is that such a beast yields parts that are burned up on the altar, and other parts that are given to the priests to eat or to the farmer, as the case may be.

Now the point is that it is the farmer who has designated a beast owned by him for sacrifice in the status of Most Holy Things or Lesser Holy Things. His disposition of the offering then places that offering into the classification that yields meat for the officiating priest out of the carcass of the sacrificial beast. Here is, in principle, something that is *surely* appropriate to the altar. But because of the designation, that is, the realization of the act of intentionality, of the householder, the owner of the beast, the beast has fallen into a classification that must yield meat to be eaten, and that meat of the carcass that is to be eaten is taken off the altar, though it is fit for being burnt up as an offering to God, and given to the owner or to the priest, as the rule may require.

It would be difficult to find a more profound difference, brought about by a keen appreciation for the power of the human will, between the Scripture's unnuanced and uncontingent rule and the Mishnah's clear revision of it. It would carry us far afield to catalogue all of the innumerable rules of the Mishnah in which intentionality forms the central concern. The rather arcane rules of Mishnah-tractate Makhshirin show us how sages thought deeply and framed comprehensive principles concerning will and intentionality and then applied these principles to exceedingly picayune cases, as we should, by now, expect. A simple conclusion seems well justified by the chapter we have examined in its broader conceptual context.

From the cases at hand, we may generalize as follows: will and deed constitute those actors of creation which work upon neutral realms, subject to either sanctification or uncleanness: the Temple and table, the field and family, the altar and hearth, woman, time, space, transactions in the material world and in the world above as well. An object, a substance, a transaction, even a phrase or a sentence is inert but may be made holy, when the interplay of the will and deed of the human being arouses or generates its potential to be sanctified. Each may be treated as ordinary or (where relevant) made unclean by the neglect of the will and inattentive act of the human being. Just as the entire system of uncleanness and holiness awaits the intervention of the human being, which imparts the capacity to become unclean upon what was formerly inert, or which removes the capacity to impart cleanness from what was formerly in its natural and puissant condition, so in the other ranges of reality, the human being is at the center on earth, just as is God in Heaven. And all of this comes to us in arguments about the status of some drops of water.

The upshot is very simple. A central problem in the interpretation of the Mishnah, the foundation-document of Judaism, is to explain this very strange mode of discourse. Specifically, we want to know why its

philosophical authorship has chosen such a strikingly concrete and
unphilosophical manner for the expression of what clearly are abstract
and profoundly reflective philosophical positions on the nature of
human intention in relationship to metaphysical reality. To answer
that question, it seems to me, sustained attention to modes of
philosophical discourse in the age of the Mishnah, which is to say, the
second century, will be required. Here then is a task awaiting
attention: to explain why philosophers have chosen the petty and
banal mode of discourse of rule-making bureaucrats.

Chapter Five

Philosophy in the Mishnaic Mode:
Mixtures, Doubts, and Establishing a Grid
for Sorting Out Relationships
among Distinct but Intersecting Principles

The authorship of the Mishnah addressed long-standing philosophical issues, taking up these issues within its own idiom. When we grasp that fact, we shall appreciate the Mishnah as not a tedious statement of details important only to an obsessive formalism, but a curious and eloquent way of talking about this and that, while addressing the great issues of intellect. Now, as I shall presently explain, two issues that were deemed intextricable, the nature of mixtures and the resolution of doubt, predominate in Mishnaic discourse. How these issues are treated then shows us the way in which, for their part, the authorship of the Mishnah chose to address matters of common concern to intellectuals of their time and place. In this chapter we shall see expositions of three basic issues: mixtures, resolution of matters of doubt, and the interplay between distinct but interrelated rules or principles of metaphysics. In the next chapter we shall address in greater detail the problem of mixtures, a standard concern of philosophy, and show how the authorship of the Mishnah makes its statement, well within the framework of the Stoic philosophy of physics, about mixtures. We first establish the basic fact that the details of the Mishnah's discourse really do concern principles of general interest and intelligibility – mixtures, resolving doubts, interrelating separate sets of abstract facts in a single unifying grid. Only then shall we turn to a very specific demonstration of the close ties between Mishnaic and Stoic discourse on physics.

In following my claim that the Mishnah's authorship talked about pots and pans so as to make an intellectually well-crafted statement about enduring issues of mind, readers will want to judge for themselves from cases and sources, rather than merely relying upon my report of what is at hand. Accordingly, we shall work our way slowly and in painstaking detail through the underbrush of Mishnaic discourse, reading texts as they should be read, and working out, from their details, the main points under discussion. Then and only then, in the direct encounter with the sources, readers can judge whether or not I have accurately portrayed the intellectual issues and characteristics of Mishnaic discourse. For if, as I hold, we deal with philosophy in a very particular idiom, then any judgment that we have in hand the mere detritus of a collectivity of obsessive formalists will fall by the wayside, not because it is (merely) wrong, but because it is uncomprehending and ignorant of what is at hand. Accordingly, the debate underway concerns the meaning of sources, and those who wish to follow the argument will have to take responsibility to judge for themselves concerning the character and conscience of those sources.

I claim that an important issue in the Mishnah concerns the nature of mixtures and how these are to be sorted out. My first piece of evidence shows that that issue occurs. It deals with a mixture of felons of various classifications and how they are to be put to death among the four modes of execution. The particular details of the case then tell us that we have the problem of sorting out a particular confusion among data that fall within four classifications.

Mishnah-tractate Sanhedrin

9:3-4

A.   A murderer who was mixed up with others – all of them are exempt.

B.   R. Judah says, "They put them all in prison."

C.   All those who are liable to death who were mixed up with one another are judged [to be punished] by the more lenient mode of execution.

D.   [If] those to be stoned were confused with those to be burned –

E.   R. Simeon says, "They are judged [to be executed] by stoning, for burning is the more severe of the two modes of execution."

F.   And sages say, "They are adjudged [to be executed] by burning, for stoning is the more severe mode of execution of the two."

G.   Said to them R. Simeon, "If burning were not the more severe, it would not have been assigned to the daughter of a priest who committed adultery."

H.   They said to him, "If stoning were not the more severe of the two, it would not have been assigned to the blasphemer and to the one who performs an act of service for idolatry."

I.   Those who are to be decapitated who were confused with those who are to be strangled –

J.   R. Simeon says, "They are killed with the sword."

K.   And sages say, "They are killed by strangling."

M. 9:3

A.   He who is declared liable to be put to death through two different modes of execution at the hands of a court is judged [to be executed] by the more severe.

B.   [If] he committed a transgression, which is subject to the death penalty on two separate counts, he is judged on account of the more severe.

C.   R. Yosé says, "He is judged by the penalty which first applies to what he has done."

M. 9:4

A-B introduce the problem of C, which sets the stage for the two disputes, D-F + G-H and I-J. M. bears its own ample exegesis, and the whole restates M. 7:1. The point of concurrence at M. 9:3C is repeated. The important point is not at A, but at B. Once more, we find ourselves engaged in the exposition of the materials of Chapter Seven, now M. 7:4K-R, the sages' view that there may be two counts of culpability on the basis of a single transgression. A's point is that if one has intercourse with a married woman and is liable for strangulation, and afterward he has sexual relations with his mother-in-law and is liable for burning, he is judged on the count of burning. If his mother-in-law had been married, we should have the problem of B. He then would be tried on the count of the mother-in-law, which produces the execution by burning, rather than on the count of the married woman, which produces the penalty of strangulation.

Yosé's clarification requires that the woman have passed through several relationships to the lover. First she was a widow, whose daughter he had married, and so she was his mother-in-law. Afterward she was married. He had sexual relations with her. He is tried for having had sexual relations with his mother-in-law, thus for burning, since that was the first aspect in which the woman was prohibited to him. If the story were reversed, he would be tried under the count of strangulation for his sexual relations with a married woman.

Let me give another example of the interest in dealing with mixtures, in this case, how a single unitary action may encompass a variety of classifications. The interest in the correct classification of things, recognition that one thing may fall into several categories now come to expression, for the authorship of the Mishnah, in diverse ways. One of the interesting ones is the analysis of the several taxa into which a single action may fall, with an account of the multiple consequences, e.g., as to sanctions that are called into play, for a single action. I offer this instance as evidence of a prevailing concern for the right taxonomy of persons, actions, and things.

Mishnah-tractate Keritot

3:9

A.   There is one who ploughs a single furrow and is liable on eight counts of violating a negative commandment:

B.   [specifically, it is] he who (1) ploughs with an ox and an ass [Deut. 22:10], which are (2,3) both Holy Things, in the case of (4) [ploughing] Mixed Seeds in a vineyard [Deut. 22:9], (5) in the Seventh Year [Lev. 25:4], (6) on a festival [Lev. 23:7] and who was both a (7) priest [Lev. 21:1] and (8) a Nazirite [Num. 6:6] [ploughing] in a grave-yard.

C.   Hanania b. Hakhinai says, "Also: He is [ploughing while] wearing a garment of diverse kinds" [Lev. 19:19, Deut. 22:11).

D.   They said to him, "This is not within the same class."

E.   He said to them, "Also the Nazir [B8] is not within the same class [as the other transgressions]."

M. 3:9

Here is a case in which more than a single set of flogging is called for. B's felon is liable to 312 stripes, on the listed counts. The ox is sanctified to the altar, the ass to the upkeep of the house (B2,3). Hanania's contribution is rejected since it has nothing to do with ploughing, and sages' position is equally flawed. The main point, for our inquiry, is simple. The one action draws in its wake multiple consequences. Classifying a single thing as a mixture of many things then forms a part of the larger intellectual address to the nature of mixtures.

My further allegation is that, when dealing with problems of mixtures, the authorship of the Mishnah further investigates the resolution of cases of doubt. For such cases, in general terms, encompass the proper classification of what is not readily subjected to taxonomy. The following sustained discussion of matters of doubt shows how, in detail, the framers address the resolution of doubt, that is to say, the sorting out of what is confused, which, I hold, forms the genus of which the issue of mixtures and how they are dealt with constitutes a subset.

Mishnah-tractate Keritot

4:1

A.   It is a matter of doubt whether or not one has eaten forbidden fat,

B.   And even if he ate it, it is a matter of doubt whether or not it contains the requisite volume –

I.   C.   Forbidden fat and permitted fat are before him,

D.   he ate one of them but is not certain which one of them he ate –

II.   E.   his wife and his sister are with him in the house,

	F.	he inadvertently transgressed with one of them and is not certain with which of them he transgressed –
III.	G.	The Sabbath and an ordinary day –
	H.	he did an act of labor on one of them and is not certain on which of them he did it –
	I.	he brings [in all the foregoing circumstances] a suspensive guilt-offering.

M. 4:1

The formal traits of M. 4:1 are of principal interest, because the point, I, is self-evident. The reason A-B are distinguished from C-D, E-F, and G-H, is that the opening statement expresses its second clause with the same language as the first, namely, SPQ...SPQ..., while the triplet uses W'YN YDW'...I see no substantive difference between the two formulations.

Mishnah-tractate Keritot

4:2-3

	A.	Just as, *if he ate forbidden fat and [again ate] forbidden fat in a single spell of inadvertence, he is liable for only a single sin-offering* [M. 3:2A],
	B.	so in connection with a situation of uncertainty involving them, he is liable to bring only a single guilt-offering.
	C.	If there was a clarification in the meantime,
	D.	just as he brings a single sin-offering for each and every transgression, so he brings a suspensive guilt-offering for each and every [possible] transgression.
	E.	Just as, *if he ate forbidden fat, and blood, and remnant, and refuse, in a single spell of inadvertence, he is liable for each and every one* [M. 3:2B],
	F.	so in connection with a situation of uncertainty involving them, he brings a suspensive guilt-offering for each and every one.
I.	G.	Forbidden fat and remnant are before him –
	H.	he ate one of them but is not certain which one of them he ate [M. 4:1C-D] –
II.	I.	His wife, who is menstruating, and his sister are with him in the house –
	J.	he inadvertently transgressed with one of them but is not certain with which one of them he has transgressed [M. 4:1E-F] –
III.	K.	The Sabbath and the Day of Atonement –
	L.	he did an act of labor at twilight, but is not certain on which one of them he did the act of labor [M. 4:1G-H] –
	M.	R. Eliezer declares him liable to a sin-offering.
	N.	And R. Joshua exempts him.

O. Said R. Yosé, "They did not dispute about the case [K-L] of him who performs an act of labor at twilight, that he is exempt.

P. – "For I say, 'Part of the work did he do while it was still this day, and part of it on the next.'

Q. "Concerning what did they dispute?

R. "Concerning one who does work wholly on one of the two days but does not know for certain whether he did it on the Sabbath or whether he did it on the Day of Atonement.

S. "Or concerning him who does an act of labor but is not certain what sort of act of labor he has done –

T. "R. Eliezer declares liable to a sin-offering.

U. "And R. Joshua exempts him."

V. Said R. Judah, "R. Joshua did declare him exempt even from the requirement to bring a suspensive guilt-offering.

M. 4:2

A. R. Simeon Shezuri and R. Simeon say, "They did not dispute about something which is subject to a single category, that he is liable.

B. "And concerning what did they dispute?

C. "Concerning something which is subject to two distinct categories.

D. "For R. Eliezer declares liable for a sin-offering.

E. "And R. Joshua exempts."

F. Said R. Judah, "Even if he intended to gather figs but gathered grapes, grapes but gathered figs,

G. "black ones but gathered white ones, white ones but gathered black ones –

H. "R. Eliezer declared liable to a sin-offering.

I. "And R. Joshua exempts."

J. Said R. Judah, "I should be surprised if R. Joshua declared him wholly exempt. If so, Why is it said, '*In which he has sinned* (Lev. 4:23)?

K. "To exclude him who was occupied [with some other matter and entirely unintentionally committed a transgression]."

M. 4:3

M. 4:2A-F complete the opening unit, linking the whole to M. 3:2, which is explicitly cited, as indicated in italics. The point is clear. If we have a single spell of inadvertence, then, when we are certain what the man has done, he brings a sin-offering, and when we are not certain, he brings a guilt-offering. Further, if in the intervals the man becomes aware of what he has done, e.g., between eating the first olive's bulk and the second, he becomes aware that he has eaten something which may be forbidden fat, he brings a suspensive guilt-offering, D, for each and every transgression. E-F are clear as given. M. 4:2G-V, continued by

M. 4:3, return us to M. 4:1, which is why I regard M. 4:1-3 as a single extended pericope. We systematically cite the triplet of M. 4:1. But there is this difference: while at M. 4:1 we have a possibility that the man has not sinned at all, when we restate the cases, G, I, and K, we make clear that there is no way that the man has *not* sinned. He does not know for sure which sin he has committed, that is, under what category of transgression his sin-offering is brought. Eliezer declared him liable, since, if it is not for one sin, it is for the other (B. Ker. 19a). Joshua exempts, since, in line with Lev. 4:23, he insists that the man who brings a sin-offering know precisely *why* he must do so, that is, for what specific sin or category of sin.

We then have two restatements of the same version of what is subject to dispute, O-U + V and M. 4:3A-I + J. Yosé corrects the statement of K-L, because, P, there is a possibility that the man did not sin at all, since liability must be for an act of completed labor. R, glossed by S which contributes nothing), then restates the matter essentially in line with the conception of M. 4:2G-N. Judah differs from Yosé, because, in Yosé's view, while the man does know for sure that he has sinned, he does not know what category of sin he has done. But, in Judah's version of Joshua's view, the suspensive guilt-offering is brought only when a man is not sure that he has sinned at all. Accordingly, *declared exempt* means *of any offering at all.* The final version presents a dispute between the two Simeons and Judah, M. 4:3A-E, F-I. The two Simeons go over the ground of Yosé and M. 4:2G-N. The disputants agree that the man is liable who has done a sin which is in a single category, e.g., inadvertently gathering on the Sabbath, with the uncertainty being whether he has gathered figs or grapes. In such a situation, Joshua concedes the man knows that he has committed the sin of gathering on the Sabbath and must bring a sin-offering. But if he has done something which may fall into two different categories, such as the cases given at M. 4:2G-N, eating either forbidden fat or remnant, which are subject to distinct prohibitions, or having intercourse with his wife who is a menstruant, as against having intercourse with his sister, again subject to two distinctive considerations, then we have the stated dispute. Accordingly, the anonymous authority of M. 4:2G-N, Yosé, and the two Simeons, concur. It is Judah who differs even on the definition of the dispute. At M. 4:3F-I, he states the difference. Even if the man is sure he has done an action subject to a single category of prohibition, but is not certain as to the details of the action, F-G, we have the stated dispute. Judah's second gloss, J, then explains the situation which, in Judah's conception of Joshua's view, leaves the man wholly exempt from an offering. It is one in which the man in no way intended to do something prohibited. But in the case Judah himself gives at F-G, Judah's Joshua will require a suspensive guilt-offering, in contrast to Judah at M. 4:2V.

Thus far, in what is a protracted account of how, specifically, our authorship carries on its philosophical discourse about philosophical issues, I have shown that issues of mixtures occur, on the one side, and that these form a subset of the question of resolving cases of doubt, e.g., as to the classification of an action, a person, or a thing. A further claim of mine in my characterization of the modes of philosophical thought of the authorship of the Mishnah is that these intellectuals concern themselves with the operation of holiness in the materials of this world. They maintain that holiness or sanctification affects the nature of things. What is holy is treated differently, in accord with different rules, from what is ordinary and secular. Since that position is not distinctive to our authorship, being held, for example, by the authorship of the Priestly Code, we forthwith proceed to the next important characterization, on my part, of these same modes of thought and, consequently, of the issues that are dealt with. I maintain that the attitude of the individual person directly affects the standing and classification of material things, which is to say, what an Israelite thinks about an object, for instance, food or drink, affects the standing and classification of that food and drink. To join these two propositions: if an Israelite regards food or drink as holy, whatever the origin and prior disposition of that food or drink (in the Temple? in the home?), then that food or drink is subjected to the rules that govern what is holy. Accordingly, we have a picture of how attitude and intentionality affect the natural world.

Now these propositions of mine, which bespeak a religion not of pots and pans, but of will, attitude, and both affective and effective intentionality, emerge in a complex and fundamental discussion, at Mishnah-tractate Tohorot 2:2-8. I shall now present in full and awesome detail that sustained discussion. What we shall see, in the details of the several positions unfolding here, is how the attitude of a person toward food and drink changes the standing and classification of that food and drink, so that the food and drink must be dealt with in accord with different rules from those that would have prevailed had that person not taken the view of the food and drink that he has taken. Specifically, if you think that a piece of bread is in the standing of food assigned to the priesthood (in accord with the rules of Leviticus 21-22), then that bread must be deemed analogous to priestly rations and treated as such. If you form the intention of treating your bread as though it were a share of the show-bread given to the priests from the altar and therefore in the standing of Holy Things of the altar, the rules that govern the handling of that bread are analogous to the rules governing the treatment of the altar's show-bread.

Not only so, but the discussion we shall now examine involves what are called "removes of uncleanness," and before we commence our slow reading of the passage, we had best consider these as well. The operative conception sees a sequence of contacts beginning with a principal source of uncleanness. One who or a thing that touches a source of uncleanness is held to be unclean in the first remove from that source; one who touches that person or thing is unclean in the second remove; one who touches that person or thing is unclean in the third remove. Now there is going to be a correlation between removes of uncleanness and levels of sanctification. The principle we shall see is that what is more holy is also more capable of being affected by uncleanness, which means, will be affected by uncleanness transmitted at a further remove from the original source of uncleanness, than what is less holy. Food that is ordinary and unconsecrated will be affected at fewer removes from the original source; food that is designated as priestly rations ("heave-offering" in what follows) is affected at more removes; food that is in the standing of Holy Things will be affected at still more removes.

These several principles are brought together in a grid, so that we can map out the entire interplay of sanctification, that is, the several stages of holiness into which food may fall, with the layers of uncleanness, unfolding from the original source of uncleanness outward to the third and fourth removes therefrom. And the mapping of that grid, like Ptolemy's map of the world by grids, allows a single and sustained picture of the two realities, holiness and uncleanness, to be superimposed upon one another. Clearly, we deal with a high level of utterly abstract thought, in which, through the issues of pots and pans, dead creeping things and bits of bread, we express the immaterial relationships among unseen givens: a world of uncleanness, a realm of the sacred. True, if we do not comprehend the stakes before us, we are going to see it all as a set of extraordinarily dull and incomprehensible rules about the ancient Israelite counterpart to stepping on the cracks in the sidewalks. But when we do see what is at stake, we understand once more how we deal with philosophers who sustain discourse in an odd and subtle idiom indeed. Now to the issue of removes from uncleanness in relationship to levels of sanctification – which is to say, establish a grid between two sets of rules, another principal interest of philosophers.

Mishnah-Tractate Tohorot

2:2

A. R. Eliezer says, "(1) He who eats food unclean in the first remove is unclean in the second remove;

"(2) [he who eats] food unclean in the second remove is unclean in the second remove;

"(3) [he who eats] food unclean in the third remove is unclean in the third remove."

B. R. Joshua says, "(1) He who eats food unclean in the first remove and food unclean in the second remove is unclean in the second remove.

"(2) [He who eats food] unclean in the third remove is unclean in the second remove so far as Holy Things are concerned,

"(3) and is not unclean in the second remove so far as heave-offering is concerned.

C. "[We speak of] the case of unconsecrated food

D. "which is prepared in conditions appropriate to heave-offering."

Mishnah-Tractate Tohorot

2:3

A. *Unconsecrated food:*

in the first remove is unclean and renders unclean;

B. in the second remove is unfit, but does not convey uncleanness;

C. and in the third remove is eaten in the pottage of heave-offering.

Mishnah-Tractate Tohorot

2:4

A. *Heave-offering:*

in the first and in the second remove is unclean and renders unclean;

B. in the third remove is unfit and does not convey uncleanness;

C. and in the fourth remove is eaten in a pottage of Holy Things.

Mishnah-Tractate Tohorot

2:5

A. *Holy Things:*

in the first and the second and the third removes are susceptible to uncleanness and render unclean;

B. and in the fourth remove are unfit and do not convey uncleanness;

C. and in the fifth remove are eaten in a pottage of Holy Things.

Mishnah-Tractate Tohorot

2:6

A. *Unconsecrated food:*
    in the second remove renders unconsecrated liquid unclean and renders food of heave-offering unfit.

B. *Heave-offering:*
    in the third remove renders unclean [the] liquid of Holy Things, and renders foods of Holy Things unfit,

C. if it [the heave-offering] was prepared in the condition of cleanness pertaining to Holy Things.

D. But if it was prepared in conditions pertaining to heave-offering, it renders unclean at two removes and renders unfit at one remove in reference to Holy Things.

Mishnah-Tractate Tohorot

2:7

A. R. Eleazar says, "The three of them are equal:

B. *"Holy Things and heave-offering, and unconsecrated food:*
    "which are at the first remove of uncleanness render unclean at two removes and unfit at one [further] remove in respect to Holy Things;
    "render unclean at one remove and spoil at one [further] remove in respect to heave-offering;
    "and spoil unconsecrated food.

C. "That which is unclean in the second remove in all of them renders unclean at one remove and unfit at one [further] remove in respect to Holy Things;
    "and renders liquid of unconsecrated food unclean;
    "and spoils foods of heave-offering.

D. "The third remove of uncleanness in all of them renders liquids of Holy Things unclean,
    "and spoils food of Holy Things."

Mishnah-Tractate Tohorot 2:2-7 presupposes knowledge of the Mishnaic system of ritual purity, to which we now turn. A review of some of its essential elements is necessary for an understanding of the arguments and analyses that follow.

In the system, ritual impurity is acquired by contact with either a primary or a secondary source of uncleanness, called a "Father" or a "Child" or "Offspring" of uncleanness, respectively. In the first category are contact with a corpse, a person suffering a flux, a leper, and the like. Objects made of metal, wood, leather, bone, cloth, or sacking become Fathers of uncleanness if they touch a corpse. Foodstuffs and liquids are susceptible to uncleanness, but will not render other foodstuffs unclean in the same degree or remove of uncleanness that they themselves suffer. Foodstuffs furthermore will not make vessels or utensils unclean. But liquids made unclean by a Father of uncleanness will do so if they touch the inner side of the vessel. That is, if they fall into the contained space of an earthenware vessel, they make the whole vessel unclean.

Food or liquid that touches a Father of uncleanness becomes unclean in the *first* remove. If food touches a person or vessel made unclean by a primary cause of uncleanness, it is unclean in the *second* remove. Food that touches *second-remove* uncleanness incurs *third-remove* uncleanness, and food that touches *third-remove* uncleanness incurs *fourth-remove* uncleanness, and so on. But liquids touching either a primary source of uncleanness (Father) or something unclean in the first or second remove (Offspring) are regarded as unclean in the first remove. They are able to make something else unclean. If, for example, the other side of a vessel is made unclean by a liquid – thus unclean in the second remove – and another liquid touches the outer side, the other liquid incurs not second, but first degree uncleanness.

Heave-offering (food raised up for priestly use only) unclean in the third remove of uncleanness, and Holy Things (that is, things belonging to the cult) unclean in the fourth remove, do not make other things, whether liquids or foods, unclean. The difference among removes of uncleanness is important. First degree uncleanness in common food will convey uncleanness. But, although food unclean in the second remove will be unacceptable, it will not convey uncleanness, that is, third degree uncleanness. But it will render heave-offering *unfit.* Further considerations apply to heave-offering and Holy Things. Heave-offering can be made unfit and unclean by a first, and unfit by a second, degree of uncleanness. If it touches something unclean in the third remove, it is made unfit, but itself will not impart fourth degree uncleanness. A Holy Thing that suffers uncleanness in the first, second, or third remove is unclean and conveys uncleanness. If it is unclean in the fourth remove, it is invalid for the cult but does not convey uncleanness. It is much more susceptible than are noncultic things. Thus, common food that suffers second degree uncleanness will render heave-offering invalid. We already know that it makes liquid unclean in the first remove. Likewise, heave-offering unclean in the third remove will make Holy Things invalid and put them into a fourth remove of uncleanness.

With these data firmly in hand, let us turn to a general discussion of M. Mishnah-Tractate Tohorot 2:2-7. Mishnah-Tractate Tohorot 2:2 introduces the removes of uncleanness. Our interest is in the contaminating effect, upon a person, of eating unclean food. Does the food make the person unclean in the same remove of uncleanness as is borne by the food itself? Thus if one eats food unclean in the first remove, is he unclean in that same remove? This is the view of Eliezer. Joshua says he is unclean in the second remove. The dispute, Mishnah-Tractate Tohorot 2:2A-B, at Mishnah-Tractate Tohorot 2:2C-D is significantly glossed. The further consideration is introduced as to the sort of food under discussion. Joshua is made to say that there is a difference between the contaminating effects upon the one who eats heave-offering, on the one side, and unconsecrated food prepared in conditions of heave-offering, on the other. This matter, the status of unconsecrated food prepared as if it were heave-offering, or as if it were Holy Things, and heave-offering prepared as if it were Holy Things, forms a substratum of our chapter, added to several primary items and complicating the exegesis. Tosefta-Tractate Tohorot 2:1 confirms, however, that primary to the dispute between Eliezer and Joshua is simply the matter of the effects of food unclean in the first remove upon the person who eats such food. The gloss, Mishnah-Tractate Tohorot 2:2C-D, forms a redactional-thematic link between Joshua's opinion and the large construction of Mishnah-Tractate Tohorot 2:3-7. Mishnah-Tractate Tohorot 2.3:5, expanded and glossed by Mishnah-Tractate Tohorot 2:6, follow a single and rather tight form. The sequence differentiates unconsecrated food, heave-offering, and Holy Things each at the several removes from the original source of uncleanness.

Eleazar, Mishnah-Tractate Tohorot 2:7, insists that, at a given remove, all three are subject to the *same* rule. The contrary view, Mishnah-Tractate Tohorot 2:3-6, is that unconsecrated food in the first remove makes heave-offering unclean and at the second remove spoils heave-offering; it does not enter a third remove and therefore has no effect upon Holy Things. Heave-offering at the first two removes may produce contaminating effects, and at the third remove spoils Holy Things, but is of no effect at the fourth. Holy Things in the first three removes produce uncleanness, and at the fourth impart unfitness to other Holy Things. Mishnah-Tractate Tohorot 2:6 then goes over the ground of unconsecrated food at the second remove, and heave-offering at the third. The explanation of Mishnah-Tractate Tohorot 2:6C is various; the simplest view is that the clause glosses Mishnah-Tractate Tohorot 2:6B by insisting that the heave-offering to which we refer is prepared as if it were Holy Things, on which account, at the third remove, it can spoil Holy Things. At Mishnah-Tractate Tohorot 2:7 Eleazar restates matters, treating all three – Holy Things, heave-offering, and unconsecrated food – as equivalent to one another at the first, second, and third removes, with the necessary qualification for unconsecrated food that it is like the other, consecrated foods in producing effects at the second and even the third removes.

Commentators read *Eliezer*. They set the pericope up against Joshua's view at Mishnah-Tractate Tohorot 2:2, assigning to Joshua Mishnah-Tractate Tohorot 2:3ff. as well. My picture of the matter is significantly different from the established exegesis. To state the upshot simply:

So far as Eleazar is concerned, what is important is not the source of contamination – the unclean foods – but that which is contaminated, the unconsecrated food, heave-offering, and Holy Things. He could not state matters more clearly than he does when he says that the three of them are exactly equivalent. And they are, because the differentiations will emerge in the food affected, or contaminated, by the three. So at the root of the dispute is whether we gauge the contamination in accord with the source – unconsecrated food, or unconsecrated food prepared as if it were heave-offering, and so on – or whether the criterion is the food which is contaminated. Mishnah-Tractate Tohorot 2:3-5 are all wrong, Eleazar states explicitly at Mishnah-Tractate Tohorot 2:7A, because they differentiate among uncleanness imparted by unclean unconsecrated food, unclean heave-offering, and unclean Holy Things, and do not differentiate among the three sorts of food *to which* contamination is imparted. It is surely a logical position, for the three sorts of food do exhibit differentiated capacities to receive uncleanness; one sort *is* more contaminable than another.

And so too is the contrary view logical: *what is more sensitive to uncleanness also will have a greater capacity to impart uncleanness.* The subtle debate before us clearly is unknown to Eliezer and Joshua at Mishnah-Tractate Tohorot 2:2. To them the operative categories are something unclean in first, second, or third *removes*, without distinction as to the relative sensitivities of the several types of food which may be unclean. The unfolding of the issue may be set forth very briefly by way of conclusion: the sequence thus begins with Eliezer and Joshua, who ask about the contaminating power of that which is unclean in the first and second removes, without regard to whether it is unconsecrated food, heave-offering, or Holy Things. To them, the distinction between the capacity to impart contamination, or to receive contamination, of the several sorts of food is unknown. Once, however, their question is raised – in such general terms – it will become natural to ask the next logical question, one which makes distinctions not only among the several removes of uncleanness, but also among the several sorts of food involved in the processes of contamination. The grid that is set forth here has allowed the philosophers to speculate about the interrelationship between distinct but intersecting principles, the one concerning removes of uncleanness, the other involving levels of sanctification.

I have established beyond all doubt that the issues of detail encompassed principles of broad interest and general intelligibility. These involve three fundamental problems of thought: how to deal with mixtures, how to confront cases of doubt, and how to show the interplay of abstract and immaterial rules, comparable in their framework to discrete and also intersecting laws of geometry, for instance. My next task, in demonstrating that in matters of detail, fundamental statements of a philosophical (or, in context, theological) character emerged, is to show a point-by-point counterpart, in the Mishnah, to a particular problem of philosophy. For that purpose I return to the issues of mixtures, which in ancient philosophy were classified as problems in physics. I shall show a point-for-point correspondence between the Mishnah's authorships classification of types of mixtures, expressed, as a matter of fact, in the context of pots and pans, with Stoic philosophers' classifications of types of mixtures.

Chapter Six

Philosophy and Physics:
The Mishnah's Mixtures and Stoic Mixtures

When the Temple stood, cleanness and uncleanness bore concrete meanings and produced practical effects. They were 'real,' in the sense of producing concrete and material results; something which touched a Father of uncleanness was *unclean*, so could not be brought to the Temple, might have to be destroyed (as in the case of unclean heave-offering). A hundred years after the destruction, by contrast, cleanness and uncleanness are represented as relative to unseen and impalpable forces, to time and circumstance, individual will and private intention. The ordinary person is assumed to be unclean. At the time of the vintage he is assumed to be clean. Liquid makes things susceptible to uncleanness. But if it is placed on dry food without the approval of the owner, the food is not susceptible to uncleanness; a *Zab* may walk on the wet olives and they remain clean as before; one may take grapes or olives to the market and bring them back, without regard to liquid on them, and toss them into the vat, for they still are clean. Clearly, a major shift has taken place in the perception of the concreteness and vividness of uncleanness, a movement from a perception of something real and capable of presenting material danger, e.g. to the cult, or to the person who proposes to eat his food as if he were in the cult, to a perception of a status which is attained or imposed without regard to material, physical realities. One might say we have moved from the realm of the absolute and religious to the world of the relative, the speculative, and the philosophical.

Indeed, if we stand back from the details of the law and ask, What is it that the second century rabbis regarded (in general terms) as subject to their speculative inquiry, we should describe their agendum as follows: In respect to society, we want to know what people usually do, how various classes of society may be expected to behave. In respect to happenings in the natural world, the world of animals for example, we ask about what are the likely principles by which we may interpret events we do not know have taken place. In respect to material processes, we wish to speculate on the nature of mixtures. If I have a substance of one sort and it is joined to a substance of another, how do the traits of the one combine with the traits of another?

This generalized way of stating the problem of M. Tohorot 1:5-9, which we shall examine in detail, for example, will not have surprised Alexander Aphrodisiensis who writes:

> Certain mixtures...result in a total interpenetration of substances and their qualities, the original substances and qualities being preserved in this mixture; this he calls specifically *krasis* of the mixed components. It is characteristic of the mixed substances that they can again be separated, which is only possible if the components preserve their properties in the mixture.... This interpenetration of the components he assumes to happen in that the substances mixed together interpenetrate each other such that there is not a particle among them that does not contain a share of all the rest. If this were not the case, the result would not be *krasis* but juxtaposition.[1]

When we hold that a substance at the first remove and one at the second remove interpenetrate and are regarded as entirely unclean at the first remove, we say much the same thing. Can they now be separated? And if they are separated, what is the result? We shall now see that our authorities raise precisely that issue, in terms of removes of uncleanness to be sure. The matter of connection is of the same order of theoretical interest. Uncleanness affecting all parts of material after they have been connected affects them all when they are separated. But if something is made unclean, then connected to something else, that latter substance is unclean just as is the former. But when it is separated, it is unclean in a lower remove, only by virtue of its contact with that which was originally contaminated. So now we have a mosaic-like mixture, in which each element in the whole preserves its own individuality. The set of pericopae turn out to be remarkably relevant to the Stoic theory of mixture, stated by S. Sambursky in the following terms:

> As far as classification is concerned, the Stoic theory is much clearer. It distinguished between three types of mixture. One of them, mingling or mechanical mixture, is identical with what Aristotle defines by 'composition' (as in the case of the mixture of barley and wheat), and it applies essentially to bodies of a granular structure where a mosaic-like mixture results, each particle of one component being surrounded by particles of the other. The other extreme is fusion, which leads to the creation of a new substance whereby the individual properties of each of the components are lost.... Between these two types lies a third case of 'mixture' proper (*krasis* for liquids, *mixis* for non-liquids), which, from the Stoic point of view, represents

---

[1]S. Sambursky, *Physics of the Stoics* (London, 1959), p. 122.

the most important category of blending. Here a complete interpenetration of all the components takes place, and any volume of the mixture, down to the smallest parts, is jointly occupied by all the components in the same proportion, each component preserving its own properties under any circumstances, irrespective of the ratio of its share in the mixture. The properties are preserved in all cases where, as opposed to the case of fusion, the components can be separated out by putting a sponge into the mixture....[2]

Certainly an example of fusion is the contamination of liquids. Once unclean, they are unclean always at a single remove; the uncleanness affects the whole equally and profoundly. An example of mingling is connection which takes place after uncleanness has affected one part of what is connected. And an example of the middle sort of mixing is the blending of solids unclean in various removes, as we saw in Chapter Five.

That is not to suggest that among the second century Galilean rabbis were Stoic philosophers, importing into the Torah of Moses, in the guise of discussions on matters of cleanness and uncleanness, the grand issues of physics. It is only to point out a curious congruence between the arcane language and problems worked out by the rabbis and the clear and lucid interest in physics and other philosophical matters under discussion elsewhere. Speculation on social behavior, on certainties and commonalities in the movement of objects and substances, on the mixture and separation of foods and liquids – that speculation, translated into more general language, surely will have proved not without its point to people familiar with the philoophical issues of the contemporary Greco-Roman world. If philosophy in time became transmuted into religion, in the case of the earlier rabbis, the opposite also may be said: the religious world of cult and cleanness generated issues remarkably pertinent to the speculations of philosophers. Now we turn to Mishnah-tractate Tohorot 1:5-9, to see in detail the texts that sustain my proposition. It is that the Mishnah's theory of mixtures corresponds to Stoic philosophy's theory of mixtures as just now spelled out.

Mishnah-tractate Tohorot 1:5-9, introducing removes of uncleanness in relation to food, is formed of three autonomous units, M. 1:5-6, M. 1:7-8, and M. 1:9. Simeon at T. 1:1 cites M. 1:5A, which certainly originates in Ushan times at the latest. M. 1:5-6 present a beautifully formed set of balanced rules, which make the point that when particles of food, unclean at different removes of uncleanness, join together they share in the uncleannness of the more lenient, or further removed, of the two removes of uncleanness. That is the case when either part by itself does

---

[2]*Ibid.*, pp. 14-15.

not form a sufficient bulk of food to be susceptible to, or to convey, uncleanness on its own. but when we have sufficient bulk of food – an egg's volume – to be susceptible to, or to convey, uncleanness on its own, then of course a mixture of two such bulks is deemed to convey uncleannness at the remove of the more stringent of the two. If we then divide such a quantity, so that we are no longer certain whether, in either part, we have a volume of food sufficient to convey uncleanness at the more stringent remove, we invoke the opening rule. This matter is fully worked out.

M. 1:7-8 exhibit the same careful attention to form and balance of detail. Now we discuss, first, pieces of dough which are stuck together and then made unclean. In this case the whole conglomerate is unclean at the same remove. We deal, second, with pieces of dough, one of which is unclean, and the others of which are then attached to the unclean one. In this case, while joined together, the whole shares in the uncleanness of the original, unclean piece, but, when separated, the parts attached after the original piece became unclean do not. Then the pieces made unclean only through their contact with the originally unclean piece now are unclean at one remove less than the originally unclean piece. This is worked out, as in M. 1:5-6, in sequence, from the first, to the second, and finally to the third remove. M. 1:7 specifies sources of uncleanness at each remove, creeping thing, a Father of uncleanness, liquid, in the first remove, and hands, in the second remove. M. 1:8 speaks only of the ordinals of remove, without giving in detail the already specified sources of uncleanness. M. asks about heave-offering, so T. (T. 1:5) adds the matter of Holy Things.

M. 1:9 is a singleton, not so carefully formulated as the foregoing, but its rule is equally cogent. It present a paradox to stress the point that liquid made unclean even in the second or third removes (in the case of Holy Things), that is, by something unclean in the first, or second removes, in any event falls into uncleanness in the first remove. This rule is worked out with reference to loaves of Holy Things touching one another; these contain water, preserved in cleanness fitting for Holy Things, in hollows of the loaves. If any one of them is made unclean by a Father of uncleanness, all are unclean. Why? Because even the loaf third in sequence contaminates the liquid in a hollow on it, the liquid falls into the first remove and forthwith renders its loaf unclean in the second remove, and the loaf fourth in sequence, because of its contact with the third loaf (which is unclean in the second remove), is in the third remove of uncleanness, and affects its liquid in the same way, and so on to infinity. This is so because we count four removes for Holy Things, so what is unclean in the third affects the fourth and thus conveys uncleannness, also, to the liquid which is on it, which liquid then falls into the first remove. In the case of heave-offering by contrast, that is not the case. To be sure, if loaves of heave-offering, which touch one another, are affected by liquid between the loaves, then the same infinite sequence is reenacted. T. 1:7B states this same rule in still clearer language.

Mishnah-tractate Tohorot

1:5-6

A.   The [solid] food which is made unclean by a Father of uncleanness and that which is made unclean by an Offspring of uncleanness join together with one another [to make up the prescribed volume] to convey the lighter degree [remove] of uncleanness of the two.

[P, Katsh #116, M, K, PB start 1:5 here:] How so?

B.   A half egg's bulk of food which is unclean in the first remove and a half egg's bulk of food which is unclean in the second remove which one mixed with one another – [the consequent mixture is unclean in the] second [remove of uncleanness].

C.   A half egg's bulk of food unclean in the second remove of uncleanness and a half egg's of food unclean in the third remove of uncleanness which one mixed together with one another – [it is unclean in the] third [remove of uncleanness].

D.   [But] an egg's bulk of food unclean in the first remove of uncleanness and an egg's bulk of food unclean in the second remove of uncleanness which one mixed together with one another – it is unclean in the first remove of uncleanness.

E.   [If] one divided them up – this is unclean in the second remove of uncleanness, and this is unclean in the second remove of uncleanness.

F.   This one fell by itself and this one by itself on (K: LTWK) a loaf of heave-offering – they have rendered it unfit [= in the third remove].

G.   [If] the two of them feel on it simultaneously [at the same time, not necessarily on the same spot (GRA)] – they have made it unclean in the second remove of uncleanness.

M. 1:5

A.   An egg's bulk of food unclean in the second remove and [V, K lack W] an egg's bulk of food unclean in the third remove which one mixed with one another – it is unclean in the second remove.

B.   [If] one divided them – this is unclean in the third remove, and this is unclean in the third remove.

C.   [If] this one fell by itself and this by itself on (V, K: LTWK) a loaf of heave-offering – they have not made it unfit.

D.   If the two of them fell simultaneously – they put it into the third remove [= render it unfit].

E.   An egg's bulk of food unclean in the first remove [V lacks W] and
        an egg's bulk of food unclean in the third remove which he mixed
        with one another – it is unclean in the first remove.

F.   [If] one divided them – this one is unclean in the second remove,
        and this is unclean in the second remove.

G.   For even that which is unclean in the third remove which touched
        something unclean in the first remove becomes unclean in the
        second remove.

H.   Two egg's bulk of food unclean in the first remove, two egg's bulks
        of food unclean in the second remove which one mixed with one
        another – it is unclean in the first remove.

I.   [If] one divided them – this is unclean in the first remove and this
        one is unclean in the first remove.

J.   [If one divided them into] three or four parts – lo, these are
        unclean in the second remove.

K.   Two egg's bulks of food unclean in the second remove, two eggs
        bulks of food unclean in the third remove, which one mixed
        together – it is unclean in the second remove.

L.   [If] one divided them – this one is unclean in the second remove,
        and this one is unclean in the second remove.

M.   [If one divided them into] three or four parts, lo, these [all] are in
        the third remove.

M. 1:6 (b. Zev. 31a)

This large and elegant unit is formulated in complete, declarative
sentences, with only slight apocopation in the examples. We have four
major subdivisions in all, (1) 1:5A-C, (2) 1:5D-G, 1:6A-D, (3) 1:6E-G, and
(4) 1:6H-M. The first opens with a generalization, 1:5A, followed by
two illustrations, B and C. The former illustration deals with the first
and second remove, the latter, the second and third remove. The second
subdivision requires but lacks an introductory generalization parallel to
A1. The important shift is that we now have food itself of a bulk
sufficient to contract and convey uncleanness. It is mixed with another
such quantity. The matter of joining together, to which A alludes, is no
longer relevant and the consequent rule shifts. No longer do we assign
the status of the consequent mixture to the lighter degree of uncleanness
of the two. Now we impose the more severe. D states that rule through
its example. E, F, and G then deal with complications of the rule, to be
explained below. M. 1:6A-D are in exactly the same model. The first
set thus presents food in the first remove mixed with food in the second,
and the second, food unclean in the second remove mixed with food
unclean in the third.

The third division carries forward this same matter, quantities of
food of requisite volume to convey uncleanness which have mixed
together. But now the mixture is between food unclean in the first

remove with food unclean in the third, thus completing the thought begun at M. 1:5D. What distinguishes the third division is the generalization at G and the absence of the issue of heave-offering after F, that in two parts, each falling by itself, then the two falling simultaneously. The final division again presents two carefully paired rules, *first/second* remove, *second/third* remove, each spelled out in the same way as the other. H-I go over familiar ground, and what is new is J and its parallel at M. In all, it would be difficult to point to a more carefully constructed set of rules. There can be no doubt that the unit, while sizeable, is unitary and harmonious, the work of a single hand. Let us now turn to the substance of the problem.

We first review the matter of removes, that is, sequences of contact with the primary source of uncleannness. A Father of uncleanness which touches something susceptible to uncleanness produces an Offspring of uncleanness. These are in four removes from the Father. That which touches the Father is unclean in the first remove. That which touches that which has touched the Father is unclean in the second remove. And so for the third and the fourth, which pertain solely to heave-offering, for the third, and Holy Things, for the fourth. Heave-offering which has touched something unclean in the second remove is rendered unfit; and Holy Things which touch something unclean in the third remove are rendered unfit, a matter resumed at M. 2:4.

The problem before us is spelled out by Maimonides (*Uncleanness of Foodstuffs* 4:12) as follows:

> An equal quantity is prescribed for all unclean foodstuffs, since no unclean foodstuff conveys uncleanness unless it is an egg's bulk in quantity; and their uncleannes is alike, since no unclean foodstuff conveys uncleanness except by contact; and it conveys uncleanness neither to persons nor to utensils; therefore they can be combined to convey the lesser uncleanness of the two of them. Thus, if there is a half egg's bulk of foodstuff suffering first-grade uncleanness and a half egg's bulk of foodstuff suffering second-grade uncleanness and they are combined, the whole suffers second-grade uncleanness; and if this touches heave-offering, it renders it invalid. If there is a half egg's bulk of foodstuff suffering second-grade uncleanness and a half egg's bulk suffering third-grade uncleanness and they are combined, the whole suffers third-grade uncleanness. And the same applies in every like case. Even if there is a half egg's bulk of foodstuff suffering first-grade uncleanness and a half egg's bulk suffering fourth-grade uncleanness, as a Hallowed Thing, and they are combined, the whole suffers only fourth-grade uncleanness.

With this in mind, the explanation of the first set, A-C is simple. Since in our combination a half of the requisite quantity is unclean in the first remove, and a half in the second, the whole mixture is unclean in the second remove, and so with a mixture of second and third.

When we come to D, however, our situation changes. Now we have a sufficient bulk to make up a contaminating quantitiy of food. That is, a whole egg's bulk is unclean in the first remove, and a whole in the second. Do we rule that they convey uncleanness in accord with the lesser or lighter degree? No, now we say the whole conveys uncleanness in accord with the more stringent remove, the first. Why? Because in fact we have in the whole mixture a sufficient quantity to convey uncleanness in the first remove. There is no reason to impose only the lesser degree of remove of uncleanness.

On the other hand, E says, if we take the mixture and divide it up, the rule of A does apply. We do not know that within either half is a sufficient quantity of unclean food in the first remove to convey uncleanness in that remove. So we rule that the two parts of the mixture, once divided, convey uncleanness in the lighter degree of uncleannness. It follows, F, that if one of the two parts fell on a loaf of heave-offering, since the part is in the second remove of uncleanness, the heave-offering is rendered unfit, that is, it is placed in the third remove. But, G points out, if the two parts simultaneously fall on heave-offering, then we invoke D, and the heave-offering, subject as it is to be food unclean in the first remove, then falls into the second. There is nothing difficult in this rule, which is simply repeated at M. 1:6A-D. Accordingly, M. 1:5C-G and 1:6A-D spell out the implications of M. 1:5A and the unstated generalization serving M. 1:5D.

This brings us to M. 1:6E-G. The important problem is at F. We have a mixture of food unclean in the first and third removes, each sufficient to convey uncleanness. E tells us what we know, which is that the whole is unclean at the first remove. But F, explains how to deal with the division. Both parts are unclean in the second remove. Why? Because what was unclean in the third remove has touched something unclean in the first remove. So we simply invoke the rule of M. 1:5A, the whole, composed of two insufficient parts, is unclean in the lighter of the two removes, the second. This is a logical extension of the opening group. The expected reference to heave-offering is absent. Why? Because it is obvious that if either of the two parts, unclean in the second remove, falls on heave-offering, it is rendered unfit, just as we have already stated at M. 1:5F, and if the two fell on it simultaneously, they make it unclean in the second remove, as M. 1:5G has said, and for the same reason.

H-J and K-M form the concluding set. Now we have two egg's bulks of food unclean in the first remove, two in the second. The reason for the specification of two egg's bulks is in J/M. The point of I and L is the same as given earlier. Since the four egg's bulks, when divided into two, still contain at least one egg's bulk unclean in the first remove, both of the divided parts, each with two egg's bulks, are unclean in the first remove. But, J asks, what if we divide the four egg's bulks into three or four parts? Then we again invoke the rule of M. 1:5A, ignoring what is spelled out at 1:6G. That is, we take account of the fact that the lesser of the two degrees is second, for J. And for M we do the same. M. 1:5A has emphasized that its rule applies when we have insufficient volume, so that either part by itself cannot convey uncleanness. While dividing the four eggs into four parts, we still have a sufficient volume to convey uncleanness, each of the three or four egg's bulks contains less than a *whole* egg's bulk of food unclean in the second remove, for K-M (or first, for H-J). Therefore we hold that the divided part is unclean in the lower, or more lenient, of the two removes. Accordingly, the point that is illustrated is not M. 1:5A, but M. 1:5D-E.

Mishnah-tractate Tohorot

1:7-8

A.   Pieces (MQRSWT) of dough [of heave-offering] stuck together,

B.   and loaves stuck together –

C.   [if] one of them is made unclean by a dead creeping thing [a Father of uncleanness],

D.   they all are unclean in the first remove [as if all had touched the insect, since they are deemed connected to one another].

E.   [If] they were separated (K: PRSH = one separated it, and so throughout) [from one another], they are all unclean in the first remove, [since they originally were connected when contaminated, so they are all affected equally by the creeping thing].

F.   [If they were made unclean by] liquid [which is always unclean in the first remove], they all are unclean in the second remove.

G.   [If] they separated [from one another], they all are unclean in the second remove.

H.   [If they were made unclean by] hands [in the second remove], they all are unclean in the third remove.

I.   [If] they separated [from one another], they all are unclean in the third remove.

M. 1:7

A.   A piece of dough [of heave-offering], which was unclean in the first remove, and one stuck others to it, – they all are unclean in the first remove.

B.   [If] they separated, it is unclean in the first remove, but all [the rest] are unclean in the second remove.

C.   [If] it was unclean in the second remove and one stuck others to it, they all are unclean in the second remove.

D.   [If] they separated, it is unclean in the second remove, but all [the rest] are unclean in the third remove.

E.   [If] it was unclean in the third remove, and one stuck others to it, it is unclean in the third remove, but all [the rest] are clean,

F.   whether they separated or whether they did not separate.

M. 1:8

Maimonides (*Uncleanness of Foodstuffs* 6:18-19) reverses the order of the rules:

> If a loaf of heave-offering suffering first-grade uncleanness is stuck to other loaves, all incur first grade uncleanness, if it is then separated from them, it still suffers first-grade uncleanness, but the rest bear only second-grade uncleanness.... If loaves of heave-offering are stuck together and one of them is rendered unclean by a dead creeping thing, all suffer first-grade uncleanness, even though they are afterward separated...*since they were a single body when they incurred uncleanness.*

The italicized words contain Maimonides' differentiation between the two cases (followed by MS, TYY, etc.). At M. 1:7, the contamination occurred when all were a single body of dough; at M. 1:8, it affected the first, to which only thereafter the others were attached. This certainly is the force of the description of the cases at M. 1:7A and 8A, *stuck together...if one is made unclean...vs. unclean in the first remove and one [then] stuck others to it...*

The point of M. 1:8F is that the third remove does not cause a fourth in the case of heave-offering, and this gloss is what necessitates our interpreting the whole as a matter of heave-offering. T. gives us Holy Things and a fourth remove, the link to M. 1:9.

The perfection of the formal articulation (except for the minor interpolation at M. 1:7B) requires little comment. Each clause is modeled in the form of the foregoing, and the whole is exquisitely balanced in form just as it is in substance. M. 1:8 clearly is harmonious with M. 1:7. The latter speaks in general terms – first remove, second, third – while the former specifies the source of uncleanness. Accordingly, the operative difference between M. 1:7 and M. 1:8 is simply the contrast between *stuck together* (NWSKWT) *vs. one stuck others* (HSYK) *to it.* The point of the difference expressed at M. 1:8 is that the original piece remains in the uncleanness to which it was originally subject, but the others, once removed, are unclean only by virtue of their (past) contact with it. In M. 1:7, by contrast, the pieces when made unclean are a unified mass. If made unclean by a Father of uncleanness, they are all in the first remove of uncleanness and remain so.

It remains to observe that the real issue before us is the nature of connection. The principle is that what is connected at the point of contamination shares in the contamination of the whole so long as it is part of the whole, but, once it is separated, it remains unclean only by virtue of its former condition. this same point is made at M. Kel. 18:7 with reference to the leg of a bed. The leg of the bed is unclean with *midras*-uncleannness and attached to a bed. The whole bed is now unclean with *midras*-uncleanness. When one removes the leg, the leg remains unclean with *midras*-uncleanness, but the bed falls into the lower remove, unclean through the uncleanness imparted by contact with *midras*-uncleanness. M. Kel. 18:8 goes over the same ground, now with reference to a phylactery which is in four parts.

Mishnah-tractate Tohorot

1:9

A.   Loaves of Holy Things [touching one another], *in* the hollows of which is water preserved in cleanness fitting for Holy Things –

B.   [if] one of them was made unclean by a creeping thing, they all are unclean. {Since even the loaf third in sequence contaminates the liquid in a hollow on it, the liquid is in the first remove and goes and renders the loaf unclean in the second remove. The loaf fourth in sequence is therefore in the third remove of uncleanness, affects *its* liquid, and so on. Thus all, however many in sequence, are made unclean].

C.   In the case of heave-offering, it [the creeping thing] renders unclean at two removes and renders unfit [but not unclean] at one [third remove]. [And liquid *on* the third is not unclean, so is not in the first remove, and the fourth loaf in sequence is unaffected.]

D.   If there is *between* them dripping liquid, even in the case of heave-offering, the whole is unclean. [The liquid is made unclean and all loaves are in the second remove.]

M. 1:9 (y. Hag. 3:2)

A.   Pieces of dough touching one another and loaves in contact with one another –

B.   and in them are holes full of liquids –

C.   [if] a dead creeping thing touched one of them –

D.   it is made unclean and renders all of them unclean.

E.   Lo, this one says, "The things that made you unclean did not make me unclean, but you made me unclean."

Sifre Zutta to Num. 19:11
(Horovitz, p. 306, ls. 3-4)

Maimonides (*Uncleanness of Foodstuffs* 9:10B) gives the rule as follows:

> If there are loaves of hallowed produce having on them hollows, and in
> the hollows liquid that is hallowed, and a dead creeping thing touches
> one of them and the first touches the second and the second the third,
> even if they are a hundred in number, they all suffer first-grade
> uncleanness; by reason of the liquid in the hollows and the reverence
> due to Hallowed Things, it counts as a liquid respecting which no
> count is made of grades of uncleanness.
>
> But if they are loaves of heave-offering, the third loaf is rendered
> invalid, and from the third onward they remain clean.
>
> Yet if there is dripping moisture on all the loaves, even though they
> are heave-offering, they all become unclean and they all suffer
> second-grade uncleanness except the first, which the creeping thing
> has touched, which suffers first grade uncleanness.

The case is parallel to the foregoing. Now we have loaves of Holy
Things. In the hollows of the loaves is water which is preserved in
cleanness fitting for Holy Things ("sanctified water"). We take for
granted we have many loaves touching one another. If a creeping thing,
a Father of uncleanness, touches one of the loaves, all are made unclean.

Why is this so? We cannot improve on Slotki's explanation (p. 367,
n.4):

> Since the first loaf that was touched by the creeping thing contracted a
> first grade of uncleanness; the second loaf contracted from the first
> one a second grade of uncleanness; the third loaf contracts from the
> second a third grade of uncleanness, and, since in the case of holy
> things a third grade may cause a fourth grade of uncleanness, it also
> imparts uncleanness to the water on it which (in accordance with the
> uncleanness of liquids) becomes unclean in the first grade and causes
> the [next] loaf to contract second grade of uncleanness and so impart
> to the next loaf third grade of uncleanness. The next loaf, for the same
> reason, imparts second grade of uncleanness to the one next to it, and
> so on *ad infinitum.*

In other words, the water on a loaf raises the degree of uncleanness
affecting that loaf, once the water is made unclean, and so each loaf in
succession affects the next.

Heave-offering, however, is subject to a different rule. The dead
creeping thing makes the first loaf unclean in the first remove, and the
loaf unclean in the first remove makes the next loaf unclean in the
second, and the one unclean in the second remove makes the third loaf
unfit as heave-offering. Here Slotki explains (p. 367, no. 7):

> Since in heave-offering a third cannot make a fourth it becomes only
> invalid but not unclean. As the loaf in the third grade cannot convey
> uncleanness, the water on it remains clean, so that neither it nor the

water can convey uncleanness to the next loaf that touched it, which (like the next loaf that touched it and the one that touched the next, and so on) consequently remains clean.

If we have dripping water *between* the loaves of heave-offering (D), however, all become unclean, Again Slotki:

> The liquid between the first loaf and second becomes, in accordance with the law of unclean liquids, unclean in the first grade and consequently conveys uncleanness of the second grade to the second loaf that touched it. Similarly the water between the second and the third loaves becomes unclean in the first grade and causes the third loaf to be unclean in the second grade, and so on *ad infinitum*.

In other words, the difference between the first case, A-B, and the second, C, is negligible, since the presence of liquid *on* heave-offering, D, imposes on heave-offering exactly the same rule as we had for A-B. However, if we had dry loaves at A, then B would read, *renders unclean at three removes and unfit at one* (the fourth), or some such language. Accordingly, A-B and C by no means contrast to one another. If C had matched A, *loaves of heave-offering between which is water preserved in cleanness fitting for heave-offering* (or, all the more so, for Holy Things), then we should have the same rule as in B – *they all are unclean*. And the point of the rule would have been exactly as at B, which is, liquid made unclean in the second remove is unclean in the first remove and conveys uncleanness accordingly, without limit. This is, therefore, an exceedingly complex way of expressing the simple rule governing contamination of liquid: whatever remove of uncleanness affects water, water, once made unclean, is always unclean in the first remove.

At this point I can offer no more persuasive argument than simply to restate what Stoic physics has already said. In my view, we have in hand nothing less, and nothing more, than a statement, in a strange idiom, of precisely the same theory of mixtures as the following:

> Certain mixtures...result in a total interpenetration of substances and their qualities, the original substances and qualities being preserved in this mixture; this he calls specifically *krasis* of the mixed components. It is characteristic of the mixed substances that they can again be separated, which is only possible if the components preserve their properties in the mixture.... This interpenetration of the components he assumes to happen in that the substances mixed together interpenetrate each other such that there is not a particle among them that does not contain a share of all the rest. If this were not the case, the result would not be *krasis* but juxtaposition.

> Whatever is carried above the Zab is unclean. And whatever the Zab is carried upon is clean, except for something which is suitable for sitting and lying, and except for man.

This rule is illustrated with cases in which the finger of a Zab is underneath stones and a clean person is above them. The clean person is made unclean so that he imparts uncleanness at two removes and unfitness at one still further remove. If food and drink, a bed or a chair, and a *maddaf*-article not used for sitting and lying – are located above the stones with the Zab below, they impart uncleanness at one remove and unfitness at one remove. If the bed and chair are below, and the Zab above, they impart uncleanness at two removes and unfitness at one. If fodd, drink, and *maddaf*-objects are below and the Zab is above, they remain clean. Now this rule is treated as beyond dispute, and its details are taken for granted. Tosefta's version (T. Zab. 5:1A) concurs that food, drink, and *maddaf*-objects above a Zab are subject to a more stringent rule than food, drink, and *maddaf*-objects underneath a Zab, while a bed or chair underneath a Zab are subject to a more strict rule than a bed or chair located above a Zab.

In asking about the origins of this rather complex notion, we find no assitance whatever either in attribution, for all parties agree on the matter, or in attestations, for there is no reference to the matter in the whole of Seder Tohorot in which the principle of *maddaf* is at issue. The important point, then, is the distinction between what is carried above the *Zab* and what is carried below. If something not used for lying or sitting, inclusive of food and drink, is located above a *Zab*, it is clean. Only a bed or chair located below a *Zab* will be unclean, only because of bearing his weight even without directly touching him (I here omit all reference to man).

When in Mishnah, we find a conception clearly present in the foundations or originating at the earliest strata of Mishnaic thought, we have to ask whether or not said conception may originate in Scripture. In the present case, by a very brief series of logical steps, I shall show that the conception of *maddaf*-uncleanness, with its distinction between a chair or a bed below, and objects not used for sitting or lying below a Zab, and a chair or a bed above, and objects not used for sitting or lying above, a *Zab*, emerges from Scripture itself. The process by which this rather complex conception emerges, moreover, is not through formal exegesis, as is the claim of Sifra Zabim III:3-7, but through the hypothetical-logical reconstruction of the analogical-contrastive mode of exegesis which I shall lay forth. That mode of exegesis rests upon the perfectly simple supposition that, when the exegetes who contribute to Oral Torah read Scripture, they come with a single, two-sided conception: rules derive from Scripture by either analogy or contrast. *That is, something (1) either is like or (2) unlike something else. If (1) it is like that other thing, it follows its rule. If (2) it is unlike that other thing, it follows the exact opposite of its rule.*

*If, again, Scripture states a rule and its condition, then the presence of
the opposite condition will generate the opposite of the stated rule.*

Let us now proceed to the relevant Scriptural passage. At the left
hand I specify the verse itself, and, to the right of it, simply restate
what the verse says. Then I produce what I call a *secondary* meaning,
which is simply a restatement of the contents of the Scriptural passage
in more general language. There then follows a *tertiary* meaning, at
which level I reproduce not the stated rule but its exact opposite: *now
the method not of analogy, but of contrast.* At the *fourth* level, I then
state the opposite of the opposite of the third level, that is, what
clearly is implied by the negative of the rule at the third level of
meaning. At his point, a mere three stages of reasoning away from the
simple sense of Scripture, we find that we have stated what is at issue
at M. Zab. 5:2, to which I shall return.

In order to distinguish among the layers of meaning, I lay matters
out in a way meant to be visually striking. At the outset, I cite the
verse and opposite it restate what it says in simple language. This is
given in italics. The secondary meaning of each verse, given in regular
type, is attained simply by generalizing upon the plain and unadorned
statement in, and restatement of, the Scriptural verse itself. There is
then the tertiary meaning, distinguished from the secondary
generalization of Scripture by boldface type. This tertiary meaning is
the point at which I introduce conceptions drawn from our tractate. I
believe that, in the main, principles at a second level of exegesis from
Scripture, that is, tertiary meanings, represent little more than a
further generalization of what Scripture says, on the one hand, and the
(now surely eisegetical) introduction of a few simple and obvious
distinctions necessitated or invited by that generalization, on the
other. In some instances there is yet a fourth level of meaning, and this
invariably is drawn by me from Mishnah-Tosefta. That too is
represented in boldface type.

Chapter Seven

The Mishnah's Generative Mode of Thought: *Listenwissenschaft* and Analogical-Contrastive Reasoning

The paramount mode of reasoning in the Mishnah is what I call "analogical-contrastive reasoning." The logic may be expressed very simply. All persons, things, or actions that fall within a single species of a given genus in a uniform system of classification follow a single rule. All persons, things, or actions, that fall within a different species of that same given genus in a uniform system of classification follow precisely the opposite rule. Stated in gross terms, therefore, something is either like or unlike something else within a single genus that validates comparison and contrast. If it is like that other thing, it follows its rule. If it is not like that other thing, it follows the opposite of its rule. That reasoning by analogy and contrast dominates in the formation of the Mishnah's rules and it is, therefore, its generative mode of thought. We can, therefore, work our way back from conclusions that the Mishnah's authorship presents through the stages of reasoning that have led to reaching those conclusions.

To explain how this logic works, I have first of all to set forth the principal mode of discourse of our document, which is to set forth rules by means of lists of like or unlike persons, actions, or things. A common rule then applies to the like, and the opposite rule to the unlike. On the surface, then, the Mishnah's philosophy is an exercise in *Listenwissenschaft*, and beneath the surface, the Mishnah's philosophy carries forward the logic of comparison and contrast, expressed through the results conveyed by lists and the rules governing their items. This analogical-contrastive logic then validates the making of lists. So let us turn to the Mishnah's *Listenwissenschaft* as the first in the two stages of the exposition of the philosophical modes of thought of the document.

The Mishnah's logic of cogent discourse establishes propositions that rest upon philosophical bases, e.g., through the proposal of a thesis and the composition of a list of facts that (e.g., through shared traits of a taxonomic order) prove the thesis. The Mishnah presents rules and treats stories (inclusive of history) as incidental and of merely taxonomic interest. Its logic is propositional, and its intellect does its work through a vast labor of classification, comparison, and contrast generating governing rules and generalizations. A simple contrasting case shows us that the stakes are very high. For that purpose, let us turn to a document we know our authorship knew well, namely, the Written Torah.

The Pentateuch appeals to a different logic of cogent discourse from the Mishnah's. It is the cogency imparted by teleology, that is, a logic that provides an account of how things were in order to explain how things are and set forth how they should be, with the tabernacle in the wilderness the model for (and modeled after) the Temple in the Jerusalem abuilding. The Mishnah speaks in a continuing present tense, saying only how things are, indifferent to the *were* and the *will-be*. The Pentateuch focuses upon self-conscious "Israel," saying who they were and what they must become to overcome how they now are. The Mishnah understands by "Israel" as much the individual as the nation and identifies as its principal actors, the heroes of its narrative, not the family become a nation, but the priest and the householder, the woman and the slave, the adult and the child, and other castes and categories of person within an inward-looking, established, fully landed community. Given the Mishnah's authorship's interest in classifications and categories, therefore in systematic hierarchization of an orderly world, one can hardly find odd that (re)definition of the subject-matter and problematic of the systemic social entity.

We may briefly dwell on this matter of difference in the prevailing logic, because the contrast allows us to see how one document will appeal to one logic, another to a different logic. While the Pentateuch appeals to the logic of teleology to draw together and make sense of facts, so making connections by appeal to the end and drawing conclusions concerning the purpose of things, the Mishnah's authorship knows only the philosophical logic of syllogism, the rule-making logic of lists. The Pentateuchal logic reached concrete expression in narrative, which served to point to the direction and goal of matters, hence, in the nature of things, of history. Accordingly, those authors, when putting together diverse materials, so shaped everything as to form of it all as continuous a narrative as they could construct, and through that "history" that they made up, they delivered their message and also portrayed that message as cogent and compelling. If the Pentateuchal writers were theologians of history, the Mishnah's aimed at composing a natural philosophy for supernatural, holy Israel. Like good Aristotelians, they would uncover the components of the rules by comparison and contrast, showing the rule for one thing by finding out how it compared with like things and contrasted with the unlike. Then, in their view, the unknown would become known, conforming to the rule of the like thing, also to the opposite of the rule governing the unlike thing.

That purpose is accomplished, in particular, though list-making, which places on display the data of the like and the unlike and implicitly (ordinarily, not explicitly) then conveys the rule. It is this resort to list-making that accounts for the rhetorical stress on groups of examples of a common principle, three or five for instance. Once a series is established, the authorship assumes, the governing rule will be perceived. That explains why, in exposing the interior logic of its authorship's intellect, the Mishnah had to be a book of lists, with the implicit order, the monothetic traits of a monothetic order, dictating the ordinarily unstated general and encompassing rule.

And all this why? It is in order to make a single statement, endless times over, and to repeat in a mass of tangled detail precisely the same fundamental judgment. The Mishnah in its way is as blatantly repetitious in its fundamental statement as is the Pentateuch. But the power of the Pentateuchal authorship, denied to that of the Mishnah, lies in their capacity always to be heard, to create sound by resonance of the surfaces of things. The Pentateuch is a fundamentally popular and accessible piece of writing. By contrast, the Mishnah's writers spoke into the depths, anticipating a more acute hearing than they ever would receive. So the repetitions of Scripture reenforce the message, while the endlessly repeated paradigm of the Mishnah sits too deep in the structure of the system to gain hearing from the ear that lacks acuity or to attain visibility to the untutored eye. So much for the logic. What of the systemic message? Given the subtlety of intellect of the Mishnah's authorship, we cannot find surprising that the message speaks not only in what is said, but in what is omitted.

The framers of the Mishnah appeal solely to the traits of things. The logical basis of coherent speech and discourse in the Mishnah then derives from *Listenwissenschaft*. That mode of thought defines way of proving propositions through classification, so establishing a set of shared traits that form a rule which compels us to reach a given conclusion. Probative facts derive from the classification of data, all of which point in one direction and not in another. A catalogue of facts, for example, may be so composed that, through the regularities and indicative traits of the entries, the catalogue yields a proposition. A list of parallel items all together point to a simple conclusion; the conclusion may or may not be given at the end of the catalogue, but the catalogue – by definition – is pointed. All of the catalogued facts are taken to bear self-evident connections to one another, established by those pertinent shared traits implicit in the composition of the list, therefore also bearing meaning and pointing through the weight of evidence to an inescapable conclusion. The discrete facts then join together because of some trait common to them all. This is a mode of classification of facts to lead to an identification of what the facts have in common and – it goes without saying, an explanation of their meaning. These and other modes of philosophical argument are entirely familiar to us all. In calling all of them "philosophical," I mean only to distinguish them from the other three logics we shall presently examine. Now we see how fundamental to thought was Sifra's authorship's insistence that Scripture, not things viewed on their own, dictates the classification of things.

The diverse topical program of the Mishnah, time and again making the same points on the centrality of order, works itself out in a single logic of cogent discourse, one which seeks the rule that governs diverse cases. And, as we now see, that logic states within its interior structure the fundamental point of the document as a whole. The correspondence of logic to system here, as in the Pentateuch viewed overall, hardly presents surprises. Seeing how the logic does its work within the document therefore need not detain us for very long. Two pericopes of the Mishnah show us the logic that joins fact to fact, sentence to sentence, in a cogent proposition, that is, in our terms, a paragraph that makes a statement. To see how this intellect does its work we return to familiar materials, those in which we have already discerned formalization of speech. We come first to Mishnah-tractate Berakhot, Chapter Eight, to see list-making in its simplest form, and then to Mishnah-tractate Sanhedrin, Chapter Two, to see the more subtle way in which list-making yields a powerfully argued philosophical theorem. In the first of our two abstracts we have a list, carefully formulated, in which the announcement at the outset tells us what is catalogued, and in which careful mnemonic devices so arrange matters that we may readily remember the conflicting opinions. So in formal terms, we have a list that means to facilitate memorization. But in substantive terms, the purpose of the list and its message(s) are not set forth, and only ample exegesis will succeed in spelling out what is at stake. Here is an instance of a Mishnah-passage which demands an exegesis not supplied by the Mishnah's authorship.

Mishnah-tractate Berakhot Chapter Eight

8:1

    A.   These are the things which are between the House of Shammai and the House of Hillel in [regard to] the meal:

[1]   B.   The House of Shammai say, "One blesses over the day, and afterward one blesses over the wine."

And the House of Hillel say, "One blesses over the wine, and afterward one blesses over the day."

8.2

[2]   A   The House of Shammai say, "They wash the hands and afterward mix the cup."

And the House of Hillel say, "They mix the cup and afterward wash the hands."

8.3

[3]   A   The House of Shammai say, "He dries his hands on the cloth and lays it on the table."

And the House of Hillel say, "On the pillow."

8.4

[4]   A   The House of Shammai say, "They clean the house, and afterward they wash the hands."

And the House of Hillel say, "They wash the hands, and afterward they clean the house."

8.5

[5]   A   The House of Shammai say, "Light, and food, and spices, and *Havdalah*."

And the House of Hillel say, "'Light, and spices, and food, and *Havdalah*."

[6]   B.   The House of Shammai say, "'Who created the light of the fire.'"

And the House of Hillel say, "'Who creates the lights of the fire.'"

As we recall, the mnemonic serving the list does its work by the simple reversal of items. If authority A has the order 1, 2, then authority B will give 2, 1. Only entry [3] breaks that pattern. What is at stake in the making of the list is hardly transparent, and why day/wine vs. wine/day, with a parallel, e.g., clean/wash vs. wash/clean, yields a general principle the authorship does not indicate. All we know at this point, therefore, is that we deal with list-makers. But how lists work to communicate principles awaits exemplification.

The next abstract allows us much more explicitly to identify the *and* and the *equal* of Mishnaic discourse, showing us through the making of connections and the drawing of conclusions the propositional and essentially philosophical mind that animates the Mishnah. In the following passage, drawn from Mishnah-tractate Sanhedrin Chapter Two, the authorship wishes to say that Israel has two heads, one of state, the other of cult, the king and the high priest, respectively, and that these two offices are nearly wholly congruent with one another, with a few differences based on the particular traits of each. Broadly speaking, therefore, our exercise is one of setting forth the genus and the species. The genus is head of holy Israel. The species are king and high priest. Here are the traits in common and those not shared, and the exercise is fully exposed for what it is, an inquiry into the rules that govern, the points of regularity and order, in this minor matter, of political structure. My outline, imposed in boldface type, makes the point important in this setting. We deal with Mishnah-tractate Sanhedrin Chapter Two:

1. The rules of the high priest: subject to the law, marital rites, conduct in bereavement

2:1

A.   A high priest judges, and [others] judge him;

B.   gives testimony, and [others] give testimony about him;

C.   performs the rite of removing the shoe [Deut. 25:7-9], and [others] perform the rite of removing the shoe with his wife.

D.   [Others] enter levirate marriage with his wife, but he does not enter into levirate marriage,

E.   because he is prohibited to marry a widow.

F.   [If] he suffers a death [in his family], he does not follow the bier.

G.   "But when [the bearers of the bier] are not visible, he is visible; when they are visible, he is not.

H.   "And he goes with them to the city gate," the words of R. Meir.

I.   R. Judah says, "He never leaves the sanctuary,

J.   "since it says, *'Nor shall he go out of the sanctuary'* (Lev. 21:12)."

K.   And when he gives comfort to others

L.   the accepted practice is for all the people to pass one after another, and the appointed [prefect of the priests] stands between him and the people.

M.   And when he receives consolation from others,

N.   all the people say to him, "Let us be your atonement."

O.   And he says to them, "May you be blessed by Heaven."

P.   And when they provide him with the funeral meal,

Q.   all the people sit on the ground, while he sits on a stool.

2. The rules of the king: not subject to the law, marital rites, conduct in bereavement

2:2

A.   The king does not judge, and [others] do not judge him;

B.   does not give testimony, and [others] do not give testimony about him;

C.   does not perform the rite of removing the shoe, and others do not perform the rite of removing the shoe with his wife;

D.   does not enter into levirate marriage, nor [do his brother] enter levirate marriage with his wife.

E.   R. Judah says, "If he wanted to perform the rite of removing the shoe or to enter into levirate marriage, his memory is a blessing."

F.   They said to him, "They pay no attention to him [if he expressed the wish to do so]."

G.   [Others] do not marry his widow.

H.   R. Judah says, "A king may marry the widow of a king.

I.   "For so we find in the case of David, that he married the widow of Saul,

J.   "For it is said, '*And I gave you your master's house and your master's wives into your embrace*' (II Sam. 12:8)."

2:3

A.   [If] [the king] suffers a death in his family, he does not leave the gate of his palace.

B.   R. Judah says, "If he wants to go out after the bier, he goes out,

C.   "for thus we find in the case of David, that he went out after the bier of Abner,

D.   "since it is said, '*And King David followed the bier*' (2 Sam. 3:31)."

E.   They said to him, "This action was only to appease the people."

F.   And when they provide him with the funeral meal, all the people sit on the ground, while he sits on a couch.

3. Special rules pertinent to the king because of his calling
2:4

A.   [The king] calls out [the army to wage] a war fought by choice on the instructions of a court of seventy-one.

B.   He [may exercise the right to] open a road for himself, and [others] may not stop him.

C.   The royal road has no required measure.

D.   All the people plunder and lay before him [what they have grabbed], and he takes the first portion.

E.   "*He should not multiply wives to himself*" (Deut. 17:17) – only eighteen.

F.   R Judah says, "He may have as many as he wants, so long as they *do not entice him* [to abandon the Lord (Deut. 7:4)]."

G.   R. Simeon says, "Even if there is only one who entices him [to abandon the Lord] – lo, this one should not marry her."

H.   If so, why is it said, "He should not multiply wives to himself"?

I.   Even though they should be like Abigail [1 Sam. 25:3].

J.   "*He should not multiply horses to himself*" (Deut. 17:16) – only enough for his chariot.

K.   "*Neither shall he greatly multiply to himself silver and gold*" (Deut. 17:16) – only enough to pay his army.

L.   *"And he writes out a scroll of the Torah for himself"* (Deut. 17:17)

M.   When he goes to war, he takes it out with him; when he comes back, he brings it back with him; when he is in session in court, it is with him; when he is reclining, it is before him,

N.   as it is said, *"And it shall be with him, and he shall read in it all the days of his life"* (Deut. 17:19).

2:5

A.   [Others may] not ride on his horse, sit on his throne, handle his scepter.

B.   And [others may] not watch him while he is getting a haircut, or while he is nude, or in the bath-house,

C.   since it is said, *"You shall surely set him as king over you"* (Deut. 17:15) – that reverence for him will be upon you.

The subordination of Scripture to the classification-scheme is self-evident. Scripture supplies facts. The traits of things – kings, high priests – dictate classification-categories on their own, without Scripture's dictate.

The philosophical cast of mind is amply revealed in this essay, which in concrete terms effects a taxonomy, a study of the genus, national leader, and its two species, [1] king, [2] high priest: how are they alike, how are they not alike, and what accounts for the differences. The premise is that national leaders are alike and follow the same rule, except where they differ and follow the opposite rule from one another. But that premise also is subject to the proof effected by the survey of the data consisting of concrete rules, those systemically inert facts that here come to life for the purposes of establishing a proposition. By itself, the fact that, e.g., others may not ride on his horse, bears the burden of no systemic proposition. In the context of an argument constructed for monothetic, taxonomic purposes, the same fact is active and weighty. The whole depends upon three premises: [1] the importance of comparison and contrast, with the supposition that [2] like follows the like, and the unlike follows the opposite, rule; and [3] when we classify, we also hierarchize, which yields the argument from hierarchical classification: if this, which is the lesser, follows rule X, then that, which is the greater, surely should follow rule X. And that is the whole sum and substance of the logic of *Listenwissenschaft* as the Mishnah applies that logic in a practical way.

If I had to specify a single mode of thought that established connections between one fact and another, it is in the search for points in common and therefore also points of contrast. We seek connection between fact and fact, sentence and sentence in the subtle and balanced rhetoric of the Mishnah, by comparing and contrasting two things that are like and not alike. At the logical level, too, the Mishnah falls into the category of familiar philosophical thought.   Once we seek regularities, we propose rules.   What is like another thing falls under its rule, and what is not like the other falls under the opposite rule. Accordingly, as to the species of the genus, so far as they are alike, they share the same rule. So far as they are not alike, each follows a rule contrary to that governing the other. So the work of analysis is what produces connection, and therefore the drawing of conclusions derives from comparison and contrast: the *and*, the *equal*. The proposition then that forms the conclusion concerns the essential likeness of the two offices, except where they are different, but the subterranean premise is that we can explain both likeness and difference by appeal to a principle of fundamental order and unity. To make these observations concrete, we turn to the case at hand. The important contrast comes at the outset. The high priest and king fall into a single genus, but speciation, based on traits particular to the king, then distinguishes the one from the other. All of this exercise is conducted essentially independently of Scripture; the classifications derive from the system, are viewed as autonomous constructs; traits of things define classifications and dictate what is like and what is unlike.

Now that we have seen how the Mishnah's fundamental mode of setting forth propositions appealed to the logic and structure deriving from *Listenwissenschaft*, specifically, the logic of analogy and contrast, let me undertake a more difficult exercise. It is to prove that analogical-contrastive logic not only accounts for the document's formal traits but also explains how the document's authorship reached the conclusions that it presents to us. For that purpose, I turn to a demonstration, which I regard as beyond refutation, that it is through appeal to analogical-contrastive logic that the Mishnah's authorship reached conclusions, deriving from Scripture, upon which it built an entire tractate. For that purpose I turn to the conception of *maddaf*-uncleanness, which is paramount in Mishnah-tractate Zabim. I shall show that that generative conception emerged in a process of analogy and contrast, through four successive steps, from a proposition set forth in Scripture. Accordingly, what we shall see in acute detail is precisely how the Mishnah's generative mode of thought, which I call analogical-contrastive reasoning, actually worked.

The exercise in analogical-contrast exegesis turns to the concept of *maddaf*-uncleanness, which is stated at Mishnah-tractate Zabim 5:2 as follows:

> Whatever is carried above the Zab is unclean. And whatever the Zab
> is carried upon is clean, except for something which is suitable for
> sitting and lying, and except for man.

This rule is illustrated with cases in which the finger of a Zab is
underneath stones and a clean person is above them. The clean person is
made unclean so that he imparts uncleanness at two removes and
unfitness at one still further remove. If food and drink, a bed or a chair,
and a *maddaf*-article not used for sitting and lying are located above
the stones with the Zab below, they impart uncleanness at one remove
and unfitness at one remove. If the bed and chair are below, and the
Zab above, they impart uncleanness at two removes and unfitness at
one. If food, drink, and *maddaf*-objects are below and the Zab is above,
they remain clean. Now this rule is treated as beyond dispute, and its
details are taken for granted. Tosefta's version (T. Zab. 5:1A) concurs
that food, drink, and *maddaf*-objects above a Zab are subject to a more
stringent rule than food, drink, and *maddaf*-objects underneath a Zab,
while a bed or chair underneath a Zab are subject to a more strict rule
than a bed or chair located above a Zab.

In asking about the origins of this rather complex notion, we find no
assistance whatever either in attribution, for all parties agree on the
matter, or in attestations, for there is no reference to the matter in the
whole of Seder Tohorot in which the principle of *maddaf* is at issue.
The important point, then, is the distinction between what is carried
above the *Zab* and what is carried below. If something not used for
lying or sitting, inclusive of food and drink, is located above a *Zab*, it is
clean. Only a bed or chair located below a *Zab* will be unclean, only
because of bearing his weight even without directly touching him (I
here omit all reference to man).

When in Mishnah, we find a conception clearly present in the
foundations or originating at the earliest strata of Mishnaic thought,
we have to ask whether or not said conception may originate in
Scripture. In the present case, by a very brief series of logical steps, I
shall show that the conception of *maddaf*-uncleanness, with its
distinction between a chair or a bed below, and objects not used for
sitting or lying below a Zab, and a chair or a bed above, and objects not
used for sitting or lying above, a *Zab*, emerges from Scripture itself. The
process by which this rather complex conception emerges, moreover, is
not through formal exegesis, as is the claim of Sifra Zabim III:3-7, but
through the hypothetical-logical reconstruction of the analogical-
contrastive mode of exegesis which I shall lay forth. That mode of
exegesis rests upon the perfectly simple supposition that, when the
exegetes who contribute to Oral Torah read Scripture, they come with a
single, two-sided conception: rules derive from Scripture by either

analogy or contrast. *That is, something (1) either is like or (2) unlike something else. If (1) it is like that other thing, it follows its rule. If (2) it is unlike that other thing, it follows the exact opposite of its rule. If, again, Scripture states a rule and its condition, then the presence of the opposite condition will generate the opposite of the stated rule.*

Let us now proceed to the relevant Scriptural passage. At the left hand I specify the verse itself, and, to the right of it, simply restate what the verse says. Then I produce what I call a *secondary* meaning, which is simply a restatement of the contents of the Scriptural passage in more general language. There then follows a *tertiary* meaning, at which level I reproduce not the stated rule but its exact opposite: *now the method not of analogy, but of contrast.* At the *fourth* level, I then state the opposite of the opposite of the third level, that is, what clearly is implied by the negative of the rule at the third level of meaning. At this point, a mere three stages of reasoning away from the simple sense of Scripture, we find that we have stated what is at issue at M. Zab. 5:2, to which I shall return.

In order to distinguish among the layers of meaning, I lay matters out in a way meant to be visually striking. At the outset, I cite the verse and opposite it restate what it says in simple language. This is given in italics. The secondary meaning of each verse, given in regular type, is attained simply by generalizing upon the plain and unadorned statement in, and restatement of, the Scriptural verse itself. There is then the tertiary meaning, distinguished from the secondary generalization of Scripture by boldface type. This tertiary meaning is the point at which I introduce conceptions drawn from our tractate. I believe that, in the main, principles at a second level of exegesis from Scripture, that is, tertiary meanings, represent little more than a *further* generalization of what Scripture says, on the one hand, and the (now surely eisegetical) introduction of a few simple and obvious distinctions necessitated or invited by that generalization, on the other. In some instances there is yet a fourth level of meaning, and this invariably is drawn by me from Mishnah-Tosefta. That too is represented in boldface type.

The exercise is meant to demonstrate that each and every proposition of Mishnah-Tosefta derives either directly or indirectly, through processes of close reasoning, generalization, and secondary logical exegesis, from Scripture itself. At each point at which our abstract exercise produces a principle found in Mishnah, the appropriate pericope is of course designated. The relationship of Mishnah's unattributed pericope to Scripture is then spelled out in detail in the following section. The net result is hypothetically to demonstrate in close detail that this aspect of the law of Zabim is little more than a logical expansion of Scripture, and that each such expansion stands in close logical expansion of Scripture, and that each such expansion stands in close logical relationship to the foregoing, so that the result, at the end, is a very tight sequence of logical-exegetical steps. (All Mishnah references are to Mishnah-tractate Zabim.)

Scriptural Verse

Lev. 15:4: *Every bed on which he who has the discharge lies shall be unclean. And everything on which he sits shall be unclean.*

Clear Implication (Plain meaning)

The Zab imparts uncleanness by lying on a bed or by sitting on a chair.

Secondary Meaning

1. The Zab imparts uncleanness to objects which can be used for lying or sitting.

2. The Zab imparts uncleanness to objects used for lying or sitting by exerting the pressure of his weight on said objects.

Tertiary Meaning

A. The uncleanness of the Zab is transmitted by pressure.

B. Pressure is exerted through lying and sitting.

C. Other modes of exerting pressure, standing, leaning, being suspended, by analogy to lying and sitting, likewise transfer the uncleanness of the Zab to another object.

D. Pressure exerted by a clean person upon an object made unclean by a Zab will in like manner transfer the uncleanness from the object or the Zab to the clean person.

Mishnah

C: M.2:4 (3:1-3, 4:1-7).

D: M. 3:1-3, 4:1, 5, 5:1-5.

Lev. 15:5: *And any one who touches his bed shall wash his clothes and bathe himself in water and be unclean until the evening.*

Touching the Zab makes a person unclean. His clothes are unclean.

Secondary Meaning

3. The Zab's uncleanness is transferred by contact,

a. either a clean person's touching the Zab

b. or the Zab's touching a clean person.

4. One who is made unclean by the Zab imparts uncleanness to his clothing.

Tertiary Meaning

E. One made unclean by the Zab makes utensils unclean.

F. Said utensils are cleaned by immersion.

G. Since Scripture specifies that touching the bed or the Zab (Lev. 15:7) effects the transfer of uncleanness, and since Scripture specifies that sitting or lying also effects the transfer of uncleanness, and therefore touching without exerting pressure or exerting pressure without touching imparts uncleanness.

Mishnah

E: M. 2:4

G: M. 5:1-9

| Lev. 15:6: *And whoever sits on anything on which he who has the discharge has sat shall wash his clothes and bathe himself in water and be unclean until the evening.* | *Sitting on the bed or chair made unclean by the Zab makes a person unclean. His clothes are unclean.* |

Secondary Meaning

5. The object used for sitting or lying to which the Zab has imparted uncleanness is unclean in exactly the same measure as the Zab himself.

Tertiary Meaning

H. Since said object is unclean exactly as the Zab, is unclean, it therefore transfers uncleanness as does the Zab, that is, if one exerts pressure on it (the plain meaning) or if one touches it, or if it touches the clean person or exerts pressure on the clean person.

I. One made unclean by the unclean bed of the Zab makes utensils unclean. Said utensils are cleaned by immersion.

Mishnah

5: M. 2:4C-D.

H: M. 2:4C-D (3:1-3, 4:1-7).

I: M. 2:4C-D.

| Lev. 15:7: *And whoever touches the body of him who has the discharge shall wash his clothes and bathe himself in water and be unclean until the evening.* | *Touching the person of the Zab imparts uncleanness. The clothes are unclean.* |

Secondary Meaning

6. There is no difference between touching the bed of the Zab (Lev. 15:5) and touching the person of the Zab (Lev. 15:7). The consequences are the same in all regards.

Mishnah

6. M. 5:1

Lev. 15:8: *And if he who has the discharge spits on one who is clean, then he shall wash his clothes and bathe himself in water and be unclean until the evening.*	*The spit of the Zab is unclean exactly as is the Zab or his bed. The clothing of the person spat upon by the Zab is made unclean.*

Secondary Meaning

7. Fluids which exude from the Zab are unclean exactly as is his body or the bed he sits upon, etc.

Tertiary Meaning

J. The ways in which the Zab and the bed made unclean by the Zab transfer uncleanness apply also to the body fluids, so far as these modes of transfer are relevant: 1. touching, 2. carrying (below, Lev. 15:10b).

Mishnah

7: M. 5:6, 5:7

Lev. 15:9: *And any saddle on which he who has the discharge rides shall be unclean.*	*The saddle ridden upon by the Zab is unclean.*

Secondary Meaning

8. Since the saddle is dealt with apart from the bed and chair, it is subject to a distinctive set of rules.

Mishnah

8: M. 5:8

Lev. 15:10a: *And whoever touches anything that was under him shall be unclean until the evening.*	*An object located underneath a Zab is unclean.*

Secondary Meaning

9. I take it that the simple meaning is derived by treating Lev. 15:10a as a continuation of Lev. 15:9, which is to say, "A saddle on which a Zab has ridden is unclean, and whoever touches anything on which a Zab rides (or: has ridden) is unclean."

But if we read the verse disjunctively, then it bears a different meaning. Mere *location* of an object beneath a Zab – even if he is not touching it, and even if he is not riding on it – imparts uncleanness to the object. Accordingly, we take account of the spatial relationships of objects to a Zab.

10. And this yields the clearly required notion (L) that an object used for sitting, lying, or riding which is located beneath a Zab is unclean, even though the Zab has not sat, lain, or ridden on said object.

Tertiary Meaning

K. Touching or carrying the saddle produces uncleanness, as specified.

L. Touching an object located underneath a Zab, even though said object is not touched by the Zab and even though said object is not directly sat, lain, or ridden upon by the Zab but merely bears the weight of his body, imparts uncleanness so that the formerly clean person is made unclean and furthermore makes his clothing unclean, and, by extension, imparts uncleanness to utensils in general.

Fourth Level of Meaning

i. An object used for sitting and lying which is located underneath the Zab is subject to the uncleanness imparted by the Zab to objects upon which he has sat or lain, etc. It follows that the same sort of object located above the Zab is *not* subject to the uncleanness imparted by the Zab to objects used for sitting and lying.

ii. An object not used for sitting and lying located *beneath* the Zab (but not touched by him or subjected to the pressure of his body-weight) is *not* unclean.

iii. And, it follows in the rule of opposites, an object not used for sitting and lying which is located *above* the Zab *will* be unclean in some way or degree, not specified.

Mishnah

9-10: M. 5:1-3.

K: M. 5:8.

L: M. 5:1-3.

i: M. 5:1-2.

ii: M: 5:1.

iii: M. 5:1-2.

Lev. 15:10b: *And whoever carries such a thing shall wash his clothes and bathe himself in water and be unclean until the evening.*	*Carrying an object used for riding, sitting, or lying, and made unclean by the Zab makes the clean person who carries said object unclean. He makes his clothing unclean.*

Secondary Meaning

11. The uncleanness of the Zab is conveyed through carriage. Specifically, if one carries an object, such as a bed or chair, made

unclean by the Zab, one is made unclean as if he touched the Zab or as if he was subjected to the weight or pressure of the Zab or of an object made unclean by the Zab. This seems to me to follow naturally from the concept of pressure, since it is not possible to carry something without bearing its weight.

Tertiary Meaning

M. A person or an object which a Zab carries is made unclean. That is, just as there is no difference between touching the Zab or being touched by him, placing pressure upon the Zab or having the Zab's pressure applied to a clean person, so there is no difference between carrying the Zab and being carried by him.

N. The person made unclean in this way imparts uncleanness to his clothing, therefore to utensils.

Fourth Level of Meaning

iv. The person made unclean in these several ways makes his clothing unclean. Clearly, that is the case when the uncleanness of the Zab is transmitted to the person. It will follow, therefore, that when the Zab touches or exerts pressure on a clean person, the person is made unclean, and the clothing on the person is made unclean. Accordingly, it is when the clean person is subject to the uncleanness of the Zab, etc., that his clothing is made unclean: "he renders utensils unclean." When the person is no longer subject to the uncleanness of the Zab, he (of course) remains unclean. But he no longer will make his clothing unclean.

Mishnah

As above, Lev. 15:10a.

iv: M. 5:1, Joshua.

Lev. 15:11: *Any one whom he that has the discharge touches without having rinsed his hands shall wash his clothes and bathe himself in water and be unclean until the evening.*

The unclean person imparts uncleanness through touching. The person made unclean thereby transmits uncleanness to clothing.

Secondary Meaning

I see nothing in this verse which is both relevant to Zabim and new.

Lev. 15:12: *And the earthen vessel which he who has the discharge touches shall be broken. And every vessel of wood shall be rinsed in water.*

Earthen, or clay, utensils cannot be cleaned by rinsing, but only by breaking. Wooden utensils can be cleaned by immersion.

Secondary Meaning

12. Wooden vessels are subject to a different rule from earthen ones. That rule, moreover, will be the same as affects any other utensil which is cleaned through immersion.

Now to the Mishnah-tractate proper the entries that follow relate to, and I think are generated by, the primary allegation of Scripture or its logical developments, as specified.

1. M. 2:4: The Zab imparts uncleanness to the bed in five ways so that the bed imparts uncleanness to man and garments: standing, and sitting, lying, suspended, and leaning. The bed imparts uncleanness to man in seven ways so that he makes clothing unclean: standing, sitting, lying, suspended, leaning, contact, and carrying.

(Compare M. Kel. 1:3.)

Sifra Mesora Zabim 3:1-3: Pressure exerted by Zab, even if he sits on top of a heavy stone, imparts uncleanness.

Sifra Mesora Zabim 2:7: If Zab lay down on chair, sat on bed, stands or is suspended, they are unclean = M. 2:4.

2. Sifra Mesora Zabim 11:1-2: Man who touches bed imparts uncleanness to clothing, but bed which touches bed does not impart uncleanness to clothing. Bed imparts uncleanness when under the Zab to impart uncleanness to man and clothing, but man under the Zab does not impart uncleanness to man and clothing.

1. The rule is specific, that the Zab imparts uncleanness to the bed in the specified five ways. The second component is distinct. How does the bed transmit uncleanness to the clean man? Omitted from consideration: How does the Zab impart uncleanness to the clean man? In point of fact, the Zab transmits uncleanness through touching and through being carried (= exerting pressure).

2. The Zab imparts uncleanness when he touches a bed. The bed touching a bed does not impart uncleanness to clothing. The bed under the Zab imparts uncleanness as a bed, man does not.

Perhaps the several contrasts are based solely upon those established in Scripture, specifically, objects used for lying and sitting located underneath the Zab impart uncleanness to clothing, Lev. 15:10a. Man is not used for sitting and lying, therefore when located under the Zab, he does not. Along these same lines, Scriptures is clear, Lev. 15:5, that man who touches the bed washes his clothes – therefore imparts uncleanness to clothing (= utensils). Scripture is silent on the affect upon clothing of a bed which touches a bed made unclean by a Zab. It will have followed that what is stated explicitly at Lev. 15:5 then deliberately means to exclude what is omitted, which is the status of the bed which touches the bed. This is, of course, rather acute, since Scripture speaks of common occurrences, and it is difficult for a bed to reach out and touch another bed; Scripture's use of touching naturally is in the context of animate creatures.

3. M. 5:2: Whatever is carried above the Zab is unclean. Whatever the Zab is carried upon, but which is not touched by him, is clean, except for something used for sitting and lying (Lev. 15:10a) and except for man who carries the Zab (Lev. 15:10b).

+ T. 5:1.

Sifra Mesora Zabim III:3-7. Food, drink, utensils not used for sitting and lying which are above the Zab are made unclean on that account, proved by Simeon.

3. The important point here is the distinction between what is carried *above* the Zab and what is carried *below* him, without touching him. In the former case, there is uncleanness, and this applies, specifically, to food, drink, and objects not used for lying and sitting (*maddaf*). If these are carried below the Zab, they are clean. Only man and bed and chair below the Zab are made unclean because of their serving to carry his weight even without directly touching him.

The illustration, M. 5:2L-M. further indicates that what is unclean above the Zab – food, drink, *maddaf* (an object not used for lying and sitting) – is unclean in the first remove.

The principle is dual (a point I shall repeat at the end): (1) What is carried *underneath* the Zab is unclean, except for lying and sitting. (2) What is carried *above* the Zab is unclean. The relationship to Scripture is not self-evident. On the one side, we may readily account for the first principle. That an object used for lying and sitting which was under the Zab is unclean is specified at Lev. 15:10a. But the rule excludes objects not used for lying and sitting. Perhaps the distinction begins at Lev. 15:9. The saddle on which the Zab rides is unclean. Lev. 15:10a, continuing this point, then specifies that whoever touches anything that was under him – thus, that has served him for sitting – is unclean. And, by exclusion therefrom, whoever touches something which has been located under the Zab but which the Zab has *not* used for sitting is not unclean. Accordingly, the object itself, if not used for sitting, does not become unclean if the Zab is located above it.

But whence the notion of *maddaf*? That is, how do we know that an object *not* used for lying and sitting and located *above* the Zab is unclean? At first glance, it appears that we come to the fourth level of meaning imputed to Lev. 15:10a (i, iii). (1) What is unclean beneath the Zab is not unclean above him. (2) Then: What is not unclean beneath the Zab *is* unclean above him. Objects not used for sitting and lying, food and drink (2) are unclean above, because they (1) are clean below, the Zab. Thus: Objects used for sitting and lying are clean above, because they are unclean below, the Zab.

But the problem of *maddaf* is not so readily settled. We have to ascertain the meaning associated with the word in the earliest assigned pericopae. With the help of Kasovsky (Chayim Yehoshua Kasovsky, *Thesaurus Mishnae* [Jerusalem, 1958], IV, p. 353a), let us rapidly review the several meanings assigned to the word *maddaf*. The word is familiar as the name of an object, which we have translated *bird trap* at M. Kel. 23:5 (Part II, p. 220); as *the smoker of the bees* (M. Kel. 16:7, Part II, p. 78), required by context in both cases. Our tractate, by contrast, knows that word to mean "an object, not used for lying or sitting, located above the Zab," and we need not review the passages in which the word appears in that meaning (M. Zab. 4:6, 5:2). The third meaning is "a status as to uncleanness," a definition to be made more precise when we return to M. Par.10:1-2, and M. Toh. 8:2. The former (Part X, pp. 164-171) requires the meaning, "A status as to uncleanness related to *midras* but of lower degree of uncleanness than *midras*." Thus M. Par. 10:1, assigned to Yavneans, on what can be made unclean with corpse-uncleanness and whether that sort of object likewise is unclean with *maddaf*-uncleanness)

Accordingly, in the context of M. Par. 10:1-2, *maddaf* can only mean, "a status of uncleanness," which, we know, is uncleanness in the first remove, effecting uncleanness for food and liquid. This same meaning is absolutely required at M. Toh. 8:2 (Part XI, p. 186): If someone deposits with an *am ha-ares* a box full of clothing, Yosé says, "When it is tightly packed, it is unclean with *midras*-uncleanness, and if it is not tightly packed, it is unclean with *maddaf*-uncleanness." Accordingly, once more, *midras*-uncleanness is set into contrast with *maddaf*-uncleanness. In this instance the point is that the *am ha-ares* is unclean as a Zab. If a Zab shifts an object not used for sitting or lying, we know, the object suffers *maddaf*-uncleanness and renders food and drink unclean. M.Ed. 6:2 (*Eliezer b. Hyrcanus. The Tradition of Man* [Leiden, 1973, I, pp. 339-340) further has a dispute of Joshua and Nehunya b. Elinathan with Eliezer, in which it is taken for granted, tangentially and within the structure of argument: "The uncleanness of living beings is greater than the uncleanness of corpses, for a living being imparts uncleanness, by lying and sitting, to what is underneath him, so that it conveys uncleanness to man and utensils, and also conveys *maddaf*-uncleanness to what is above him, so that it conveys uncleanness to food and liquid, a mode of transferring uncleanness which a corpse does not convey." The same authorities – Joshua and Eliezer – are at M. Par. 10:1-2, and moreover, Yosé continues the matter, at M. Toh. 8:2, taking the rule for granted, just as do Joshua and Eliezer. We need not review in detail Tosefta's usages of the same word, since all occur in the context of the correlative Mishnaic pericopae (T. Par. 10:2, 3, T. Toh. 9:4, T. Zab. 3:3, 5:1).

The two senses in which the word is used (now omitted: references to the occurrences in M. Kel.) of course are complementary. M. Par. and M. Toh. know *maddaf* as a status as to uncleanness contrasted to *midras*, and M. Zab. uses the word to refer to objects which can enter that very same status as to uncleanness. Our translation in the present tractate has been required by its context. But the meaning in point of fact is complementary to that necessitated by the context of M. Par. and M. Toh.: What can become unclean with *maddaf*-uncleanness – an object not used for lying and sitting and hence not susceptible to *midras*-uncleanness (a point familiar throughout our order e.g., Kelim Chapter Twenty-Four) – here is called *maddaf*. And M. Par. and M. Toh. know *maddaf* as that uncleanness imparted to something from something (used for lying and sitting) susceptible to *midras*. Our tractate, moreover, hastens to add: The status of *maddaf*-uncleanness is attained when an object not used for lying or sitting (also food or drink, explicitly included as well) is located above a Zab. *Maddaf* as the opposite of *midras*, of course, is contained in the pericopae of M. Toh. in particular, but also, with slight eisegesis, at M. Par.

The contrast between *midras* and *maddaf*, strikingly, is precisely the same contrast as I have hypothetically imputed to the exegetes of Lev. 15:10A at i, iii. Indeed, *midras* and *maddaf* express exactly the same idea as is spelled out in the circumlocutions above. Our invocation, at that point, of the rule of opposites therefore is justified by the result of the present analysis of the consistent contrast, drawn in M., between *midras* and *maddaf*. The concept of *maddaf*, in its two, complementary senses, most certainly is attested by Joshua and Eliezer at M. Ed. and M. Par. Because of the givenness of the idea of M. Par., at both pericopae assigned to Eliezer and Joshua, I am inclined to suppose that the concept of *maddaf*-uncleanness and of objects susceptible not to *midras*, because they are not used for lying and sitting, but, under the specified circumstance, to *maddaf*-uncleanness, hence *maddaf*-objects, originates before 70.

4. M. 5:6: He who touches the Zab, Zabah, menstruating woman, woman after childbirth, mesora, or a bed or chair on which any of these have lain or sat. Touching and shifting, carrying and being carried, are equivalent.

+ T. 5:3: utensils are in the first remove.

4. The pericope so far as it deals with modes of transfer makes two points.

First, while one is touching these sources, he is able to impart uncleanness at two removes, unfitness at one. That is to say, just as at M. 5:1, he is like a Father of uncleanness, so far as food for heave-offering is concerned.

Second, touching is deemed equivalent to shifting, carrying, and being carried.

That the uncleanness of the Zab is transferred to one who touches the Zab (etc.) is stated explicitly at Lev. 15:5. That one who carries such a thing is made unclean is stated at Lev. 15:10b.

The sole new point has to do with the inclusion of shifting as a mode of transfer of uncleanness. This is probably generated by the analogy to bearing the weight of the Zab, that is, carrying. the inclusion of shifting as a mode of transfer of uncleanness derives simply from the extension of Scripture's stated modes. One can hardly carry without shifting the object. The sole open question is whether we include even derivatives of the pressure of the Zab or of pressure upon the Zab, that is, vibration, movement which takes place indirectly and not directly. We do not, as the Ushans state.

5. M. 5:7: He who touches the flux of the Zab, his spit, his semen, his urine, and the blood of the menstruating woman (imparts uncleanness at two removes, etc.) All the same is touching and moving. Eliezer: Also carrying.

5. 1. The specified excretions are unclean just as the Zab is unclean.

2. They transfer uncleanness just as the Zab transfers uncleanness, that is, through contact.

3. Shifting is equivalent to contact.

Touching the spit of the Zab effects the transfer of the Zab's uncleanness, so Lev. 15:8. The secondary point is the inclusion of other substances. The issue of carrying as equivalent to contact of course is not of equivalent antiquity.

6. T. 5:2B: Phlegm, mucous, saliva, and snot of Zab are like his spit. Tear, blood of wound, milk of woman, blood of mouth and penis are unclean only in the first remove. Flux, spit, urine are unclean as Fathers. Semen of Zab: Eliezer – does not impart uncleanness when carried; and sages – imparts uncleanness when carried, because urine is contained therein.

Sifra Mesora Zabim 1:7-8: Zab imparts uncleanness through white flux, not through red flow (blood from penis).

Sifra Mesora Zabim 1:9-13: Flux itself is unclean. Blood which exudes form the penis is not unclean as flux. His urine is unclean. Sweat, rancid moisture, excrement are not unclean. Nine liquids apply to Zab: secretion, putrid sweat, excrement are clean in all respect; tear, blood, milk impart susceptibility to uncleanness as liquids; flux, spit, urine are unclean as flux.

Sifra Mesora Zabim 3:8: Phlegm, slaver, and snot are equivalent to spit. Sifra Mesora Zabim 1:3: Flux derives solely from the genitals, not from the nose or mouth.

There are two issues in the present set, first of all, the notion that the transfer of the Zab's uncleanness takes place not solely through touching the Zab, but also through touching other substances which exude from him. Second, other modes of transfer besides direct contact are of the same effect as direct contact. The matter of touching the Zab's spit is explicit at Lev. 15:8. Accordingly, not only the flux, but also spit is unclean. Then spit supplies an analogy for other such substances which are like it. Flux is like semen; urine derives from the same location. Phlegm, mucus, saliva, snot, all are treated as analogous to spit. The second issue is the analogy between touching and moving, on which all parties agree. Eliezer wishes to treat carrying as equivalent mode of transfer of uncleanness. His basis, surely, will be the diverse rulings which treat touching, shifting, and carrying as equivalent. At T. 5:2B, an Eliezer wishes to exclude semen of the Zab. If this is the same Eliezer, then M. 5:7 should contain the equivalent qualification, that is, adding *carrying* as a mode of transfer of uncleanness, and detaching *semen* from the opening list. We do not know which Eliezer is before us, one of the Yavneans or one of the Ushans. That is why we cannot adduce the present set as evidence that discussion of the interrelationships of the diverse modes of transfer uncleanness was carried forward at Yavneh, with the secondary notion that the issues were still live at that time. This is suggested by the pointed claim, intruded at M. 5:6, 7, etc., that the diverse modes do produce equivalent effects, or are the same as one another, which suggests that in the background are efforts seriously to distinguish among them. But the main point in Mishnah is that there are diverse modes, and that point derives from the obvious sense of Scripture, which specifies touching or contact, carrying, lying or sitting, generalized into exerting pressure.

7. M. 5:8: He who carries saddle, is carried on it, and moves it, etc.

7. Carrying, being carried on, and moving, the saddle imparts uncleanness as if one were made a Father of uncleanness.

Carrying carrion, purification water sufficient for sprinkling.

Here, too, the man is as if he were a Father of uncleanness.

+ T. 5:5A.

M. 5:9: He who eats carrion of clean bird, while it is in his gullet, etc.

This item is not relevant to Zabim.

+ T. 5:10-12

Sifra Mesora Zabim 4:2-3: Bed and chair impart uncleanness when they are carried.

Sifra Mesora Zabim 4:1: Whoever touches saddle is unclean, but whoever touches what is under the saddle is not unclean on that account.

Carrying the saddle or being carried on it make a person unclean, so Lev. 15:10 states explicitly. That the bed and chair which are carried impart uncleanness is also at Lev. 15:10b. Touching the saddle produces uncleanness, so Lev. 15:10a. Lev. 15:10b then specifies that whoever carries something which has been underneath a Zab is unclean, which then is exclusive of merely *touching* the saddle. Nothing in this set brings us significantly outside the boundaries of Scriptural meaning, so far as I can see. (We omit reference to the matter of carrion, which is not within the thematic limits of our tractate.)

8. M. 5:10: He who touches a dead creeping thing, semen, one made unclean by corpse-uncleanness, mesora during period of counting clean days, purification water insufficient for sprinkling, carrion, and saddle...This is the general rule: Whatever touches any of all the Fathers of uncleanness listed in the Torah imparts uncleanness at one remove and renders unfit at one. Man in contact with a Father of uncleanness, imparts uncleanness at two removes, unfitness at one. Or: except for man, who, as a corpse, makes that which touches it into a Father of uncleanness and so that which is in contact with a corpse imparts uncleanness at two removes and unfitness at one more.

M. 5:11: He who has a seminal emission is like one who has touched a dead creeping thing. He who has sexual relations with a menstruating woman is like one who is unclean by reason of corpse-uncleanness to bed and chair so that they render food and drink unclean, which the former does not accomplish.

M. 5:12: Ten items which are in the second remove of uncleanness and therefore render heave-offering unfit. Sifra Mesora Zabim 2:8-13: Seminal emission does not cause uncleanness. Person unclean through *nega*, corpse, does not impart uncleanness to bed and chair.

8. In all these cases, the one who touches the source of uncleanness is unclean only in the first remove, not functioning as if he were a Father of uncleanness.

Any object, other then man, in contact with a Father of uncleanness, is in the first remove of uncleanness.

The last units, M. 5:10-12, complete the construction of M. 5:6-9 by specifying sources of uncleanness, touching which leaves a person unclean only in the first remove, then in the second. The set contains no attestations, but in fact goes over the specifications of Scripture. What is pointed is the distinction between "whatever touches any of the Fathers of uncleanness" and "*man* who touches a Father of uncleanness," which is to say, the important point of M. 5:1, 6-9, upon which Joshua's further observation, about the difference between one's state while touching such a Father and after one has ceased to touch the Father, is based. It is, of course, the specification at Lev. 15:5, for the Zab, Lev.

15:21, for the menstruating woman, Lev. 15:27, for the Zab, and the comparison of the woman after childbirth to the menstruating woman, Lev. 12:2, 5, that the person who touches things on which the aforenamed have lain or sat washes his clothes, which leads to the stated conclusion.

Let us now, as I promised, relate the foregoing to M. Zab. 5:2.

M. Zab. 5:2: Whatever is carried above the Zab is unclean. Whatever the Zab is carried upon, but which is not touched by him, is clean, except for something used for sitting and lying (Lev. 15:10a) and except for man who carries the Zab (Lev. 15:10b).

The important point here is the distinction between what is carried *above* the Zab and what is carried *below* him, without touching him. In the former case, there is uncleanness, and this applies, specifically, to food, drink, and objects not used for lying and sitting (*maddaf*). If these are carried below the Zab, they are clean. Only man and bed and chair below the Zab are made unclean because of their serving to carry his weight even without directly touching him. The illustration, M. Zab. 5:2L-M, further indicates that what is unclean above the Zab – food, drink, *maddaf* (an object not used for lying and sitting) – is unclean in the first remove.

Now to repeat, this is how analogical-contrastive reasoning works:

The principle is dual:

(1) What is carried *underneath* the Zab is clean, except for an object used for lying and sitting.

(2) What is carried *above* the Zab is unclean. The relationship to Scripture is not self-evident. On the one side, we may readily account for the first principle. That an object used for lying and sitting which was under the Zab is unclean is specified at Lev. 15:10a. But the rule excludes objects not used for lying and sitting. To review what has been suggested: The distinction begins at Lev. 15:9.

The saddle on which the Zab rides is unclean.

Lev. 15:10a, continuing this point, then specifies that whoever touches anything that was under him – thus, that has served him for sitting – is unclean.

And, by exclusion therefrom, whoever touches something which has been located under the Zab but which the Zab has *not* used for sitting is not unclean.

Accordingly, the object itself, if not used for sitting, does not become unclean if the Zab is located above it.

But, whence the notion of *maddaf*? That is, how do we know that an object *not* used for lying and sitting and located *above* the Zab is unclean?

We come to the fourth level of meaning imputed to Lev. 15:10a.

(1) What is unclean beneath the Zab is not unclean above him.

(2) Then: What is *not* unclean beneath the Zab *is* unclean above him. Objects not used for sitting and lying, food and drink (2) are unclean above, because they (1) are clean below, the Zab.

Thus: Objects used for sitting and lying are clean above, because they are unclean below, the Zab.

This exercise can readily be repeated for the principles and generative rules of three tractates, Negaim, Niddah, and the remainder of Zabim, all of which to begin with draw out and spell out Scripture's rules and principle for the *mesora'*, the menstruating woman, Zabah, woman after childbirth, and finally, for the Zab, respectively. All deal with sources of uncleanness.[1] Here the Oral Torah is contented to restate and develop through logical exegesis (not merely through formal exegesis, such as at Sifra, which is post facto) what is said in the Priestly Code. The reason is that at the outset the people among whom the Oral Torah, that is, Mishnah, originates have no intention whatsoever to augment and enrich the laws of the *sources* of uncleanness and even those of the transfer of the uncleanness of those sources of uncleanness to men and utensils, food and drink, objects purified by immersion and objects purified by breaking, food which is unconsecrated, which is heave-offering, and which is Holy Things.

Their original and fresh proposition concerns the *locus* of uncleanness, which is the world as well as the cult, and the means of removing uncleanness, in the world as well as in the cult. Accordingly, tractates on these matters begin in conception wholly autonomous of, and alien to, the Written Torah, because the Priestly Code, in its ultimate redaction, claims that cleanness and uncleanness are categories of the cultic metaphysic, not of the world outside the cult. The ultimate redactors who make such a claim in behalf of the Temple of course obscure the worldly locus of the laws of uncleanness, e.g., the corpse which lies in the tent imparts uncleanness to the utensils which are in the tent, and this without regard to the use of said utensils in the

---

[1] The same is so of M. Ohalot Chapters One-Three and Sixteen-Eighteen, that is, the prologue and epilogue of Ohalot, which deal with substances unclean like the corpse.

cult. Menstrual impurity has primary implications for the home, not only for the cult, despite the ultimate redactional claim stated in connection with the pericope of the Zab, the menstruating woman, and the Zabah at Lev. 15:31: *Thus you shall keep the people of Israel separate from their uncleanness, lest they die in their uncleanness by defiling my tabernacle that is in their midst* (see *Purities* XVI, pp. 208-211.

It would be an error, however, to conclude that the Oral Torah represented by Mishnah bears an essentially dual relationship to the written one, that is, partly exegetical, partly autonomous. Even though Kelim, Ohalot, Parah-Yadayim, Tohorot-Uqsin, Miqvaot-Tebul Yom, and Makhshirin begin in conceptions essentially autonomous of Scripture, while Negaim, Niddah, and Zabim (merely) spell out and develop rules laid down in Scripture, all the tractates, whatever the character of their fundamental presuppositions in detail, share an approach which is distinctive to Mishnah in its very origins. All of them take an intense interest in details of cleanness. This fact is what marks them all, whatever their relationship to Scripture, as particular and Pharisaic. Even though everyone in the Land of Israel concurred that the *Zab* was unclean, not everyone developed the layers of exegesis, the secondary and tertiary conception, producing a tractate such as *Zabim*. So far as our extant sources tell us, whether or not others, e.g., in the Essene community at Qumran, observed the purity-laws, no on else took equivalent interest in developing the laws of Leviticus Chapters Twelve through Fifteen. The detailed principles of Negaim, Niddah, and Zabim in no way express conceptions definitive of and distinctive to Pharisaism, such as we observe at Kelim, Parah, Tohorot, Miqvaot, and Makhshirin, and (possibly) at the shank of Ohalot (M. Oh. 3:6-16:2) as well. Authorities before 70, whom we assume are Pharisees, devote time and attention to the elucidation and extension of Scripture's rules. Extant evidence does not suggest that others did so. What is distinctive to the "Oral Torah" which we assume characterizes Pharisaism is detailed attention to matters of uncleanness. Others either took for granted and observed them or took for granted and ignored them. Accordingly, there are two aspects to the analysis of the relationship of Zabim to Scripture, exegetical and eisegetical. Exegesis of a straightforward, and (hypothetically) highly logical, sequential character produces Zabim. Not exegesis, but eisegesis imparts to Lev. 15:1-15 such importance that the exegetical enterprise to begin with is undertaken. A religion of pots and pans? What a contemptible conception!

Part Two

A PROGRAM
PAST AND FUTURE

Chapter Eight

Explaining an *Ouevre:*
After Thirty Years and Two Hundred Books

Religions form social worlds and do so through the power of their rational thought, that is, their capacity to explain data in a (to an authorship) self-evidently valid way. The framers of religious documents answer urgent questions, framed in society and politics to be sure, in a manner deemed self-evidently valid by those addressed by the authorships at hand. For at stake in my *ouevre*, now in print in more than two hundred books of various classifications and serving diverse purposes and audiences, are striking examples of how people in writing explain to themselves who they are as a social entity. Religion as a powerful force in human society and culture is realized in society, not only or mainly theology; religion works through the social entity that embodies that religion. Religions form social entities – "churches" or "peoples" or "holy nations" or monasteries or communities – that, in the concrete, constitute the "us," as against "the nations" or merely "them." And religions carefully explain, in deeds and in words, who that "us" is – and they do it every day. To see religion in this way is to take religion seriously as a way of realizing, in classic documents, a large conception of the world. But how do we describe, analyze, and interpret a religion, and how do we relate the contents of a religion to its context? These issues of method are worked out through the reading of texts, and, I underline, through taking seriously and in their own terms the particularity and specificity of texts.

The formative writings of a particular Judaism serve as an example of how such work might be done. My *ouevre* has concerned exemplary classics of Judaism and how they form a cogent statement. These classical writings, produced from the first to the seventh centuries A.D., form the canon of a particular statement of Judaism, the Judaism of the Dual Torah, oral and written. That canon defined Judaism in both Christendom and Islam from the seventh century to the present. The circumstances of its formation, in the beginnings of Western civilization, the issues important to its framers, the kind of writings they produced, the modes of mediating change and responding to crisis – these form the center of interest. To expound my method for systemic description, analysis, and interpretation on the basis of written evidence, I wrote the book, *From Writing to Religion: The Documentary Method in the Study of Judaism* (Nashville, 1989: Abingdon). But the larger context in which my method has taken shape requires explanation in its own terms. That is what I propose to explain concerning my *ouevre*, now three decades in the making.

To undertake systemic analysis on the strength of written evidence, I have systemically reread the classic documents of the Judaism that took shape in the first through sixth centuries A.D. and that has predominated since then, the Judaism of the Dual Torah. These documents – the Mishnah, Midrash-compilations, the two Talmuds – represent the collective statement and consensus of authorships (none is credibly assigned to a single author and all are preserved because they are deemed canonical and authoritative) and show us how those authorships proposed to make a statement to their situation – and, I argue, upon the human condition. What I want to do is in three stages. First, I place a document on display in its own terms, examining the text in particular and in its full particularity and immediacy. Here I want to describe the text from three perspectives: rhetoric, logic, and topic (the standard program of literary criticism in the age at hand). Reading documents one by one represents a new approach in this field. Ordinarily, people have composed studies by citing sayings attributed to diverse authorities without regard to the place in which these sayings occur. They have assumed that the sayings really were said by those to whom they are attributed, and, in consequence, the generative category is not the document but the named authority. But if we do not assume that the documentary lines are irrelevant and that the attributions are everywhere to be taken at face value, then the point of origin – the document – defines the categorical imperative, the starting point of all study.

Second, I seek to move from the text to that larger context suggested by the traits of rhetoric, logic, and topic. Here I want to compare one text to others of its class and ask how these recurrent points of emphasis, those critical issues and generative tensions, draw attention from the limits of the text to the social world that the text's authorship proposed to address. Here too the notion that a document exhibits traits particular to itself is new with my work, although, overall, some have episodically noted traits of rhetoric distinctive to a given document, and, on the surface, differences as to topic – observed but not explained – have been noted. Hence the movement from text to context and how it is effected represents a fresh initiative on my part.

Finally, so far as I can, I want to find my way outward toward the matrix in which a variety of texts find their place. In this third stage I want to move from the world of intellectuals to the world they proposed to shape and create. That inquiry defines as its generative question how the social world formed by the texts as a whole proposes to define and respond to a powerful and urgent question, that is, I want to read the canonical writings as response to critical and urgent questions. Relating documents to their larger political settings is not a commonplace, and, moreover, doing so in detail – with attention to the traits of logic, rhetoric, and topic – is still less familiar.

That brings us to the systemic approach to the reading of the formative documents of Judaism, which I have invented. Spelling it out is not difficult. Writings such as those we read have been selected by the framers of a religious system, and, read all together, those writings are deemed to make a cogent and important statement of that system, hence the category, "canonical writings." I call that encompassing, canonical picture a "system," when it is composed of three necessary components: an account of a world-view, a prescription of a corresponding way of life, and a definition of the social entity that finds definition in the one and description in the other. When those three fundamental components fit together, they sustain one another in explaining the whole of a social order, hence constituting the theoretical account of a system. Systems defined in this way work out a cogent picture, for those who make them up, of *how* things are correctly to be sorted out and fitted together, of *why* things are done in one way, rather than in some other, and of *who* they are that do and understand matters in this particular way. When, as is commonly the case, people invoke God as the foundation for their world-view, maintaining that their way of life corresponds to what God wants of them, projecting their social entity in a particular relationship to God, then we have a religious system. When, finally, a religious system appeals as an important part of its authoritative literature or canon to the Hebrew Scriptures of ancient Israel or "Old Testament, we have a Judaism.

I recognize that in moving beyond specific texts into the larger world-view they join to present, I may be thought to cross the border from the humanistic study of classical texts to the anthropological reading of those same texts. I therefore emphasize that I take most seriously the particularity and specificity of each document, its program, its aesthetics, its logic. I do not propose to commit upon a classic writing an act of reductionism, reading a work of humanistic meaning merely as a sociological artifact. And, further, as between Weber and his critics, I take my place with Weber in maintaining that ideas constitute, in their context and circumstance, what sociologists call independent variables, not only responding to issues of society, but framing and giving definition to those larger issues. In this way I make a stand, in the systemic reading of the classic writings of Judaism in its formative age, with those who insist upon the ultimate rationality of discourse.

The movement from text to context and matrix is signalled by use of the word "system." For reading a text in its context and as a statement of a larger matrix of meaning, I propose to ask larger questions of systemic description of a religious system represented by the particular text and its encompassing canon. Colleagues who work on issues of religion and society will find familiar the program I am trying to work out. But, I underline, the success of that program is measured by its power to make the texts into documents of general intelligibility for the humanities, to read the text at hand in such a way as to understand its statement within, and of, the human condition. That seems to me not only the opposite of reductionism but also a profoundly rationalist mode of inquiry.

Systems begin in the social entity, whether one or two persons or two hundred or ten thousand – there and not in their canonical writings, which come only afterward, or even in their politics. The social group, however, formed, frames the system, the system then defines its canon within, and addresses its politics to the larger setting, the *polis* without. We describe systems from their end products, the writings. But we have then to work our way back from canon to system, not to imagine either that the canon is the system, or that the canon creates the system. The canonical writings speak, in particular, to those who can hear, that is, to the members of the community, who, on account of that perspicacity of hearing, constitute the social entity or systemic community. The community then comprises that social group the system of which is recapitulated by the selected canon. The group's exegesis of the canon in terms of the everyday imparts to the system the power to sustain the community in a reciprocal and self-nourishing process. The community through its exegesis then imposes continuity and unity on whatever is in its canon.

While, therefore, we cannot account for the origin of a successful system, we can explain its power to persist. It is a symbolic transaction, as I said just now, in which social change comes to expression in symbol-change. That symbolic transaction, specifically, takes place in its exegesis of the systemic canon, which, in literary terms, constitutes the social entity's statement of itself So, once more, the texts recapitulate the system. The system does not recapitulate the texts. The system comes before the texts and defines the canon. The exegesis of the canon then forms that ongoing social action that sustains the whole. A system does not recapitulate its texts, it selects and orders them. A religious system imputes to them as a whole cogency, one to the next, that their original authorships have not expressed in and through the parts, and through them a religious system expresses its deepest logic, *and it also frames that just fit that joins system to circumstance.*

The whole works its way out through exegesis, and the history of any religious system – that is to say, the history of religion writ small – is the exegesis of its exegesis. And the first rule of the exegesis of systems is the simplest, and the one with which I conclude: *the system does not recapitulate the canon. The canon recapitulates the system.* The system forms a statement of a social entity, specifying its worldview and way of life in such a way that, to the participants in the system, the whole makes sound sense, beyond argument. So in the beginning are not words of inner and intrinsic affinity, but (as Philo would want us to say) the Word: the transitive logic, the system, all together, all at once, complete, whole, finished – the word awaiting only that labor of exposition and articulation that the faithful, for centuries to come, will lavish at the altar of the faith. A religious system therefore presents a fact not of history but of immediacy, of the social present.

The issue of why a system originates and survives, if it does, or fails, if it does, by itself proves impertinent to the analysis of a system but of course necessary to our interpretation of it. A system on its own is like a language. A language forms an example of language if it produces communication through rules of syntax and verbal arrangement. That paradigm serves full well however many people speak the language, or however long the language serves. Two people who understand each other form a language-community, even, or especially, if no one understands them. So too by definition religions address the living, constitute societies, frame and compose cultures. For however long, at whatever moment in historic time, a religious system always grows up in the perpetual present, an artifact of its day, whether today or a long-ago time. The only appropriate tense for a religious system is the present. A religious system always *is*, whatever it was, whatever it will be. Why so? Because its traits address a condition of humanity in society, a circumstance of an hour – however brief or protracted the hour and the circumstance.

When we ask that a religious composition speak to a society with a message of the *is* and the *ought* and with a meaning for the everyday, we focus on the power of that system to hold the whole together: the society the system addresses, the individuals who compose the society, the ordinary lives they lead, in ascending order of consequence. And that system then forms a whole and well-composed structure. Yes, the structure stands somewhere, and, indeed, the place where it stands will secure for the system either an extended or an ephemeral span of life. But the system, for however long it lasts, serves. And that focus on the eternal present justifies my interest in analyzing why a system works (the urgent agenda of issues it successfully solves for those for whom it solves those problems) when it does, and why it ceases to work (loses self-evidence, is bereft of its "Israel," for example) when it no longer works. The phrase, the *history* of a *system*, presents us with an oxymoron. Systems endure – and their classic texts with them – in that eternal present that they create. They evoke precedent, they do not have a history. A system relates to context, but, as I have stressed, exists in an enduring moment (which, to be sure, changes all the time). We capture the system in a moment, the worm consumes it an hour later. That is the way of mortality, whether for us one by one, in all mortality, or for the works of humanity in society. But systemic analysis and interpretation requires us to ask questions of history and comparison, not merely description of structure and cogency. So in this exercise we undertake first description, that is, the text, then analysis, that is, the context, and finally, interpretation, that is, the matrix, in which a system has its being.

Let me now specify the discipline within which my method is meant to find its place. It is the history of religion, and my special area, history of Judaism in its formative period, the first six centuries A.D. I am trying to find out how to describe a Judaism in a manner consonant with the historical character of the evidence, therefore in the synchronic context of society and politics, and not solely or mainly in the diachronic context of theology which, until now, has defined matters. The inherited descriptions of the Judaism of the Dual Torah (or merely "Judaism") have treated as uniform the whole corpus of writing called "the Oral Torah". The time and place of the authorship of a document played no role in our use of the allegations, as to fact, of the writers of that document. All documents have ordinarily been treated as part of a single coherent whole, so that anything we find in any writing held to be canonical might be cited as evidence of views on a given doctrinal or legal, or ethical topic. "Judaism" then was described by applying to all of the canonical writings the categories found imperative, e.g., beliefs about God, life after death, revelation, and the like. So far as historical circumstance played a role in that description, it was assumed that everything in any document applied pretty much to all cases, and historical facts derived from sayings and stories pretty much as the former were cited and the latter told.

Prior to the present time, ignoring the limits of documents, therefore the definitive power of historical context and social circumstance, all books on "Judaism" or "classical," "Rabbinic," "Talmudic" Judaism, have promiscuously cited all writings deemed canonical in constructing pictures of the theology or law of that Judaism, severally and jointly, so telling us about Judaism, all at once and in the aggregate. That approach has lost all standing in the study of Christianity of the same time and place, for all scholars of the history of Christianity understand the diversity and contextual differentiation exhibited by the classical Christian writers. But, by contrast, ignoring the documentary origin of statements, the received pictures of Judaism have presented as uniform and unitary theological and legal facts that originated each in its own document, that is to say, in its distinctive time and place, and each as part of a documentary context, possibly also of a distinct system of its own. I had of course corrected that error by insisting that each of those documents be read in its own terms, as a statement – if it constituted such a statement – *of* a Judaism, or, at least, *to* and so in behalf of, a Judaism. I maintained that each theological and legal fact was to be interpreted, to begin with, in relationship to the other theological and legal facts among which it found its original location.

The result of that reading of documents as whole but discrete statements, as I believe we can readily demonstrate defined their original character, is in such works as *Judaism: The Evidence of the Mishnah, Judaism and Society: The Evidence of the Yerushalmi, Judaism and Scripture: The Evidence of Leviticus Rabbah,* as well as *Judaism and Story: The Evidence of The Fathers According to Rabbi Nathan.* At the conclusion of that work, for reasons spelled out in its own logic, I stated that the documentary approach had carried me as far as it could. I reached an impasse for a simple reason. Through the documentary approach I did not have the means of reading the whole all together and all at once. The description, analysis, and interpretation of a religious system, however, require us to see the whole in its entirety, and I had not gained such an encompassing perception. That is why I recognized that I had come to the end of the line, although further exercises in documentary description, analysis, and interpretation and systemic reading of documents assuredly will enrich and expand, as well as correct, the picture I have achieved in the incipient phase of the work.

I have worked on describing each in its own terms and context the principal documents of the Judaism of the Dual Torah. I have further undertaken a set of comparative studies of two or more documents, showing the points in common as well as the contrasts between and among them. This protracted work is represented by systematic accounts of the Mishnah, tractate Avot, the Tosefta, Sifra, Sifré to

Numbers, the Yerushalmi, Genesis Rabbah, Leviticus Rabbah, Pesiqta deRab Kahana, The Fathers According to Rabbi Nathan, the Bavli, Pesiqta Rabbati, and various other writings (listed presently). In all of this work I have proposed to examine one by one and then in groups of afines the main components of the Dual Torah. I wished to place each into its own setting and so attempt to trace the unfolding of the Dual Torah in its historical manifestation. In the later stages of the work, I attempted to address the question of how some, or even all, of the particular documents formed a general statement. I wanted to know where and how documents combined to constitute one Torah of the Dual Torah of Sinai.

Time and again I concluded that while two or more documents did intersect, the literature as a whole is made up of distinct sets of documents, and these sets over the bulk of their surfaces do not as a matter of fact intersect at all. The upshot was that while I could show interrelationships among, for example, Genesis Rabbah, Leviticus Rabbah, Pesiqta deRab Kahana, and Pesiqta Rabbati, or among Sifra and the two Sifrés, I could not demonstrate that all of these writings pursued in common one plan, defining literary, redactional, and logical traits of cogent discourse, or even one program, comprising a single theological or legal inquiry. Quite to the contrary, each set of writings demonstrably limits itself to its distinctive plan and program and not to cohere with any other set. And the entirety of the literature most certainly cannot be demonstrated to form that one whole Torah, part of the still larger Torah of Sinai, that constitutes the Judaism of the Dual Torah.

Having begun with the smallest whole units of the Oral Torah, the received documents, and moved onward to the recognition of the somewhat larger groups comprised by those documents, I reached an impasse. On the basis of literary evidence – shared units of discourse, shared rhetorical and logical modes of cogent statement, for example – I came to the conclusion that a different approach to the definition of the whole, viewed all together and all at once, was now required. Seeing the whole all together and all at once demanded a different approach. But – and I state with heavy emphasis: *it has to be one that takes full account of the processes of formation and grants full recognition to issues of circumstance and context, the layers and levels of completed statements.* That is what I propose to accomplish in the exercise of systemic analysis, which the seminar is meant to illustrate and carry forward. My explanation of the movement from text, to context, to matrix, now takes on, I believe, more concrete meaning.

It may help to specify current work. I am trying to find out how to describe that "Judaism" beyond the specific texts – now beyond the text and the context and toward the matrix of all of the canonical texts – that each document takes for granted but no document spells out. And that research inquiry brings me to the matter of category-formation, which, in this context, requires me to specify the categorical imperative in the description of a Judaism. As I see it, there are three components of any Judaism, deriving their definition from the systemic model with which I began: world-view, way of life, social entity. As is clear, "Israel" forms the social entity. The documents at hand, as I shall show, demand that we focus upon that same matter. So the category comes to me both from the theoretical framework I have devised, but also from the inductive reading of the sources as I have now read the bulk of them. Two further categories that will occupy my attention in time to come may be stated in Judaic and also in abstract theoretical terms. The Judaic category, God "in our image" corresponds to the theoretical component of the world-view, and the Judaic category of the human being "after our likeness" corresponds – though not so self-evidently – to the theoretical component of the way of life. The correspondence will strike the reader as a simple one, when we recall that, in any Judaism, "we" are what "we" do. To all Judaic systems known to me, one's everyday way of life forms a definitive element in the system, and if we wish to know how a Judaic system at its foundations defines its way of life, we do well to translate the details of the here and the now into the portrait of humanity "after our likeness." I have now spelled out in my studies the systemic social entity and the systemic world-view in, respectively, *"Israel:" Judaism and its Social Metaphors* (Cambridge, 1988: Cambridge University Press), and *The Incarnation of God. The Character of Divinity in Formative Judaism* (Philadelphia, 1988: Fortress Press). My account of the systemic way of life in due course will be *In Our Image: Judaism and its Anthropological Metaphors* (not andropological!). My sense is that the planned study is full of self-evident propositions, which is why I have been reluctant to carry it out. What these studies set forth, then, are the systemic social entity, world-view, and, in the anthropology, way of life.

To explain these two works and the anticipated completion of the project: I therefore determined to pursue through the formative documents, as I had traced the stages of their unfolding, the formation and function of the principal systemic components of the world-view of the Judaism at hand. Since any Judaism will make a statement concerning world-view, way of life, and social entity or "Israel," I see three choices and plan to work on all three of them. "World-view" begins with Heaven, not earth, since that is the world, up there, upon which Judaic sages fix their gaze. So I wrote a work on the personality of God, "in our image." "Social entity" of course requires us to examine

"Israel." As to "way of life," I see that category as representing, in a Judaic system, the systemic theory of humanity or anthropology. I identify as anthropological the metaphors through which the authorships of the documents of the Dual Torah speak in concrete terms of that abstraction treated as a thing when we speak of "way of life." The seminar will work on these three matters and how we may learn to identify appropriate data and critically – in the correct social and historical context – to describe, analyze, and interpret those data.

There is a larger program for the study of religion to which, in the unfolding of my *ouevre*, I now turn. It concerns the social scientific setting for the academic study of religion, with special reference to the three principal components of the program of a social system, politics, economics, and philosophy. My most current work has called me to study the economics, politics, and philosophy of the Judaic systems in their successive unfolding in late antiquity. Let me set this present project forth. I have undertaken the development of the field of the political economy of religion, exemplified through the case of Judaism in its classical age.

Political economy joins the study of the institutions of the management of power we know as the politics of a society with the analysis of the disposition of scarce resources we know as economics. In prior ages, the ideas that governed collective life and conduct, that is, political ideas, encompassed issues of material life generally deemed economic, and in the interstices and interplay of both politics and economics, large-scale conceptions of the public interest and of society took shape. Plato's *Republic* and Aristotle's *Politics*, particularly the latter, pay ample attention to economics in the setting of politics, and, in the case of Aristotle, what the system says about economics forms a chapter within the larger statement of the system as a whole. And that is the point at which religion becomes a matter of acute interest. For religious systems may make statements not only about matters we identify as theology but also about economics and political behavior.

Religions are today studied as modes of making social worlds, but that language very commonly veils considerable uncertainty about what we wish to know about the "making of a social world" that a religion proposes to accomplish (and may actually effect). In any event one universal criterion for the differentiation and classification of religious systems is whether or not a religious system addresses, encompasses within its system, the realm of political economy. Some do, some don't. Christianity in late antiquity had virtually nothing to say about economics and cannot be said to have affected political economy at all, while in medieval times, with its encounter with Aristotle in particular, Christianity in the West worked out a political economy that predominated until the eighteenth century, when politics went its way, and economics became disembedded from the political world. It is perfectly self-evident that, from antiquity, Judaism, and from its beginning in early medieval times, Islam, have taken as critical the issues of political economy and have assumed a powerful role in the organization of politics and the management of economics. And other religious systems do as well. That is why the political economy of religions, how it is to be described, analyzed, and interpreted, forms a central concern for anyone interested in how humanity in the past, and the world today, sort out the issues of public policy for politics and economics alike.

Not only so, but until World War I, considerable interest attached to generalizations about political economy of religion. The field does not have to be invented, only renewed and reworked in light of things we have learned about religion and about the academic study of religion. For one major example, Weber's *Protestant Ethic and the Spirit of Capitalism* was only a chapter in public discussion, alongside Sombart's work on the theory that capitalism arose not from the Protestants but from the Jews. Weber, as you recall, worked on China, India, and ancient Israel as well, asking about the relationships between religious belief and the conduct of political economy, that is, rational economic action within a defined political framework of power relationships, all read against the backdrop of beliefs about "the sacred" or other religious concerns. So we may say that the political economy of religions is an old subject. But it has to be reworked, since we now realize that belief-systems of religion form only one part of the whole, and not, as even Weber posited, the centerpiece of interest. Since Weber we have learned much about religion and how to study religion, but we have not pursued Weber's questions. And that is why, through the reengagement with political economy as a dimension of religious systems and their construction of societies and world-views, I have undertaken to renew a discipline that, well over half a century ago, proved its worth.

But political economy of religion assuredly requires renewal, and available work guides only as to goal, but not as to method, and that is for two reasons. First, because none of the inherited work accomplished the useful description of the religions under study. The ways in which religions were described have vastly changed. My work on systemic description, analysis, and interpretation of religions, focused on Judaism, shows in the contrast with Weber's *Ancient Judaism* that we have made many steps forward since that time and has rendered utterly obsolete every word in Weber's book on the same subject. Second, because, in point of fact, while the issues of political economy in relationship to religion retain their urgency, in Islam, Christendom, and the worlds of India and Southeast Asia, for example, so that we cannot speak of Latin America without its Liberation Theology, a vast statement upon issues of political economy, systematic and critical work is virtually unknown. In the range of theory and accurate description, analysis, and interpretation of the political economy of a religious world, and in the comparison of the political economy of one religious system with that of another, so far as I know, scholarship in the study of religion has fallen silent. And yet, as we now recognize, there is simply no coping with the world today without the intellectual tools for understanding religion, not as a theory of another world, but as a power and force in the shaping of this world. Events in Iran and Afghanistan, as to Islam, Latin America and Poland, as to Roman Catholic Christianity, the State of Israel and the USA, as to Judaism, only illustrate that simple fact that most (though not all) of humanity does what it does by reason of religious conviction. And since public policy falls silent before that fact, it is time to reenter discourse with issues long dormant on the relationship between religious systems and the world of politics and of economics.

But in universities, this is done in a way particular to scholarship, in full recognition that, beyond universities, what we learn will be put to good use by others in the framing of public policy, a partnership of learning. And that is the point at which my proposed five-year research program becomes pertinent. What we do is address not concrete and practical issues of the other, but matters of theory that may guide those who do make policy. In my federal career I have seen how much we in the bureaucracy (for our citizens' councils are part of the bureaucracy) depend upon research done on contract, and that involves not merely collecting and analyzing facts, but gaining a long perspective and working out a useful theory that will guide our staff in collecting and analyzing facts and so working out the everyday policy that the bureaucracy effects. What we require is hypotheses and the testing of hypotheses against facts, and hypotheses emerge, to begin with, in the trial and error of particular cases: asking questions, attempting answers, testing hypotheses, explaining things. So long as a case is meant to exemplify, so long as we ask of a case, why this, not that? with a sustained answer meant to generate a theory, the case is not the mere collecting and arranging of facts but an exercise in description, analysis, and interpretation.

I use as my case the Judaism of late antiquity, because that is one religious system that did, indeed, develop a large-scale conception of political economy, that is to say, that is a religious system that made its encompassing statement, also, through what it had to say about the household as the irreducible unit of production, about the market and its role in rationing scarce goods, and about wealth and its relationship to money (and to land, as a matter of fact). In this regard, that Judaism carried forward in a way, so far as I know unique in ancient times the systematic thought of Aristotle, the only figure in antiquity who had anything important to say about economics. The system of that Judaism, further, paid ample attention also to the disposition of issues and institutions of power we know as political science, once again, a remarkable labor of large-scale social thought. The study, therefore, of the political economy of ancient Judaism, beginning in the law-codes and other writings of that Judaism, seems to me a promising area in which to develop the intellectual tools – points of inquiry, modes of thought – that will serve as a useful model in studying the political economy of Islam, in its varieties and rich diversity, as well as of Christianities of medieval and modern times. It goes without saying that the reading of the law for other than legal theory, so far as the study of antiquity is concerned, also is not a commonplace inquiry.

My own preparation for this work began with my study of the logical structures of the writings of ancient Judaism, yielding *The Making of the Mind of Judaism. The Formative Age* and *The Formation of the Jewish Intellect.* When I finish *Formation,* I turned to economics, which is now *The Economics of Judaism: The Initial Statement.* Reading for this work and conversations with colleagues here have broadened my conception and made me realize that Aristotle is the model for this system as a whole, combining as he did the issues of the material sustenance of society and the political organization of society, and, of course, exercising a sustaining influence nearly down to the eighteenth century Physiocrats, founders of economics as we now know it. It was with my study of Plato and Aristotle in the setting of economics, as I looked for the affinities and influences on the thought of the writers of the formative documents of Judaism, that my notion of the "re-founding" of political economy of religion as a subfield of the academic study of religion came up. I now work on the next two studies of the initial system, which are *The Politics of Judaism* and *The Philosophy of Judaism.* When this systematic account of the economics, politics, and philosophy embedded in the initial system have been completed, I shall turn to the next system, connected to, but not continuous or wholly symmetrical with the first, which is the system of the Talmuds of the Land of Israel and Babylonia and related writings.

To conclude this account, let me turn to undergraduate education, for, I maintain, one important concern of all methods worked out for the academy is the impact of scholarship on undergraduate education. In our shared work, we did not neglect that consideration. In my *ouevre* I see two important results for the teaching of religion as an academic subject. First, I am trying to learn how to read a text in such a way as to highlight the human situation addressed by an authorship. If I can do so, I can show undergraduates of diverse origin what this text has to say to people in general, not only to Jews (of a quite specific order) in particular. In other words, my entire enterprise is aimed at a humanistic and academic reading of classics of Judaism, yet with full regard for their specific statements to their own world. People wrote these books as a way of asking and answering questions we can locate and understand – that is my premise – and when we can find those shared and human dimensions of documents, we can relate classic writings to a world we understand and share. That imputes a common rationality to diverse authorships and ages – theirs and ours – and, I believe, expresses the fundamental position of the academic humanities.

The second lesson draws us from text to context. Treating a religion in its social setting, as something a group of people do together, rather than as a set of beliefs and opinions, prepares colleagues to make sense of a real world of ethnicity and political beliefs formed on the foundation of religious origins. Indeed, if colleagues do not understand that religion constitutes one of the formative forces in the world today, they will not be able to cope with the future. But how to see precisely the ways in which religion forms social worlds? In the small case of Judaism, a set of interesting examples is set forth. Here they see that diverse Judaic systems responded to pressing social and political questions by setting forth cogent and (to the believers) self-evidently valid answers. That is one important aspect of the world-creating power of religion, and one nicely illuminated in the formation of Judaic systems.

The more critical academic issue should be specified. We are living in an age in which the old humanities are joined by new ones; women's studies (in their humanistic mode), black studies, Jewish studies, and a broad variety of other subjects enter the curriculum. The universities require them, because we now know that the humanities encompass a world beyond the European, religions in addition to the Christian, for instance. But how are we to make our own and academic what appears at first encounter to be alien and incomprehensible? One solution accepts as special and particular the new humanities, treating as general and normal the old ones. Hence – in the settlement accepted by some – Jews teach Jewish things to Jews, and form a segregated intellectual community within the larger academic world. But I think that the subject-matter at hand is too urgent and important – and altogether too interesting – to be left to the proprietors or to be permitted to be segregated. To deprive interested colleagues and students of access to the rich human experience and expression contained within the cultural artifacts of hitherto excluded parts of humanity diminishes the academic program and misrepresents the condition of humanity. But how to afford access to what is strange and perceived as abnormal is not readily explained. I have spent nearly thirty years trying to find appropriate access for colleagues and students alike to one of the new humanities. In the terms of Judaic studies I have insisted that the ghetto walls, once down, may not be reconstructed in the community of intellect. And, in that same framework, I have spent my life trying to explore the dimensions of a world without walls. That is the context in which the entire program now spelled out finds its shape and motivation.

Chapter Nine

The Social Foundations of Judaism in Classical and Modern Times A Programmatic Statement

By
Calvin Goldscheider and Jacob Neusner

Religion and Civilization

Religion is important because the story of civilization is written by religion, which so forms attitudes and viewpoints as to move nations, societies, and communities to act in one way, rather than some other. What people believe God wants of them, approves or disapproves, rewards or punishes, tells them how to live and what to do together. Whether the consequent deeds are private and individual or public and social, Heaven's dictates inform and enthuse humanity in society. Since, moreover, the social world forms the matrix for the individual and family, it is the power of religion to define and inform society that matters in framing the story of civilization. For society endures, social continuities defining the range of choice for individual and family alike. Accordingly, if we propose to describe religion, to analyze its traits and effects, and to interpret its character as a formative force in civilization, we ask about the social world framed and formed by religion. At stake in the answer is the understanding of how humanity forms society, creates culture, sustains civilization. That understanding comes to us when we grasp the way religion informs society, frames the possibilities of culture, and defines what it means to live in civilization. In this paper we propose a research-program on the problem of religion and society, specifically exemplified by the inquiry into the social foundations of Judaism, viewed as a suggestive case.

For the whole then has held together, and now holds together, in a great many societies, by reason of the social imagination of religion. We need hardly point to the power of religion in the social order of whole nations, east and west alike, or to the capacity of religion to destroy the social order in countries as disparate as Ireland and Iran. Religion as a social force comprises an act of shared imagination concerning the social world. Seen as a formative and definitive structure, religion encompasses three components and holds all three together: ethos, ethics, and ethnos. That is to say, religion is made up of the mentality, the world-view, above all, the world-defining view, that religion sets forth to link Heaven to earth and holds all together and all at once, in proper balance, proportion, and composition, all things that live or have ever lived in the here and now of the social world we know. True, that forms no small claim for religion, but it is a claim well substantiated in the history of religion and in the contemporary sociology and politics of religion too. Accordingly, to make sense of civilization as humanity has known it for the brief moment in which humanity has formed the consciousness to want to know itself, religion takes center-stage. Its sense of things, its explanations, its modes of sorting things out and placing all things into perspective – these acts of imagination define and dictate the traits of those social worlds that have endured over time.

Accordingly, in trying to make sense of civilization we propose to ask ourselves how religion forms and informs social worlds. But the answer comes from the study of psychology, history, philosophy, sociology, and anthropology, the principal intellectual tools at our disposal in the study of religion, as well as from the study of religion as a world-defining force and fact. The social scientific and humanistic orientations to the study of religion treat the subject matter of religion as an independent variable. The question of civilization as now framed requires answers from the facts of society but also from the fantasies of humanity imagining, thinking, wondering. Out of the results of both the social order and the imaginative life come the attitudes and viewpoints that impart shape and structure to the social life. Because people believe things, they do things, define their lives and give them up, for instance. True, we may describe a society by appeal to diverse indicative traits. But if we hope to make sense of that society and explain what holds it together, imparts purpose and cogency to the whole, gives to the parts that symmetry and balance, composition and order, that makes society social and enduring, we must interrelate the facts of sociology and the fantasies of faith.

In the intersection of the social world and the realm of imagination we find the (to the outsider) nonsense that (to the engaged person) makes sense of the this and the that of everyday social life. We claim that religion stands in conjunction with, not separate from, the social world that appeals to religion. Religion sets forth the account and explanation for how things are and ought to be: what God wants.

Explaining the parts and making them whole and coherent, religion then stands for the power of imagination to account for reality. And, as everyone knows, the inner eye shapes vision, and imagination dictates how history is made and people make their lives.

The Study of Religion

Wanting to know how and why the story of civilization is written by religion, we naturally find our way to the study of religion. And what, in religion, we want to investigate is the power of religion so to form attitudes and viewpoints as to move nations and societies to act as they do – however that is. But when we take up the systematic study of religion, we find ourselves bound by the limitations of the sorts of evidence to which, over time and in the present, we gain access. The evidence, concerns not religion but religions. Religion, after all, does not exist in abstract form except in the imagination of the academic scholar of religion. Religion in the world exists only as religions, one by one. We then propose to generalize about religion out of the data of religions. And religions moreover testify to their qualities not in generalities but in concrete kinds of evidence. Religions speak through diverse media, for diverse purposes, to diverse issues. Religions in the here and now come to concrete expression in many ways. To study one religion or a set of religions, we require knowledge of philosophy; to investigate another, we need to know the possibilities of the theater; a third will require us to know about visual arts, a fourth, about music, a fifth, about dance, a sixth, about story-telling. As many as there are religions, so many are the modes of paramount expression, hence the types of evidence, that demand analysis.

The System of Judaism

Before proceeding, let us now offer definitions for terms that have already made their appearance. In all that follows, two usages predominate, first "system," then "religious" or "Judaic" system. By "system," we refer to three things that are one, ethos, ethics, and ethnos:

1. *ethos:* a world-view, which by reference to the intersection of the supernatural and the natural worlds accounts for how things are and puts them together into a cogent and harmonious picture;
2. *ethics:* a way of life, which expresses in concrete actions the world-view and which is explained by that world-view;
3. *ethnos:* a social group, for which the world-view accounts, which is defined in concrete terms by the way of life, and therefore which

gives expression in the everyday world to the world-view and is defined as an entity by that way of life.

A religious system is one that appeals to God as the principal power. A Judaic system is a religious system – ethos, ethics, ethnos – that identifies the Hebrew Scriptures or "Old Testament" as principal component of its canon and appeals to those writings for authority. A Judaism, then, comprises not merely a theory – a book or a set of ideas or ideology or theology – distinct from social reality. A Judaism is an explanation for the group (an "Israel") that gives social form to the system and an account of the distinctive way of life of that group. A Judaism, that is, a Judaic system, derives from and focuses upon a social entity, a group of Jews who (in their minds at least) constitute not an Israel but Israel. How Judaisms relate to the social circumstances of Jews then forms the problem of this programmatic proposal.

What makes the study of the interplay of context and content interesting is the quest for the points of interrelationship and connection. A religious system holds together on its own and at the same time holds in cogent balance the society that understands itself by appeal to that system. But how to find a way of holding together the three components of a religious system – ethos, ethics, ethnos? What serves is a hypothesis that reads these components as elements of an answer to a question. If we can propose a single encompassing statement that constitutes the system's recurrent message and judgment, then we can claim to formulate a theory of the answer to the question of cogency and coherence, both for the system and for the society that the system represents. From that knowledge, we can make a good guess at the question to which the answer responds. So in studying the interplay of religion and society, we aim to formulate indirectly and by inference a theory on the description of the system – ethos, ethics, social entity – and the analysis of that system – urgent question, compelling answer.

Religion is often adduced as an explanation of why a social system sustains itself. We see the issue of why a system originates and survives, if it does, or fails, if it does, by itself as impertinent to the analysis of a system. A system on its own is like a language. A language forms an example of language if it produces communication through rules of syntax and verbal arrangement. That paradigm serves full well however many people speak the language, or however long the language serves. Two people who understand each other form a language-community, even, or especially, if no one understands them. So too by definition religions address the living, constitute societies, frame and compose cultures. For however long, at whatever moment in historic time, a religious system always grows up in the perpetual present, an artifact of its day, whether today or a long-ago time. The only appropriate tense for a religious system is the present. A religious system always *is*, whatever it was, whatever it will be. Why so? Because its traits address a condition of humanity in society, a circumstance of an hour – however brief or protracted the hour and the circumstance.

When we ask that a religious composition speak to a society with a message of the *is* and the *ought* and with a meaning for the everyday, we focus on the power of that system to hold the whole together: the society the system addresses, the individuals who compose the society, the ordinary lives they lead, in ascending order of consequence. And that system then forms a whole and well-composed structure. The structure stands somewhere, and, indeed, the place where it stands will secure for the system either an extended or an ephemeral span of life. But the system, for however long it lasts, serves. And that focus on the eternal present justifies our interest in analyzing why a system works (the urgent agenda of issues it successfully solves for those for whom it solves those problems) when it does, and why it ceases to work (loses self-evidence, is bereft of its "Israel," for example) when it no longer works. The phrase, the *history* of a *system*, presents us with an oxymoron. Systems endure in that eternal present that they create. They evoke precedent, but they do not have a history. A system relates to context, but, as we have stressed, exists in an enduring moment (which, to be sure, changes all the time). We capture the system in a moment, the worm consumes it an hour later. That is the way of mortality, whether for us one by one, in all mortality, or for the works of humanity in society. But systemic analysis and interpretation requires us to ask questions of history and comparison, not merely description of structure and cogency. So in this exercise we undertake first description, that is, the text, then analysis, that is, the context, and finally, interpretation, that is, the matrix, in which a system has its being. That explains one of the basic methods of this program. We call for the presentation of successive examples of systems, past and present, as these illustrate the question we have taken as primary: the interplay of systems and circumstances. By this we mean the discovery of how an urgent question finds its self-evidently valid answer and generates a Judaism. Within the program we set forth, we do not ask for a continuous history of Judaism in the Jew's society, but examples of Judaisms in societies of Jews, for we do not conceive a single Judaism, therefore a single linear and harmonized history of that one Judaism, to characterize the data we choose to analyze.

The Ecology of Judaism

What is at stake in this reading of religion, in the case of Judaism, as the statement of a society's fundamental system? The answer to that question brings us to the ecology of Judaism. For what we propose to exemplify is how to investigate, through the case of Judaism, what we call the ecology of religion, that is, the interplay between a religious system and the social world that gives to that system its shape and meaning. When we understand a religious system in the context of the social order, we grasp whatever in this world we are likely to understand about religion in the shaping of the civilization of humanity. And no other generative force in civilization has exceeded in power and effect the formative force of religion. Accordingly, in this method we have meant to exemplify in a very particular setting the larger problem of how to relate the content of a religion to its context, social culture to religious conviction, above all, social change, which is public and general, to symbol change, which is particular and invariably distinctive to its setting. The study of the ecology of religion is therefore whether and how religion forms an independent variable in the shaping of civilization.

We draw upon a metaphor from the natural and social sciences for the study of religion. Our inquiry concerns whether, in the analysis of the interrelated components of civilization, religion constitutes a singular constituent of the whole. Ecology is a branch of science concerned with the interrelationships of organisms and their environments. By "ecology of..." we mean the study of the interrelationship between a particular, religious way of viewing the world and living life, and the historical, cultural, social, economic, and especially political situation of the people who view the world and live life in accord with the teachings of their religion. The Jews have formed ongoing groups, existing over time in various places, and hence describing, analyzing, and interpreting in context a Judaism does not conclude the work of studying the ecology of Judaism as exemplar of the ecology of religion. An ongoing social entity, after all, yields more than a single system, but the ecology of the social entity in its indicative traits requires attention not only for its change but also for its enduring qualities.

But what can we say of the ecology of not a Judaism but of Judaism, now meaning *all* Judaisms? We see two fundamental traits to that ecology, one social and political, the other religious and fundamentally autonomous of the material realities of society altogether. In so stating, we lay down our claim that religion constitutes an independent variable in the study of society and culture.

The former fact of the ecosystem encompassing all Judaisms – the politics that will affect all Judaisms – is readily identified. The Jewish people form a very small group, spread over many countries. One fact of their natural environment is that they form a distinct group in diverse societies and have been so over time. A second is that they constitute solely a community of fate and, for many, of faith, in that they have few shared social or cultural traits. A third is that they do not form a single political entity. A fourth is that they look back upon a very long and in some way exceptionally painful history. A world-view suited to the Jews' social ecology must make sense of their unimportance and explain their importance. It must define an ethos that will sustain and not only explain the continuing life of the group and persuade people that their forming a distinct and distinctive community is important and worth carrying on. The interplay between the political, social, and historical life of the Jews and their conceptions of themselves in this world and the next – that is, their world-view, contained in their canon, their way of life, explained by the teleology of the system, and the symbolic structure that encompasses the two and stands for the whole all at once and all together – these define the focus for the inquiry into the political side of the ecology of the religion at hand, that is, the ecology of Judaism.

The Religious Component of All Judaisms

What about the religious component of the ecology of Judaism? If we claim that when we study religion, we deal with what is among the most important force in the formation of the life of civilization, we have also to ask about the religious component of the enduring ecology of the social entity. What we want to know about religion, as exemplified by the ecology of Judaism, therefore, is how religion forms an uncontingent force in society and politics and what is the nature of the religious system per se. In asking about the political and social problem addressed by matters of belief, we do not treat religion as merely instrumental, that is, a way of saying something else altogether. The fundamental allegation of our method is that religion stands at the center of the world of humanity in society.

In part, we claim that when we study the ecology of religion, we study written evidence about how through religious systems – ethos, ethics, ethnos – humanity in society responded to challenge and change, mediated between the received tradition of politics and social life and the crisis of the age and circumstance. Religion is not trivial, not private, not individual, not simply a matter of the heart. Religion is public, political, social, economic. The religious component of the ecosystem in which a Judaism finds its place derives from the fundamental and generative religious structure to which all Judaisms have conformed, a religious structure that persists and applies ubiquitously because, under diverse circumstances, that deep structure shaping all Judaisms precipitates a crisis and also resolves that crisis.

Every Judaism finds its indicative trait as a Judaism in its appeal to a single scripture, the Pentateuch in particular. And it is – for reasons that pertain to its very structuring of the consciousness of all Israels in relationship to their diverse circumstances – the Pentateuch that forms the other ecosystem for a Judaism. Accordingly, we have now to take account of the ongoing, inherited realities that frame any given Judaic system and that invariably for all Judaisms define the setting for the systemic authorship that produces the writings. A religious system, e.g., a Judaism seen as a subset of Judaism, takes a place within a larger set of affined religious systems. In the present context a Judaism can be shown to relate to prior Judaisms, all Judaisms forming a diachronic fact, one framed by matters of attitude and conviction, as much as (for a given moment) a synchronic fact. True enough, there is not now, and never has been, a single Judaism. There have been only Judaisms, each with its distinctive system and new beginning, all resorting to available antecedents and claiming they are precedents, but in fact none with a history prior to its birth. Each system begins on its own, in response to a circumstance that strikes people as urgent and a question they find ineluctable. But all Judaisms not only address a single social-ecological system, that of the Jews.

The Pentateuch, the Five Books of Moses, framed out of inherited materials, sets forth certain attitudes and viewpoints that would define for all Judaisms to follow a single structure of experience and expectation. And that structure stood autonomous of the social and political facts of any given group of Jews to whom, and for whom, a Judaism was meant to speak. Accordingly, while we identify one ecosystem of the religion, Judaism, as social and political, the other, in our view, must be classified as religious: the religious eco-system for a religion, a Judaism. All Judaisms have addressed resentments in their respective "Israels," and these resentments are precipitated by the Pentateuchal theory of its "Israel," that is, the social entity of the Pentateuchal Judaism, and the concommitant world-view and way of life of that same system. All Judaisms have not only dealt with, but also have resolved, those resentments. All Judaisms in one way or another sorted out whatever social experience their "Israels" proposed to explain by appeal to the tension of exile and the remission of return, and Judaisms in general appeal to the fixed paradigm of Israel's exile and return. That singular and indicative appeal formed an ecological fact for all Judaisms, as much as the Jews' minority status and utopian situation defined issues to be addressed by any Judaism.

Exile and Return in Judaism

The original reading of the Jews' existence as exile and return derives from the Pentateuch which was composed as we now have them (out of earlier materials, to be sure) in the aftermath of the destruction of the Temple in 586 B.C. and in response to the exile to Babylonia. The experience selected and addressed by the authorship of the document is that of exile and restoration. The framing of events into the pattern at hand represents an act of powerful imagination and interpretation. It is an experience that is invented, because no one person or group both went into "exile" and also "returned home." Diverse experiences have been sorted out, various persons have been chosen, and the whole has been worked into a system by those who selected history out of happenings, and models out of masses of persons. Since no Jews after 586 B.C. actually experienced what in the aggregate Scripture says happened, the materials within Scripture were "selected". Since Scripture does not record a particular person's experience, it is not autobiographical; writing for society at large the personal insight of a singular figure is also not an account of a whole nation's story. Many Jews in the Judea of 586 B.C. never left. And, as is well known, a great many of those who ended up in Babylonia stayed there. Only a minority went back to Jerusalem. Consequently, the story of exile and return to Zion encompasses what happened to only a select number of families, who identified themselves as part of the family of Abraham, Isaac, and Jacob, and their genealogy as the history of Israel. Those families that stayed and those that never came back had they written the Torah would have told as normative and paradigmatic a different tale altogether.

The experiences of the few that formed the paradigm for Israel beyond the restoration taught as normative lessons that in fact generated profound alienation. Let us state with emphasis the lessons people claimed to learn out of the events they had chosen for their history: *the life of the group is uncertain, subject to conditions and stipulations.* Nothing is set and given, all things a gift: land and life itself. But what actually did happen in that uncertain world – exile but then restoration – marked the group as special, different, select. There were other ways of seeing things, and the Pentateuchal picture was no more compelling than any other. Those Jews who did not go into exile, and those who did not "come home" had no reason to take the view of matters that characterized the authorship of Scripture. The life of the group need not have appeared more uncertain, more subject to contingency and stipulation, than the life of any other group. The land did not require the vision that imparted to it the enchantment, the personality, that, in Scripture, it received: "The land will vomit you out as it did those who were here before you." And the adventitious circumstance of Iranian imperial policy – a political happenstance – did not have to be recast into return. So nothing in the system of Scripture – exile for reason, return as redemption – followed necessarily and logically. Everything was invented: interpreted.

The uncertainty of the life of the group in the century or so from the destruction of the First Temple of Jerusalem by the Babylonians to the building of the Second Temple of Jerusalem by the Jews, with Persian permission and sponsorship returned from exile, formed the paradigm. With the promulgation of the "Torah of Moses" under the sponsorship of Ezra, the Persians' viceroy, at ca. 450 B.C., all future Israels would then refer to that formative experience as it had been set down and preserved as the norm for Israel in the mythic terms of that "original" Israel. The Israel was not of Genesis and Sinai and the end at the moment of entry into the promised land, but the "Israel" of the families that recorded as the rule and the norm the story of both the exile and the return. In that minority genealogy, that story of exile and return, alienation and remission, imposed on the received stories of pre-exilic Israel and adumbrated time and again in the Five Books of Moses and addressed by the framers of that document in their work over all, we find that paradigmatic statement in which every Judaism, from then to now, found its structure and deep syntax of social existence, the grammar of its intelligible message.

In theological terms, that experience rehearsed the conditional moral existence of sin and punishment, suffering and atonement and reconciliation, and, in social terms, the uncertain and always conditional national destiny of disintegration and renewal of the group. That moment captured within the Five Books of Moses, that is to say, the judgment of the generation of the return to Zion, led by Ezra, about its extraordinary experience of exile and return would inform the attitude and viewpoint of all the Judaisms and all the Israels beyond. Accordingly, we identify as a fact of the diachronic ecology of all Judaisms that generative and definitive moment precisely as all Judaisms have done, that is, by looking into that same Scripture. All Judaisms identify the Torah or the Five Books of Moses as the written-down statement of God's will for Israel, the Jewish people (which, as a matter of fact, every Judaism also identifies as its own social group). We suppose that on the surface, we should specify that formative and definitive moment, recapitulated by all Judaisms, with the story of Creation down to Abraham and the beginning of his family, the children of Abraham, Isaac, and Jacob. Or perhaps we are advised to make our way to Sinai and hold that that original point of definition descends from Heaven. But allowing ourselves merely to retell the story deprives us of the required insight. Recapitulating the story of the religion does not help us understand the religion. Identifying the point of origin of the story, by contrast, does. For the story tells not what happened on the occasion to which the story refers (the creation of the world, for instance) but how (long afterward and for their own reasons) people want to portray themselves. The tale therefore recapitulates that resentment, that obsessive and troubling point of origin, that the group wishes to explain, transcend, transform.

Every Judaism found as its task the recapitulation of the original Judaism: exile and return, resentment of circumstance and reconciliation with the human condition of a given "Israel." Each made its own distinctive statement of the generative and critical resentment contained within that questioning of the given, that deep understanding of the uncertain character of the existence of the group in its normal location and under circumstances of permanence that (so far as the Judaic group understood things) characterized the life of every other group but Israel. What for everyone else (so it seemed to the Judaisms addressed to the Israels through time) was a given, for Israel was a gift. What all the nations knew as how things *must* be Israel understood as how things *might not be*: exile and loss, alienation and resentment, but, instead of annihilation, renewal, restoration, reconciliation, and (in theological language) redemption. That pattern, permanently inscribed in the Torah of God to Moses at Sinai, would define for all Israels over all time that matter of resentment demanding recapitulation: leaving home, coming home. What is that one systemic trait that marks all Judaisms and sets them apart from all other religious systems, viewed jointly and severally? The religious ecology of Judaisms is dictated by that perpetual asking of the question, who are we? That trait of self-consciousness, that incapacity to accept the group as a given and its data – way of life, world-view, constituting the world of an Israel, a Jewish people, in the here and now – is the one thing that draws together Judaisms from beginning to end. Jews' persistent passion for self-definition characterizes all of the Judaisms they have made for themselves. What others take as the given, the Jews perceive as the received, the special, the extraordinary. And that perception of the remarkable character of what to other groups is the absolute datum of all being requires explanation.

Since the formative pattern imposed that perpetual, self-conscious uncertainty, treating the life of the group as conditional and discontinuous, Jews have asked themselves who they are and invented

Judaisms to answer that question. Accordingly, no circumstances have permitted Jews to take for granted their existence as a group. Looking back on Scripture and its message, Jews have ordinarily treated as special, subject to conditions and therefore uncertain what (in their view) other groups enjoyed as unconditional and simply given. Why the paradigm renewed itself is clear: this particular view of matters generated expectations that could not be met, hence created resentment – and then provided comfort and hope that made possible coping with that resentment. Specifically, each Judaism retells in its own way and with its distinctive emphases the tale of the Torah, the story of a no-people that becomes a people, that has what it gets only on condition, and that can lose it all by virtue of its own sin. It is a terrifying, unsettling story for a social group to tell of itself, because it imposes acute self-consciousness, chronic insecurity, upon what should be the level plane and firm foundation of society. That is to say, the collection of diverse materials joined into a single tale on the occasion of the original exile and restoration because of the repetition in age succeeding age also precipitates the recapitulation of the interior experience of exile and restoration – always because of sin and atonement.

Hence, the power of religion to form an independent variable, alongside politics, economics, and the facts of social organization and structure, derives from its capacity (in the case at hand) to form a permanent paradigm and to perpetuate a single attitude and experience. And how was and is this done? Promising what could not be delivered, then providing solace for the consequent disappointment, the system at hand precipitated in age succeeding age the very conditions necessary for its own replication. Precipitating resentment and then remitting the consequent anguish, religion itself forms a self-perpetuating fact of the ecology of religion. Religion is not only a category of the life of society, politics, economics. An irreducible fact of humanity, there is a dimension of the social power of religion that is uniquely religious.

From Judaism to Judaisms

While the permanent paradigm that perpetuates a single experience shaped Judaism as a religion, the social scientific approach focuses on Judaisms in context. Following the long and distinguished tradition of Weber, Marx, and Durkheim, social scientists place the study of variation and change in Judaism in the context of the comparative and historical analysis of Jews and their communities. This orientation goes beyond the description of historical patterns by testing propositions about historical processes; rather than focusing solely on country or community case studies, it emphasizes systematic cross-national comparisons of Judaisms. Multiple comparisons of Judaisms and non-Judaisms, over time and in different societies, are the basis for understanding Judaisms in their contexts. And through systematic comparisons, it becomes possible to analyze the translation of the Judaism of "exile and return" into the Judaisms of the societies.

What do we examine when we study Judaisms? Four major dimensions of religion are encompassed within the social scientific investigation of Judaisms: (1) the religious behavior, beliefs, and values of Jews; (2) the religious institutions of the Jews; (3) the linkages between Judaism and other aspects of social life – family, economy, polity, and culture; and (4) particular religious ideologies and religious social movements. Within each of these areas of investigation, social scientists emphasize historical and cross-national comparisons and comparisons between Jews and others. We treat the extent of change in Jewish religious values as part of those processes that require explanation, investigating empirically their role in shaping Judaism and Jewish life, without assuming their centrality on theoretical grounds. The social scientific study of Judaism, therefore, treats the religion of the Jew as a complex set of variables, not as a constant.

In the areas of behavior, beliefs, and values, the focus is on changes in the patterns of religious observances and religious ritual, variations in what Jews do religiously, what they believe and their attitudes toward Judaism and ritual observance, and the importance of religious observances and activities for them and their communities. Of central importance are changes and variations in religious values, ideologies, and the ideals expressed by an elite, whether and how these ideals and values are transmitted to the Jewish community. The methodological emphasis on systematic comparisions between the religions of Jews and of non-Jews, using theoretical frameworks common to both and applying general models to the study of Judaisms, allows us to identify that which is particular to Judaism in a specific context and that which is a more generalizable feature of the religion of groups under similar conditions. Most importantly, comparisons facilitate the analysis of how the content of Judaism, exile and return, is translated into the Judaisms of particular contexts. Each Judaism reinterprets the core themes of exile and return, in its form and in its idiom, in reponse to contexts that are social, economic, and political as well as cultural and ideological.

By necessity, comparisons are made in historical and cross-national community studies. Social science questions relate to how the religion of the Jews is related to other institutional, cultural, political, economic, and social patterns of Jews and to the broader societies of which they are a part; and how these linkages are different for Jews and others. As such, the analysis of Judaism focuses on the ways religion changes over time and varies with different social, economic, political, and cultural contexts; it includes, as well, how new institutions – religious and secular – emerge in different settings as responses to religious change.

Since the social scientific study of Judaism deals with the life of Jews and the institutions of the Jewish community, comparisons between the religions of Jews and non-Jews require as well comparisons of the social-community contexts of Jews and others. A key research issue concerns how the changing configurations of religion and religious institutions are related to the changing cohesion of the Jewish community, over time and among the societies where Jews live. Do changes in religious observances result in the declines in the extent to which economic and family networks are Jewish? Does the shift in religious ideology lead to changes in the stability of Jewish families? Are religious ideological changes associated with shifts in occupational concentration, migration, and educational attainment? Do religious values influence the political and cultural expressions of Jews? In what ways is Judaism central or marginal to the lives of Jews and the institutions of their communities? In short, the social scientific study of Judaism attempts to examine systematically (i.e., theoretically, methodologically, and empirically) the changing determinants and consequences of Judaism (in its multidimensional forms and expressions) for the lives of Jews and the structure of their communities. Analytically, research on these questions necessities multiple comparisons over time, cross-culturally and cross-societally, among Jews and between Jews and non-Jews. These are the ways the social scientist treats religion as a set of variables.

The goal is to use the social scientific mode to ask new questions about Judaism in context, to reshape our understanding of changes in the expressions and institutions of Judaism, comparatively and historically. We thus have to move beyond a description of the internal workings of religious institutions and the expressed ideals of a religious elite for understanding the Judaisms of contemporary societies. Two major limitations characterize an emphasis on studying the internal workings of religious institutions and concentrating on the religious elite: the error of assuming a cross-cultural commonality of one Judaism (i.e., that context does not matter for content) and the error of assuming the disintegrative forces of change (i.e., that the newly formed contents are weaker, not only different, than earlier forms). Let us explain. Studying the internal structure of Jewish institutions and focusing solely on the elite, we center analytic attention solely on the Jews and assume that there is cross-cultural religious commonalities among Jews and that Jewish values are monolithic. Religious uniformity and continuity are assertions, rather than the objects of systematic study. The core paradigm of Judaism, of exile and return, does not assume that the ways in which the paradigm of Judaism is worked out is identical for all the Judaisms. Indeed, our argument is that each Judaism works out the paradigm of the Judaism of exile and return in its context and in its mode, moving the content of Judaism into context of each Judaism. Thus, the social scientific study of Judaism always involves the study of the new formulations of the Judaic system in context and is not primarily the study of the more conspicuous forms of variation and change in the religious movements of Judaism (Hasidism and Reform Judaism, for example).

The focus on the internal structure of the institutions of Judaism and on the values expressed as norms by the religious elite results in the interpretation of change in the context of religious decline. It is often implicitly assumed or asserted as a "given" of analysis that the forces of modernization have had a negative impact on Judaism and traditional values since these are what most manifestly have changed. It has always been the case that the values of the religious elite, always in their specific contexts, have changed, and the religious institutions of one context have been altered to fit into a new context. It would be untenable in the social science mode to assume that change and variation was unusual or exceptional. Change and variation in Judaism has been an integral part of the variety of communities, societies, and cultures of the Jewish experience. Judaisms have emerged to interpret and reinterpret the Judaic paradigm of exile and return in the multiplicity of forms generated by the experiences of the Jewish context. In this sense, it is a limiting assumption to treat change as distintegration and crisis without allowing for the possibility that change might also represent opportunity and challenge.

Thus, for example, a classic work in the social history of the Jews begins by describing "traditional society" as one "based upon a common body of knowledge and values handed down from the past". It is further asserted that the traditional society "accurately describes the whole of world Jewry, at least from the talmudic era (200 C.E.) up to the age of European Emancipation (during the first half of the nineteenth century), and it applies to some part of Jewish society even in more recent times."[1] The analysis further assumes that there is an

---

[1] J. Katz, *Tradition and Crisis: Jewish Society at the End of the Middle Ages*, New York: Schocken Books, 1961, p. 3.

"underlying national unity of the Jewish people in the lands of their dispersion." "This unity", it is asserted, "is an indisputable fact."[2] It is not surprising that the focus of that social history is on Judaic values and ideals, assuming that they will reveal the reality of Judaism and Jewish life; the internal structure of the community and its religious institutions are examined trusting that they will convey the religiosity of the community. There are no systematic comparisons among Jewish communities given the "fact" of underlying unity. It follows from these premises that change is described as "crisis" and transformation as "disintegration".

In contrast, the thrust of our argument is that the social scientific study of Judaism focuses on general theoretical frameworks, methodological strategies, and empirical evidence about Judaisms in comparative and historical perspectives. These general theories about social change and ethnic continuity, about the general sociology of religion and of culture, are applied to the study of Judaism in context, to the analysis of Jews and their communities. While there are specific features of Judaism that relate to the Judaism of Scriptures, reinventing core themes of Judaism in new contexts, the sociology of Judaism focuses precisely on those new contexts to study how each Judaism is shaped and reshaped as a Judaism. Each new form of Judaism requires analysis; each needs to be identified and studied systematically. Each new Judaism responds to context and shapes it.

The general assertion or assumption that Jewish culture is a constant over time and place treats cultural variation as the description of the exotic or radically different form of ritual or religious observance. In anthropological work this often involves comparing "eastern" (e.g., Yemenite, Morrocan) Jewish cultures with a "western" ashkenasic model and is the prelude to dealing with the changes generated by migration to new places where older cultural forms are disrupted and new forms of cultural blends are emerging.

Judaism in the Context of Culture

We do not in any way deny the need to study Judaism in the context of culture, nor do we denigrate the importance of values in the lives of Jews and in the expressions of their Judaism. We also do not deny that values play a role in the perpetuation of group continuity and in the manifestation of Judaism. Rather we argue for the following social science principles:

---

[2]Ibid., p. 7

1. Treat the role of religious values as part of structural as well as cultural contexts;

2. Question explanations that focus solely on culture and test with evidence the often unstated assumption that values are the major determinants of social and religious change;

3. Demonstrate whether and how religious ideologies are the major factors shaping the ways in which people express their commitments to community;

4. Examine whether declines in some forms of religious or cultural expression by necessity imply the disintegration of all forms of religious expressions;

5. Challenge the notion that the ideals of Judaism are the only basis for measuring the current behavioral expressions of Judaism (or even the behavioral expressions of past generations);

6. Investigate whether religious change implies a decline in religion and under what conditions alternatives to one form of religious expression weakens the social fabric of the community;

7. Assume that Judaism in particular contexts is relative and changing, testing always whether the ideals of the elite reflect the behavior of the people, and whether norms and behavior are identical.

These are fundamental premises of social science but are often rejected by those who study Judaism when they assume the "uniqueness" of the Jewish people, the "continuity" of Judaism from the past to the diverse communities of the present, without specifying what is content and what is context, and assuming always that there is a "decline" of Judaism and hence of the Jewish people in the context of modern, open, pluralistic societies.

While it is clear that specific features of Judaism may influence the shape of Jewish communities and the responses of Jews to the communities they live in, it is also clear that these specific features operate in a social structural context, requiring an analysis of social situations in order to disentangle how and where these factors are important, what they determine and how they work. To argue that the "Jewish condition" is mainly or solely determined by abstract religious values and Jewish culture or by non-Jews (e.g., anti-Semitism) is to misread the complexities of Judaism in context and to ignore the social, economic, political, and cultural variation among Jewish communities; it is to fail to specify the conditions under which the core themes of all Judaisms are shaped by the particular contexts of each Judaism.

Transformation and Judaism

Sociology, in particular, and the social sciences, more generally, provide a perspective that is fundamental not only for the study of Judaism and Jewry but for understanding human society in all of its manifestations, one that can be applied to all societies at all points in time. Some have applied them to the study of the Biblical period; others have used social scientific theories to map out issues of the Mishnah and the Talmud and to study Jews, their communities and cultures, at distant times and places. The application of social scientific perspectives to study contemporary manifestations of Judaisms need not be, indeed cannot be, ahistorical. A central sociological question, perhaps the master theme, in the social scientific study of contemporary Judaisms is the impact of the transformation or "modernization" of society on the religion of the Jews. We have noted earlier the multidimensionality of Judaism and discussed the various elements involved in studying Judaism in behavioral, institutional, and communal terms. Here we need to clarify issues associated with transformation and modernization as master contexts translating Judaism into Judaisms. We focus on transformation in the social-scientific, not the historical, sense. Thus, our question of transformation and Judaism is not addressed to when "modern" society begins, a question of the periodization of history,[3] but rather, How do the processes of modernization, secularization, and transformation unfold and, in turn, how these processes relate to changes in the lives of people, in the institutions of society, in the structure of social relations, and the generational transmission of Jewish values and culture? How do these transformations alter Judaism to form new systems of Judaisms?

What, then, are the major analytic themes in the social scientific study of Judaism in the context of the transformation of Jews and their communities? The master theme of contemporary social science is the analysis of the transformation of societies and the variety of groups within them as a result of modernization. Industrialization, urbanization, political and social mobilization, cultural change and secularization are among the major elements. The key processes involve structural differentiation and the expansion of political and economic opportunities. New structures and values, new institutions, new ways of behaving and thinking, new jobs, residences, political movements, cultures, and ideologies, as well as new sources of conflict, competition, and inequality have emerged in the modern era. Our master question then becomes: What has been the impact of these transformations on

---

[3]L. Kochan, "The Methodology of Modern Jewish History," *Journal of Jewish Studies* 36 (1985), pp. 185-194.

the Jews, generally, and on their religious systems, specifically? How has the modernization of the societies in which Jews lived affected their Judaism? Are the consequences of modernization for the transformation of the Jewish community and Judaism similar to the consequences for others in terms of direction, extent, and pace of change? How have Jews, their leaders and elites, religious and secular, their organizations and institutions, responded to the sweep of modernization? With the dissolution of the older bases of cohesion, what new types of communal bonds, associational ties, and cultural forms link Jews to each other? In turn, what are the relationships of new forms of communal cohesion and religious transformations? What are the bases of solidarity, in the Durkheimian sense, among Jews and their communities as they were transformed by modernization? And, in turn, how does Judaism transformed relate to these changes? Since it is not tenable to assume that Judaism will not respond to the dramatic changes transforming traditional to modern society, the question becomes, How do the Judaisms of modern society shape and reshape the themes of exile and return of Judaism?

These questions focus our attention on broad changes over time and their effects on Jews and their communities. They are directed to the broader issue of how modernization has transformed Judaism into Judaisms. History has a central place in sociological analyses of Jews; not the four-thousand-year history of Jews everywhere, but historical processes associated with the transformation of Jews in modern societies. We are concerned about those particular processes associated with modernization, not about all historical change. So our focus is not on an abstract and oversimplified notion of historical events and sequences but on the processes associated with the modernization of societies, communities, families, and individuals. In our context, we want to link these to the transformation of Judaism in all its dimensions.

Our questions, therefore, involve, first and foremost, a focus on historical change of a particular sociological kind and analytic type. They also require a second type of comparison in addition to changes over time – variation across communities within and between countries. The objective of cross-community and historical comparisons is not to isolate the exotic and unique; rather it is to frame analytic questions (why these religious changes and not others; why particular religious changes occur in community X and not in community Y; why at time B and not time A; why for some Jews and not for others in the same society at the same time) and provide a comparative basis for testing theories and hypotheses with empirical evidence. So the first analytic issue is to place the study of Judaism and Jews in the framework of theories of transformation and change.

Judaism and the Role of Others

A second analytic strategy is to incorporate the systematic comparison of Jews and others as an integral part of our research agenda. We can focus solely on the Jews and their communities, analyzing their patterns over time and in various communities. We can learn much from such "internal" group comparisons but these alone are insufficient to address analytic themes in the social sciences. Ideally, we would want to compare systematically the religions of Jews and the many groups of non-Jews over time and in various societies. Such comparisons provide the basis for evaluating the structural and cultural sources of Jewish distinctiveness and assessing whether differences between Jews and non-Jews are temporary and transitory or whether they are embedded in the social structure. Comparisons between the religions of non-Jews and Jews are essential in identifying how the particular manifestations of Judaism are shaped by contexts.

It is clearly not appropriate analytically to compare Jews with non-Jews without taking into account and disentangling differential structural *and* cultural patterns. Thus, for example, comparing the development of religious institutions and religious ideologies among Jews in Germany in the nineteenth century with all Germans, without taking into account the specific jobs, urban location, and education of the Jews would be misleading. Such a crude comparison would reveal differences between Jews and non-Jews, reflecting in large part social class and rural-urban residential differences but not necessarily specific factors associated with Jewishness or Judaism, the place of Jews in German society or their "culture". On the one hand, to know that differences between Jews and non-Jews in nineteenth century Germany are primarily the consequence of socioeconomic and demographic differences shapes a series of specific analytic questions regarding the determinants and consequences of the particular socioeconomic and demographic characteristics of German Jewry. On the other hand, in neutralizing the socioeconomic and demographic effects, we are able to focus on other powerful structural and cultural factors. But to simply attribute crude differences between Jews and non-Jews to "culture" and "values" particular to Jews without studying non-Jews directly and without taking into account the social, political, demographic, and economic contexts of our comparisons, results in a series of distortions in our understanding of social change among Jews in Europe and America over the last century. Only through systematic comparison do we begin to understand how and why the core themes of Judaism are translated into the particular forms of Judaic expressions.

In the analysis of religious reform in nineteenth century Western Europe, in the comparisons between the religious transformations of Judaism and other religions in Europe during the nineteenth century and America in the twentieth century, and in the comparisons of religious and political transformations in various countries including the State of Israel, analysis has revealed consistently the value of comparisons, yielding new insights derived from comparative analysis.[4] For example, comparative analysis allows us to interpret why some aspects of Reform Judaism emerged in Germany and not in France and points to the underlying similarity of diffusion processes of political ideologies in Russia and religious ideologies in Germany in the nineteenth century.[5] Furthermore, we are able to disentangle the relative importance of changes in religious ideology, economic, demographic, and political factors to account for the differential spread of religious reform throughout Germany. The comparative similarities in the levels of synagogue attendance, to take another example, among Jews in the State of Israel and in the United States suggested general processes of secularization in two very different Jewish communities in distinct socio-cultural contexts. These and related analytic findings emerge when multiple comparisons – historical, cross-community, and with non-Jews – are the bases for the systematic social scientific analysis of Judaism. Without comparisons, we are left with description, not analysis, and no basis for testing theories and hypotheses.

But why focus on the Jews? Are there analytic considerations, beyond issues of self interest and ethnocentrism, which justify our investigation of the Jews? If not, general sociologists will learn little from our sociology of the Jews and we will address only each other. The Jews form a useful subject for research, because they are a small group, well documented, with a long history, and also they exhibit enormous diversity. The diversity allows for the introduction of various factors in explaining facts, and where and when religious belief or practice forms one of those factors, there are sufficient variables for testing the importance of the religious factor. Because of their role in diverse political and economic entities, it proves fruitful analytically to address questions about the processes of transformation to the Jewish group than to total societies. A more reasonable, managable unit of

---

[4]For examples see the discussion in C. Goldscheider and A. Zuckerman, *The Transformation of the Jews*. University of Chicago Press, 1984.
[5]See the selection in this anthology Chapter X.

analysis than a total heterogeneous society, the Jews prove accessible and important.

Moreover, comparative analysis is facilitated by the central role Jews have played in places of earlier and later modernization within Europe and in the new nations of America and Israel. The comparative study of Jews thus provides an analytic handle for understanding general processes of western development just as it does for understanding the role of religions in society. The location of Jews in various societies makes it efficient to examine changes across societies comparatively while focusing at the community level. There is significant internal variation when the total society is used as the unit of analysis, so that crucial patterns are oftened neutralized by countervailing processes; cross-societal comparisons only compound these analytic difficulties. And while the Jews occupy a unique position in western societies, insights derived from a sociological analysis of the Jews are generalizable to others when the focus is on analytic issues within comparative and historical perspectives.

Issues of modernization apply to Jews and their communities as they apply to total societies and to other ethnic and minority groups. The examination of the transformation of the Jews yields insight as well into critical theories associated with the social, political, economic, and cultural integration of minority, ethnic, and religious groups in the processes associated with modernization, including social differentiation, communal cohesion, intergroup relations, and the structural and cultural dimensions of assimilation. Important aspects of the core theories of ethnicity in pluralistic societies can be systematically tested within the framework of the sociology of the Jews.[6] There are, in addition, particular Jewish issues of modernization that are of importance in exploring modern Jewish society. These include the specifics of Judaism, anti-Semitism, and the internal structure and organization of the Jewish community.

Specific Features of Judaism in Context

In the modernization of the Jews, Judaism was transformed. The normative and communal centrality of Judaism declined. As the older order changed so did the institutions legitimating that order. As religion changed, it was redefined and new forms of communal identification emerged. How these changes evolve, what becomes the bases of the new forms of legitimacy and consensus, and how cultural and value consensus emerge are key issues. The responses of religious

---

[6]See for example, C. Goldscheider, *Jewish Continuity and Change*, Indiana University Press, 1986.

movements and ideologies to the challenges of modern secular society
and how they relate to other social-religious movements require
clarification. The transformation from religious centrality to communal
hnic diversity poses the fundamental concern for Jewish continuity
discontinuity at the community and individual levels. Clearly,
iosity (or religiousness) is not only or primarily an issue of personal
itment to specifically religious institution or ideologies. It is
and communal. These broader contexts are often lost when the
ogies of Judaisms are discussed solely in the context of their
l ideologies and organizational patterns and not in terms of the
definitions of membership and identification, family and
ration patterns. The "Jewish *verstehende*" requires a sociological
tehende grounded in the rich sociological tradition of Weber, Marx,
d Durkheim, among others.

A second particular feature in the analysis of modern Jewish society
relates specifically to anti-Semitism and ethnic-religious
discrimination in general. How important are attitudes, policies, and
ideologies of governments and of non-Jews in understanding the
transformation of Judaism? How does political anti-semitism relate to
various ideologies and governments? How does anti-semitism in its
political and attitudinal forms relate to conflict, competition, and
inequality within societies? How is anti-semitism affected by the
presence of other minorities in the society? How are political and
attitudinal dimensions of anti-Semitism related to each other and to
the general attitudes and values of non-Jews and Jews? How do these
dimensions relate to the size and structure of the Jewish community?
These questions are particular to Jews, in ways that are perhaps
different than for religious, ethnic, and racial minorities in general.
There cannot be a comprehensive sociology of Judaism without taking
into consideration the political, social, and attitudinal context of the
non-Jewish "other". But again, social structural and cultural contexts
are critical for understanding the "other" and in evaluating the
relative importance of "others" in determining variation and change
among Jews. How modern forms of anti-Semitism, and its most extreme
form, the Holocaust, reshaped the Judaism of exile and return and
generated new forms of Judaism in the post-Nazi era is of critical
importance.

The changing internal structure of the Jewish community, its
variation across societies, and the relationship of Jews to religious
institutions and organizations which are the formal network of the
community is the final arena of specific analytic concern. Clearly the
organization of the Jewish community is transformed in the process of
modernization. How and why the formal structure changes and what

the role of ideological factors is in shaping those changes are major questions. How these institutional changes are linked to, determine, and are the consequence of changes in the social structure of the Jewish community are critical issues. How does the organizational structure of the Jewish community link to the formal organizational and institutional structure of the general community and the formal institutional structure of its religious organizations? In short, the sources of growth, expansion, and competition among organizations and the emergence of new institutions need to be analyzed in the broader contexts of organizational theory and other institutional developments occurring in society. As organizations and institutions change, so do elites; as the centrality of religion declines, so does the authority and power of the rabbis; as religion takes on new forms and new secular and religious organizations are shaped, new organizational elites emerge with new sources of power and new bases of resources. The linkages between religious and secular organizational developments within the Jewish community and the changing relationships between ethnic and religious dimensions of Jewish identity and identification are prime theoretical and empirical areas of inquiry.

These are complex issues which relate to Jews specifically and to changes in the place of Jews in modern society. In large part, these issues revolve around the forces shaping why particular changes occur among Jews and how Jews respond relative to non-Jews. But we ask questions not only about the determinants of changes among Jews but about the consequences of these changes for Jewish continuity. More particularly, we focus on the implications of the transformation of the Jewish community for the relative cohesion of the Jewish community. We analyze the relative cohesion of communities under different conditions; we should not infer the *implications* of change from the changing characteristics of the Jewish community. Thus, for example, the increasing secularization of Judaism, in terms of the reduction in traditional religious ritual observances and ritual practices, has been documented in almost every study of modern Jewish communities. Often, the inference has been made that patterns of secularization have negative consequences for the cohesion of the Jewish community; from the point of view of the community, therefore, secularization is treated as one indicator of the decline of the Jewish community in modern society. That is the case only when we confuse Judaism with Jewishness and equate the religion of the Jews with the strength of the Jewish community. These dimensions were more interchangeable in the past, when religion was more central in the lives of Jews and connected in integral ways to social, economic, family, cultural, and political aspects of Jewish communities. In modern pluralistic societies, the two questions have to be untangled: (1) How are changes in religion linked to other processes of transformation? and (2) What are the implications of the new emerging Judaisms for the cohesion of the community? Only if the cohesion of the Jewish community is defined by the religiosity of the Jewish community, then, by definition, would a change in religiosity imply a decrease in Jewish cohesion. The more profound question is phrased differently: How do the new forms of Judaism in modern society link to the nature of Jewish cohesion? And, in turn, how have the new Judaisms translated the Judaism of exile and return in the new contexts of modernity?

Emphasis on the religious behavior and on the characteristics of Jews and their communities needs to be separated from an analysis of values and attitudes, if only to see how behavior and values are related. The study of elites, norms, ideologies, and ideas is important but should not be viewed as substitutes for analyzing the behavior of the masses and the characteristics of their communities. The elite, by definition, is not a cross-section of the community. To study the elite, comparatively and historically, is a most engaging area of investigation but it is not the same as studying the Jewish community. Norms, values, and ideas are not synonomous with behavior. Values, ideologies, and culture need to be studied as phenomena to be explained no less than as sources of explanation. Indeed, there is a critical need to test the relative importance of structural and cultural explanations of social processes, no less among Jews than as part of the general sociological analyses of groups. Elite ideas are but one of many determinants of mass behavior; they are rarely the only determinants of the behavior even of elites.

We need to ask theoretical questions to guide our empirical inquiries and identify new areas of comparative research among contemporary Jews and their communities. It is a grand intellectual challenge and a complex scholarly agenda to place the sociological study of the Jews and Judaism in the broader context of the societies of which they are a part, to examine the unique and the general, to test theories and hypotheses, to investigate the general social, economic, cultural, political patterns of the Jews and their communities, and to see connections among communities, comparing Jews and others systematically and over time. It is the agenda of the social sciences in general. It is doubly difficult when the focus is on Jews and their communities because of the need to investigate one group among many and to link their analysis with other groups, other Jews, and societal patterns in general. The permutations are extensive. Nevertheless, and perhaps because of it, it is an intellectual challenge of the highest order and worth pursuing. When the social scientific study of Jews is connected to the humanistic orientation to religion, each perspective generates new maps to discover new linkages by raising new questions.

The systematic study of Judaism is linked to the study of the Jews and their communites. To understand these links we need to place the analysis of the Jews in the perspectives not only of the social sciences but of the humanities. By specifying those theoretical and methodological linkages we put the issues of social science in systematic order. Then can we begin to connect these to the study of religion in general and Judaism in particular within the humanities. Combining social science and humanistic perspectives is thus the first step toward the ongoing search for grand integrative theories.

Index